Math in Focus

Singapore Math®
by Marshall Cavendish

Student Edition

Program Consultant and Author
Dr. Fong Ho Kheong

Authors
Gan Kee Soon
Dr. Ng Wee Leng

Marshall Cavendish
Education

U.S. Distributor
Houghton Mifflin Harcourt.
The Learning Company™

Course 1A

Contents

Chapter

1 Whole Numbers, Prime Numbers, and Prime Factorization

Chapter Opener   1

? How do you express a whole number as a product of its factors

RECALL PRIOR KNOWLEDGE   2

Finding factors of a whole number • Finding multiples of a whole number
• Identifying prime numbers • Using order of operations to simplify
numerical expressions

1	**Prime Factorization**	**5**
	Write a composite number as a product of its prime factors ▶	5–8
	INDEPENDENT PRACTICE	9
2	**Common Factors and Multiples**	**11**
	Identify the common factors of two whole numbers	11
	Find the greatest common factor of two whole numbers ▶	12–14
	Use the greatest common factor with the distributive property	15
	Identify the common multiples of two whole numbers	16
	Find the least common multiple of two whole numbers	17–18
	INDEPENDENT PRACTICE	19
3	**Squares and Cubes**	**23**
	Find the square of a whole number	23–24
	Find the cube of a whole number	24–25
	Evaluate numerical expressions that contain exponents	25–26
	INDEPENDENT PRACTICE	27

▶ Activity

MATH JOURNAL   31

PUT ON YOUR THINKING CAP!   32

CHAPTER WRAP-UP   34

CHAPTER REVIEW   35

PERFORMANCE TASK   39

STEAM PROJECT WORK   42

Chapter

 2 Number Lines and Negative Numbers

Chapter Opener

43

❓ **How do you express and compare numbers less than 0?**

RECALL PRIOR KNOWLEDGE
44

Comparing numbers to 1,000,000

1 The Number Line		**45**
Represent whole numbers on a number line, and compare two numbers using > or <		45–47
Represent fractions, mixed numbers, and decimals on a number line		48–50
Use > or < to write statements of inequality involving fractions and decimals		51–52
INDEPENDENT PRACTICE		53
2 Negative Numbers		**57**
Recognize and use negative numbers in real-world situations		57–59
Represent negative numbers on a number line		59–61
Use > or < to write statements of inequality involving negative numbers ▶		62–63
Interpret and explain statements of order involving negative numbers in real-world situations		63–64
INDEPENDENT PRACTICE		65
3 Absolute Value		**69**
Write the absolute value of a number		69–70
Use absolute values to interpret real-world situations		71–72
INDEPENDENT PRACTICE		73

▶ Activity

MATH JOURNAL   75

PUT ON YOUR THINKING CAP!   75

CHAPTER WRAP-UP   76

CHAPTER REVIEW   77

PERFORMANCE TASK   83

Chapter

3 Fractions and Decimals

Chapter Opener

85

How do you add, subtract, multiply, or divide fractions and decimals?

RECALL PRIOR KNOWLEDGE **86**

Adding and subtracting decimals • Expressing improper fractions as mixed numbers • Expressing mixed numbers as improper fractions • Multiplying fractions by fractions • Dividing fractions by a whole number • Dividing whole numbers by a unit fraction

1	**Dividing Fractions**	**89**
	Divide a whole number by a proper fraction 	89–92
	Divide a proper fraction by a unit fraction 	93–95
	Divide a proper fraction by a proper fraction 	96–99
	Divide a fraction by an improper fraction or a mixed number	99–100
	INDEPENDENT PRACTICE	101
2	**Real-World Problems: Fractions**	**103**
	Divide a whole number by a proper fraction to solve real-world problems	103–104
	Divide a proper fraction by a unit fraction to solve real-world problems	104–105
	Divide a fraction by a whole number to solve multi-step real-world problems	105–108
	Divide a whole number by a fraction to solve multi-step real-world problems	108–111
	Divide a fraction by a fraction to solve real-world problems 	112–116
	INDEPENDENT PRACTICE	117
3	**Adding and Subtracting Decimals Fluently**	**121**
	Add multi-digit decimals	121–122
	Subtract multi-digit decimals	123–124
	INDEPENDENT PRACTICE	125
4	**Multiplying Decimals Fluently**	**127**
	Multiply a decimal by a whole number	127–129
	Multiply tenths by tenths	130
	Multiply two decimals with one decimal place	131
	Multiply decimals with one or more decimal places	132
	MATH SHARING	132
	INDEPENDENT PRACTICE	133

 Activity

5 Dividing Decimals Fluently — **135**
Divide a whole number by a decimal — 135–137
Divide tenths by tenths — 137–138
Divide hundredths by hundredths — 138–139
Divide decimals with one or more decimal places — 140
INDEPENDENT PRACTICE — 141

6 Real-World Problems: Decimals — **143**
Add or subtract decimals to solve real-world problems — 143–144
Multiply decimals to solve real-world problems — 145
Divide decimals to solve real-world problems — 146
INDEPENDENT PRACTICE — 147

MATH JOURNAL — 151

PUT ON YOUR THINKING CAP! — 151

CHAPTER WRAP-UP — 152

CHAPTER REVIEW — 153

PERFORMANCE TASK — 161

Chapter

Ratio

Chapter Opener

165

How does the use of ratio help you compare quantities?

RECALL PRIOR KNOWLEDGE **166**

Expressing fractions as equivalent fractions by multiplication • Expressing fractions as equivalent fractions by division • Writing equivalent fractions • Writing fractions in simplest form • Converting measurements given in one unit of measure to another • Interpreting a comparison bar model

1	Comparing Two Quantities	169
	Write ratios to compare two quantities with the same unit	169–171
	Write ratios to compare two quantities with different units	171–172
	Use a part-part or a part-whole bar model to show ratios	173–174
	Use a bar model to show fractions or ratios 	175–177
	Use ratios to find how many times one number or quantity is as great as another	177–178
	MATH SHARING	178
	INDEPENDENT PRACTICE	179
2	**Equivalent Ratios**	**183**
	Write equivalent ratios to show the same comparisons of numbers and quantities	183–186
	Find equivalent ratios by division	187–188
	Use the greatest common factor to write ratios in simplest form	188–189
	Find the missing term in a pair of equivalent ratios	189–190
	Work with tables of ratios	190–191
	Work with descriptions of ratios to find quantities	191–195
	Find equivalent ratios involving two sets of ratios	196
	INDEPENDENT PRACTICE	197

Activity

3 Real-World Problems: Ratios	**201**
Solve real-world problems involving ratios	201–202
Solve real-world problems involving ratios of three quantities	203–204
Solve real-world problems involving two sets of ratios	205–206
Solve before-and-after problems involving changing ratios	207–210
LET'S EXPLORE	210
INDEPENDENT PRACTICE	211

MATH JOURNAL	**217**
PUT ON YOUR THINKING CAP!	**218**
CHAPTER WRAP-UP	**220**
CHAPTER REVIEW	**221**
PERFORMANCE TASK	**227**
STEAM PROJECT WORK	**230**

5 Rates and Speed

Chapter Opener   231

How does the use of a rate help you compare one quantity to another quantity?

RECALL PRIOR KNOWLEDGE   232

Multiplying whole numbers • Multiplying fractions or mixed numbers by a whole number • Multiplying fractions • Dividing with fractions and whole numbers • Dividing fractions • Finding the quantity represented by a number of units • Finding ratios • Finding ratios in simplest form

1	Rates and Unit Rates	237
	Identify a unit rate	237–238
	Express and compute unit rates in terms of time and other quantities	238–239
	Find a unit rate	239–240
	Find and compare unit rates	241–243
	Find a quantity given the unit rate	243–244
	INDEPENDENT PRACTICE	245
2	Real-World Problems: Rates and Unit Rates	247
	Solve simple real-world problems involving rates and unit rates	247–248
	Solve two-part real-world problems involving rates and unit rates	249–250
	Read a table to find the information to solve multi-step rate problems	251
	Solve multi-step real-world problems involving comparison of unit rates	252–253
	Read a graph to find the information to solve rate problems	253–256
	INDEPENDENT PRACTICE	257
3	Distance and Speed	261
	Read, interpret, and write speed	261–262
	Find the speed or rate of travel given the distance and time	262–263
	Find the distance given the speed and time	263–265
	Find the time given the distance and speed	266–268
	MATH SHARING	268
	INDEPENDENT PRACTICE	269

Activity

4	**Average Speed**	**271**
	Find the average speed given the total distance traveled and total time taken	271–274
	INDEPENDENT PRACTICE	275
5	**Real-World Problems: Speed and Average Speed**	**277**
	Draw and use diagrams to solve real-world problems involving speed, distance, and time	277–279
	Draw and use diagrams to find the average speed given the time taken and distance traveled for a proportion of the journey	279–281
	Draw and use diagrams to solve average speed problems involving a fixed distance	282–283
	Draw and use diagrams to solve constant speed problems involving two objects or persons moving towards the same end point	284–285
	Draw and use diagrams to solve constant speed problems involving two objects or persons moving away from each other 	286–288
	INDEPENDENT PRACTICE	289

MATH JOURNAL	**291**
PUT ON YOUR THINKING CAP!	**292**
CHAPTER WRAP-UP	**294**
CHAPTER REVIEW	**295**
PERFORMANCE TASK	**301**

6 Percent

Chapter Opener   **303**

How does the use of a percent help you compare quantities?

RECALL PRIOR KNOWLEDGE   **304**

Finding equivalent fractions using multiplication • Finding equivalent fractions
using division • Writing fractions with a denominator of 100 as a decimal
• Multiplying fractions by a whole number

1	**Understanding Percent**	**307**
	Express a part of a whole as a fraction and a percent	307–309
	Express percents as fractions or decimals ▶	310–312
	INDEPENDENT PRACTICE	313
2	**Fractions, Decimals, and Percents**	**315**
	Express fractions or mixed numbers as percents ▶	315–317
	Express decimals as percents	318–319
	Express percents as fractions	319–320
	INDEPENDENT PRACTICE	321
3	**Percent of a Quantity**	**323**
	Find the quantity represented by the percent	323–325
	Find the whole given a quantity and its percent ▶	325–326
	INDEPENDENT PRACTICE	327
4	**Real-World Problems: Percent**	**331**
	Solve real-world problems involving finding the percent represented by a quantity	331–333
	Solve real-world problems involving taxes	334–335
	Solve real-world problems involving finding the whole given a quantity and its percent	336
	Solve real-world problems involving interest	337–338
	LET'S EXPLORE	338
	INDEPENDENT PRACTICE	339

▶ Activity

MATH JOURNAL   341

PUT ON YOUR THINKING CAP!   341

CHAPTER WRAP-UP   342

CHAPTER REVIEW   343

PERFORMANCE TASK   347

Glossary   **349**

Index   **351**

Photo Credits   **357**

Manipulative List

Fraction circle

Preface

Welcome!

Math in Focus® is a program that puts **you** at the center of an exciting learning experience! This experience is all about equipping you with critical thinking skills and mathematical strategies, explaining your thinking to deepen your understanding, and helping you to become a skilled and confident problem solver.

What's in your book?

Each chapter in this book begins with a real-world situation of the math topic you are about to learn.

In each chapter, you will encounter the following features:

THINK introduces a problem for the whole section, to stimulate creative and critical thinking and help you hone your problem-solving skills. You may not be able to answer the problem right away but you can revisit it a few times as you build your knowledge through the section.

ENGAGE consists of tasks that link what you already know with what you will be learning next. The tasks allow you to explore and discuss mathematical concepts with your classmates.

LEARN introduces new mathematical concepts through a Concrete-Pictorial-Abstract (C-P-A) approach, using activities and examples.

Activity comprises learning experiences that promote collaboration with your classmates. These activities allow you to reinforce your learning or uncover new mathematical concepts.

TRY supports and reinforces your learning through guided practice.

INDEPENDENT PRACTICE allows you to work on a variety of problems and apply the concepts and skills you have learned to solve these problems on your own.

Additional features include:

RECALL PRIOR KNOWLEDGE	Math Talk	MATH SHARING	Caution and Math Note
Helps you recall related concepts you learned before, accompanied by practice questions	Invites you to explain your reasoning and communicate your ideas to your classmates and teachers	Encourages you to create strategies, discover methods, and share them with your classmates and teachers using mathematical language	Highlights common errors and misconceptions, as well as provides you with useful hints and reminders
LET'S EXPLORE	MATH JOURNAL	PUT ON YOUR THINKING CAP!	CHAPTER WRAP-UP
Extends your learning through investigative activities	Allows you to reflect on your learning when you write down your thoughts about the mathematical concepts learned	Challenges you to apply the mathematical concepts to solve problems, and also hones your critical thinking skills	Summarizes your learning in a flow chart and helps you to make connections within the chapter
CHAPTER REVIEW	Assessment Prep	PERFORMANCE TASK	STEAM
Provides you with ample practice in the concepts learned	Prepares you for state tests with assessment-type problems	Assesses your learning through problems that allow you to demonstrate your understanding and knowledge	Promotes collaboration with your classmates through interesting projects that allow you to use math in creative ways

Are you ready to experience math the Singapore way? Let's go!

Whole Numbers, Prime Numbers, and Prime Factorization

How many guests?

Have you ever organized a party? How did you decide how many guests to invite? Did you calculate the cost of assorted room decorations, and the number of tables and chairs your guests might need? How did you decide how much food to prepare?

Perhaps you decided that your guests would enjoy a variety of finger foods. Suppose you considered preparing 80 sandwiches and 60 miniature pies. If each person ate the same amount of each finger food, how many guests could you feed? Your answer told you how many guests you could invite.

In this chapter, you will learn how to use prime factorization and greatest common factors to answer a variety of questions like these.

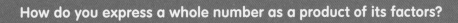

How do you express a whole number as a product of its factors?

Name: _____ Date: _____

Finding factors of a whole number

Find the factors of 24.

$24 = 1 \times 24$

$24 = 2 \times 12$

$24 = 3 \times 8$

$24 = 4 \times 6$

The factors of 24 are 1, 2, 3, 4, 6, 8, 12, and 24.

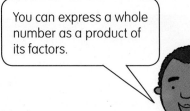

You can express a whole number as a product of its factors.

▶ **Quick Check**

Find the factors of each number.

1. 30

2. 63

3. 56

4. 84

Finding multiples of a whole number

Find the first six multiples of 7.

1 × 7 = 7

2 × 7 = 14

3 × 7 = 21

4 × 7 = 28

5 × 7 = 35

6 × 7 = 42 …

Write the multiples in order from least to greatest.

7, 14, 21, 28, 35, and 42 are the first six multiples of 7.

▶ **Quick Check**

Find the first five multiples of each number.

5 4

6 6

7 9

8 13

Identifying prime numbers

A prime number has only two different factors, 1 and the number itself.
Decide whether 11 and 14 are prime numbers.

Find the factors of 11.

$11 = 1 \times 11$

The factors of 11 are 1 and 11.
11 is a prime number.

Find the factors of 14.

$14 = 1 \times 14$
$14 = 2 \times 7$

The factors of 14 are 1, 2, 7, and 14.
14 is not a prime number.

▶ **Quick Check**

Identify all the prime numbers in the following set of numbers.

⑨   2, 5, 13, 21, 23, 39, 47, 51, 53, 57

Using order of operations to simplify numerical expressions

STEP 1 Evaluate inside parentheses.

STEP 2 Multiply and divide from left to right.

STEP 3 Add and subtract from left to right.

Find the value of $(98 + 34) - 6 \times 7$.

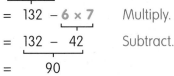

$\mathbf{(98 + 34)} - 6 \times 7$ Perform operations inside parentheses.

$= 132 - \mathbf{6 \times 7}$ Multiply.

$= 132 - 42$ Subtract.

$= 90$

▶ **Quick Check**

Find the value of each expression.

⑩ $(40 - 28) + 8 \times 7$

⑪ $75 \times (45 \div 5) - 70$

1 Prime Factorization

Learning Objective:
• Express a composite number as a product of its prime factors.

New Vocabulary
prime factor
prime factorization

THINK

Sean thinks that a whole number can only be a prime number or a composite number. Explain why you agree or disagree with him.

ENGAGE

Amy has 24 goldfish and a number of bowls. Use 24 counters and a number of plates to show the different ways she can divide the goldfish equally into the bowls.

LEARN Write a composite number as a product of its prime factors

Activity Classifying whole numbers greater than 0 based on their number of factors

Work in pairs.

(1) Write the factors of each number in the tables.

Number	Factors
1	
2	
3	
4	
5	
6	
7	
8	
9	
10	

Number	Factors
11	
12	
13	
14	
15	
16	
17	
18	
19	
20	

(2) Classify each number from 1 to 20 based on the number of factors it has. Write your answers in the table.

Number of Factors	Numbers
1	
2	
3 or more	

1 You can represent a whole number as a product of its factors.

$18 = 1 \times 18$ $18 = 2 \times 9$ $18 = 3 \times 6$

The factors of 18 are 1, 2, 3, 6, 9, and 18.
18 has 6 factors. It is an example of a composite number.

> A composite number has more than two different whole-number factors.

2 Recall that a prime number has only two factors, 1 and the number itself.

$3 = 1 \times 3$

The factors of 3 are 1 and 3.
3 has only 2 factors. It is an example of a prime number.

Math Talk
Are 0 and 1 primes, composites, or neither? Explain.

2 and 3 are the only prime numbers in the list of factors of 18.
2 and 3 are the prime factors of 18.

3 You can express a composite number as a product of its prime factors. For example, you can write 18 as a product using only its prime factors.

$18 = 2 \times 3 \times 3$

This is known as prime factorization.

Math Note
Finding the prime factorization of a number is not the same as finding the factors of a number. A composite number can be written as the product of different pairs of its factors. But there is only one prime factorization for a given composite number.

4 Express 60 as a product of its prime factors.

▶ **Method 1**

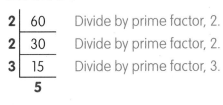

2 | 60   Divide by prime factor, 2.
2 | 30   Divide by prime factor, 2.
3 | 15   Divide by prime factor, 3.
    5

> Start dividing the number by its least prime factor. Continue dividing by the next prime factor until the quotient is a prime number.

The prime factors of 60 are 2, 3, and 5.

$60 = 2 \times 2 \times 3 \times 5$

▶ **Method 2**

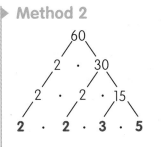

The prime factors of 60 are 2, 3, and 5.

$60 = 2 \cdot 2 \cdot 3 \cdot 5$

Math Note

Another multiplication symbol is the multiplication dot.
So, $60 = 2 \cdot 2 \cdot 3 \cdot 5$ means
$60 = 2 \times 2 \times 3 \times 5$.

Math Talk

James found the prime factorization of 60 this way:

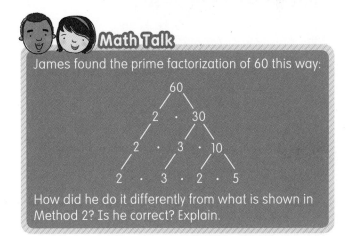

How did he do it differently from what is shown in Method 2? Is he correct? Explain.

TRY Practice writing a composite number as a product of its prime factors

Express each number as a product of its prime factors.

1   48

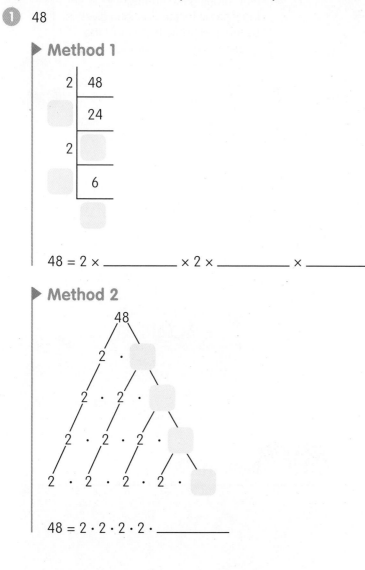

▶ Method 1

$$48 = 2 \times \underline{\hspace{2cm}} \times 2 \times \underline{\hspace{2cm}} \times \underline{\hspace{2cm}}$$

▶ Method 2

$$48 = 2 \cdot 2 \cdot 2 \cdot 2 \cdot \underline{\hspace{2cm}}$$

2   30   3   72   4   150

INDEPENDENT PRACTICE

Circle all the prime numbers.

1

1	2	3	4	5	6
7	8	9	10	11	12
13	14	15	16	17	18
19	20	21	22	23	24
25	26	27	28	29	30

Express each number as a product of its prime factors.

2 6

3 15

4 36

5 78

6 81

7 144

8 245

9 510

10 250

11 1,089

12 4,725

13 27,000

Solve.

14. **Mathematical Habit 6** Use precise mathematical language
Describe the steps for writing 42 as a product of its prime factors.

15. 400 is 2 × 2 × 2 × 2 × 5 × 5 when written as a product of its prime factors.
Write 800 as a product of its prime factors.

16. 320 is 2 × 2 × 2 × 2 × 2 × 2 × 5 when written as a product of its prime factors.
Write 3,200 as a product of its prime factors.

17. 2,700 is 2 × 2 × 3 × 3 × 3 × 5 × 5 when written as a product of its prime factors.
Write 270 as a product of its prime factors.

18. 4,800 can be expressed in terms of its prime factors as
2 × 2 × 2 × 2 × 2 × 2 × 3 × 5 × 5.

    a Write 1,200 as a product of its prime factors.

    b Now, write 120 as a product of its prime factors.

Common Factors and Multiples

Learning Objectives:
- Find the common factors and the greatest common factor of two whole numbers.
- Find the common multiples and the least common multiple of two whole numbers.

> **New Vocabulary**
> greatest common factor
> least common multiple

THINK

Ms. Jones wants to use square patches to make a rectangular sail that measures 36 feet by 52 feet. She wants to use the fewest square patches without cutting any of them. What is the length of each side of a square patch?

ENGAGE

List the factors of 6 and 15. Which number has more factors, 6 or 15? Which factors do they have in common?

If two numbers have the common factors 1, 2 and 4 only, what possible numbers can they be? Explain your thinking.

LEARN Identify the common factors of two whole numbers

1   Find the common factors of 12 and 30.

$12 = 1 \times 12$ $30 = 1 \times 30$ Factors of 12: ①, ②, ③, 4, ⑥, and 12

$12 = 2 \times 6$ $30 = 2 \times 15$ Factors of 30: ①, ②, ③, 5, ⑥, 10, 15, and 30

$12 = 3 \times 4$ $30 = 3 \times 10$ 1, 2, 3, and 6 are all factors of both 12 and 30.

                    $30 = 5 \times 6$ 1, 2, 3, and 6 are called the common factors of 12 and 30.

TRY Practice identifying the common factors of two whole numbers

Fill in each blank.

1   Use the multiplication facts to find the common factors of 10 and 28.

$10 = 1 \times 10$ $28 = 1 \times 28$

$10 = 2 \times 5$ $28 = 2 \times 14$

                 $28 = 4 \times 7$

The factors of 10 are _____, _____, _____, and _____.

The factors of 28 are _____, _____, _____, _____, _____, and _____.

The common factors of 10 and 28 are _____ and _____.

ENGAGE

There are 18 girls and 24 boys at a summer camp. The campers are placed in groups. The number of boys in each group is the same. The number of girls in each group is also the same. What is the greatest possible number of groups possible? Show and explain your strategy to your partner. Discuss if there are other strategies.

LEARN Find the greatest common factor of two whole numbers

1 Find the greatest common factor of 45 and 75.

▶ **Method 1**

$45 = 1 \times 45$ $75 = 1 \times 75$

$45 = 3 \times 15$ $75 = 3 \times 25$

$45 = 5 \times 9$ $75 = 5 \times 15$

Factors of 45: ①, ③, ⑤, 9, ⑮, and 45

Factors of 75: ①, ③, ⑤, ⑮, 25, and 75

The common factors of 45 and 75 are 1, 3, 5, and 15.

Of these four common factors, 15 is the greatest.

So, 15 is the greatest common factor of 45 and 75.

▶ **Method 2**

By prime factorization,

$45 = ③ \cdot 3 \cdot ⑤$ Identify the prime factors that are common to both 45 and 75, and circle them.

$75 = ③ \cdot ⑤ \cdot 5$

Greatest common factor $= 3 \cdot 5$

$= 15$

The greatest common factor of 45 and 75 is 15.

▶ **Method 3**

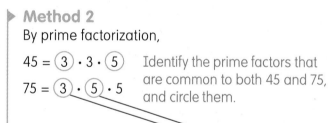

3	45, 75	Divide by common prime factor, 3.
5	15, 25	Divide by common prime factor, 5.
	3, 5	Stop dividing here as 3 and 5 have no common factor other than 1.

$3 \times 5 = 15$ Multiply the common factors.

The greatest common factor of 45 and 75 is 15.

Work in pairs.

① Shuffle a set of number cards (from 10 to 100) and place them face down.

② Turn over a number card each and write each number as the product of its prime factors.

Example:

20 = 2 · 2 · 5

42 = 2 · 3 · 7

③ Work together to identify the greatest common factor (GCF) of the two numbers. Then, put the number cards aside.

④ Continue the activity until you have used all the number cards.

TRY Practice finding the greatest common factor of two whole numbers

Find the greatest common factor of each pair of numbers.

1 20 and 32

▶ **Method 1**

$20 = 1 \times 20$ $32 = 1 \times 32$

$20 = 2 \times 10$ $32 = 2 \times 16$

$20 = 4 \times 5$ $32 = 4 \times 8$

The factors of 20 are _____, _____, _____, _____, _____, and _____.

The factors of 32 are _____, _____, _____, _____, _____, and _____.

The common factors of 20 and 32 are _____, _____, and _____.

The greatest common factor of 20 and 32 is _____.

▶ **Method 2**

By prime factorization,

$20 = 2 \cdot$ _____ $\cdot$ _____

$32 = 2 \cdot$ _____ $\cdot$ _____ $\cdot$ _____ $\cdot$ _____

Greatest common factor $= 2 \cdot$ _____

                            $=$ _____

The greatest common factor of 20 and 32 is _____.

▶ **Method 3**

$$\begin{array}{r|ll} 2 & 20, & 32 \\ \hline & \boxed{}, & \boxed{} \\ \hline & 5, & 8 \end{array}$$

$2 \times$ _____ $=$ _____

The greatest common factor of 20 and 32 is _____.

2 15 and 27

3 36 and 54

ENGAGE

a List all the factors of 12, then list all the factors of 18.

b What are possible side lengths of a rectangle that has an area of 12 square units? What about a rectangle that has an area of 18 square units? What about connected rectangles that have a combined area of (12 + 18) square units? Draw a sketch to show your thinking.

LEARN Use the greatest common factor with the distributive property

1 Express 12 + 20 as a product of the greatest common factor of the numbers and another sum.

First, find the greatest common factor of the two numbers.

$12 = ②·②·3$

$20 = ②·②·5$

Greatest common factor of 12 and 20 = 2 · 2
= 4

Then, write the sum a different way. You know that

$12 = 4·3$ $\qquad\qquad$ $20 = 4·5$

So, 12 + 20 = 4 · 3 + 4 · 5
= 4(3 + 5).

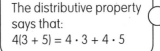

The distributive property says that:
4(3 + 5) = 4 · 3 + 4 · 5

TRY Practice using the greatest common factor with the distributive property

Express the sum of each pair of numbers as a product of the greatest common factor of the numbers and another sum.

1 18 + 45

By prime factorization,

18 = 2 · _____ · _____ $\qquad\qquad$ 45 = 3 · _____ · _____

Greatest common factor of 18 and 45 = _____ · _____

= _____

18 + 45 = _____ · _____ + _____ · _____

= _____ (_____ + _____)

2 35 + 91 $\qquad$ 3 60 + 85 $\qquad$ 4 24 + 64

ENGAGE

a Make a list of multiples of 5 and a list of multiples of 3.

b A green light flashes every 5 seconds. A yellow light flashes every 3 seconds. In one minute, how many times will the two lights flash together? Explain your thinking.

LEARN Identify the common multiples of two whole numbers

1 Find the first two common multiples of 8 and 12.

Find the multiples that are common to both 8 and 12.

1 × 8 = 8	1 × 12 = 12
2 × 8 = 16	2 × 12 = 24
3 × 8 = 24	3 × 12 = 36
4 × 8 = 32	4 × 12 = 48
5 × 8 = 40	5 × 12 = 60
6 × 8 = 48	6 × 12 = 72
7 × 8 = 56	7 × 12 = 84
8 × 8 = 64	8 × 12 = 96
9 × 8 = 72	9 × 12 = 108
10 × 8 = 80	10 × 12 = 120

Multiples of 8: 8, 16, (24), 32, 40, (48), 56, 64, (72), 80, ...

Multiples of 12: 12, (24), 36, (48), 60, (72), 84, 96, 108, 120, ...

24, 48, 72, ... are multiples of both 8 and 12.

24, 48, 72, ... are called the common multiples of 8 and 12.

The first two common multiples of 8 and 12 are 24 and 48.

TRY Practice identifying the common multiples of two whole numbers

List the first ten multiples of each pair of numbers. Then, find the common multiples of each pair of numbers from the list.

1 3 and 5
The first ten multiples of 3 are _____, _____, _____, _____, _____, _____,

_____, _____, _____, and _____.

The first ten multiples of 5 are _____, _____, _____, _____, _____, _____,

_____, _____, _____, and _____.

The first two common multiples of 3 and 5 are _____ and _____.

2 6 and 12   3 7 and 11

ENGAGE

a Make a list of the first 10 multiples of 4 and 6. Which are the common multiples?

b Mason and Davi are training for a triathlon. Mason swims every 4th day. Davi swims every 6th day. Today, they both swam. When is the next time they swim together? Explain your thinking.

LEARN Find the **least common multiple** of two whole numbers

1 Find the least common multiple of 6 and 9.

▶ **Method 1**

1 × 6 = 6	1 × 9 = 9
2 × 6 = 12	2 × 9 = 18
3 × 6 = 18	3 × 9 = 27
4 × 6 = 24	4 × 9 = 36
5 × 6 = 30	5 × 9 = 45
6 × 6 = 36	6 × 9 = 54
7 × 6 = 42	7 × 9 = 63
8 × 6 = 48	8 × 9 = 72
9 × 6 = 54	9 × 9 = 81
10 × 6 = 60	10 × 9 = 90

Multiples of 6: 6, 12, (18), 24, 30, (36), 42, 48, (54), 60, ...

Multiples of 9: 9, (18), 27, (36), 45, (54), 63, 72, 81, 90, ...

The common multiples of 6 and 9 are 18, 36, 54, ...

Of these common multiples, 18 is the least.

So, 18 is the least common multiple of 6 and 9.

▶ **Method 2**

By prime factorization,

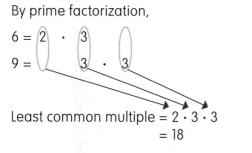

Least common multiple = 2 · 3 · 3
          = 18

The least common multiple of 6 and 9 is 18.

> 6   9
> /\   /\
> 2 · 3   3 · 3
> 2 · 3 · 3 is the least product containing 2 · 3 and 3 · 3. So, 2 · 3 · 3 is the least common multiple of 6 and 9.

Method 3

3 | 6, 9   Divide by common prime factor, 3.

    2, 3   Since 2 and 3 have no common factor other than 1, stop dividing.

$3 \times 2 \times 3 = 18$ Multiply the factors.

The least common multiple of 6 and 9 is 18.

TRY Practice finding the least common multiple of two whole numbers

Find the least common multiple of each pair of numbers.

1 8 and 10

Method 1
The multiples of 8 are _____, _____, _____, _____, _____, _____,

_____, _____, _____, _____, …

The multiples of 10 are _____, _____, _____, _____, _____, _____,

_____, _____, _____, _____, …

The common multiples of 8 and 10 are _____, _____, …

The least common multiple of 8 and 10 is _____.

Method 2
By prime factorization,

$8 = 2 \cdot$ _____ $\cdot$ _____ $10 = 2 \cdot$ _____

Least common multiple $= 2 \cdot$ _____ $\cdot$ _____ $\cdot$ _____

              $=$ _____

The least common multiple of 8 and 10 is _____.

Method 3
2 | 8, 10

    □ , □

$2 \times$ _____ $\times$ _____ $=$ _____

The least common multiple of 8 and 10 is _____.

2 3 and 7   **3** 5 and 12

Solve.

23 Sarah has two ropes that she wants to use to tie butterfly knots. To start, she wants to cut the two ropes into pieces of the same length.

84 inches

116 inches

a Find the greatest possible length of each piece, so that no rope will be left unused.

b Write the sum of the two lengths and factor out the number you found in **a**. What do the numbers inside the parentheses represent?

24 A florist combined 48 pink roses and 56 white lilies to make identical bouquets, with no flowers left over.

a Find the greatest number of bouquets that the florist made.

b Find the number of pink roses and white lilies in each bouquet.

25 A red light flashes every 14 minutes. A blue light flashes every 24 minutes. When will the two lights flash together again, if they last flashed together at 8 A.M.?

26 a Find the product of 84 and 90.

b Find the product of the greatest common factor and the least common multiple of 84 and 90.

c What do you observe about your answers to parts a and b?

d Choose two other numbers and repeat parts a and b. Do you get the same results?

3 Squares and Cubes

Learning Objectives:
- Find the square and cube of a whole number.
- Write the square and cube of a whole number using exponents.
- Evaluate numerical expressions involving whole-number exponents.

> **New Vocabulary**
> perfect square
> perfect cube

THINK

Charles wants to use small cubes with 2-inch edges to build a tower with two sections. The lower section is a cubic base with edges of length 30 inches whereas the upper section has a square base of side 18 inches. The total height of the tower is 50 inches. How many 2-inch cubes does he need?

ENGAGE

Use a 100-square grid. How many squares of different sizes can you find on the grid? Compare your squares to your partner's.

LEARN Find the square of a whole number

1. A square has sides that are each 8 centimeters long. Find the area of the square.

   Area of the square = 8 × 8
                      = 64 cm^2

   8 × 8 is called the square of 8.
   You can write 8 × 8 as 8^2.

   So, 8^2 = 64.

   The number 2 in 8^2 is called the exponent.

   The number 8 is called the base of the expression.

   > The square of a whole number is called a **perfect square**.
   > Since 64 = 8 × 8, 64 is a perfect square.

   > 8^2 is read as "8 squared."

   8 cm

2. Find the square of 5.

   5^2 = 5 × 5
       = 25

   The square of 5 is 25.

   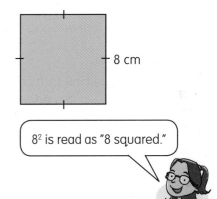

   > I can relate this to finding the area of a square with sides that are each 5 units long.

   5 units

   > 5 is called the square root of 25. We can write $\sqrt{25} = 5$.

TRY Practice finding the square of a whole number

Find the square of each number.

1. 6

2. 7

3. 9

4. 11

5. 14

6. 25

Solve.

7. Given that $39^2 = 1,521$, find the square of 390.

ENGAGE

Show how you use connecting cubes to make solids with volumes of 5, 6, 7, 8, or 9 cubic units. Discuss with your partner which volume can form a cube.

LEARN Find the cube of a whole number

1. A cube has edges that are each 4 centimeters long. Find its volume.

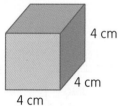

4 cm
4 cm
4 cm

Volume of cube = $4 \times 4 \times 4$
= 64 cm³

$4 \times 4 \times 4$ is called the cube of 4.
You can write $4 \times 4 \times 4$ as 4^3.

So, $4^3 = 64$.

The number 3 in 4^3 is the exponent.
The number 4 is the base.

4^3 is read as "4 cubed."

The cube of a whole number is called a perfect cube.
Since $64 = 4 \times 4 \times 4$, 64 is a perfect cube.

② Find the cube of 7.

$7^3 = 7 \times 7 \times 7$
$ = 343$

The cube of 7 is 343.

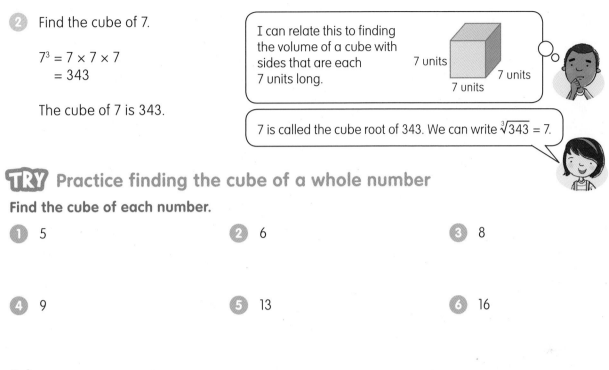

I can relate this to finding the volume of a cube with sides that are each 7 units long.

7 units
7 units
7 units

7 is called the cube root of 343. We can write $\sqrt[3]{343} = 7$.

TRY Practice finding the cube of a whole number

Find the cube of each number.

① 5

② 6

③ 8

④ 9

⑤ 13

⑥ 16

Solve.

⑦ Given that $21^3 = 9,261$, find the cube of 210.

ENGAGE

a. Write a perfect square and a perfect cube using exponents. Work with a partner to determine how you find their sum, difference, product, and quotient.

b. Alyssa is thinking of a whole number within 12. The difference between the square and the cube of the number is a perfect square. What are the possible numbers Alyssa is thinking of?

LEARN Evaluate numerical expressions that contain exponents

① In order to evaluate expressions with exponents, you need to follow the order of operations.

Order of Operations

 Evaluate inside parentheses.

 Evaluate exponents.

 Multiply and divide from left to right.

STEP 4 Add and subtract from left to right.

② Find the value of $3^2 + 4^2$.

$3^2 = 3 \times 3$
$\quad = 9$

$4^2 = 4 \times 4$
$\quad = 16$

> ⚠️ **Caution**
> $3^2 + 4^2$ does not have the same value as $(3 + 4)^2$.

So, $3^2 + 4^2 = 9 + 16$ Evaluate terms with exponents first.
$\qquad\qquad = 25$ Then, add.

③ Find the value of $7^2 \times 2^2 + 3^3$.

$\mathbf{7^2 \times 2^2 + 3^3} = \mathbf{49 \times 4 + 27}$ Evaluate terms with exponents first.
$\qquad\qquad\qquad\qquad\qquad$ Then, multiply.
$\qquad\qquad = \quad 196 + 27$ Finally, add.
$\qquad\qquad = 223$

④ Find the value of $10^3 - 4^2 \times 5^2$.

$\mathbf{10^3 - 4^2 \times 5^2} = \mathbf{1{,}000 - 16 \times 25}$ Evaluate terms with exponents first.
$\qquad\qquad\qquad\qquad\qquad$ Then, multiply.
$\qquad\qquad = 1{,}000 - 400$ Finally, subtract.
$\qquad\qquad = 600$

TRY **Practice evaluating numerical expressions that contain exponents**

Find the value of each expression.

① $5^2 + 5^3$

$5^2 = $ _____ $\times$ _____

$\quad = $ _____

$5^3 = $ _____ $\times$ _____ $\times$ _____

$\quad = $ _____

So, $5^2 + 5^3 = $ _____ $+$ _____

$\qquad\qquad = $ _____

$5 \cdot 5 \cdot 5 \cdot 5 \cdot 5$

$5 \cdot 5 \cdot 5 \cdot 5 \cdot 5 = $ _____

② $6^3 + 4^2$

③ $7^3 - 4^3$

④ $3^2 \times 5^3 + 9^2$

⑤ $8^3 \div 4^2 - 5^2$

⑥ $7^2 + 6^3 \div 2^3$

⑦ $9^3 - 4^2 \times 3^3$

INDEPENDENT PRACTICE

Find the square of each number.

1 3

2 7

3 10

4 12

Find the cube of each number.

5 2

6 3

7 10

8 11

Solve.

9 List the perfect squares that are between 25 and 100.

10 List the perfect cubes that are between 100 and 600.

11 **Mathematical Habit 6** **Use precise mathematical language**
Find the value of each expression. Then, describe any pattern(s) you see.

a $2^2 - 1^2$

b $3^2 - 2^2$

c $4^2 - 3^2$

d $5^2 - 4^2$

12. Find two consecutive numbers whose squares differ by 17.

Find the value of each expression.

13. $8^3 + 5^2$

14. $10^3 - 6^2$

15. $3^3 \times 9^2$

16. $9^3 \div 3^2$

17. $7^2 + 8^3 - 4^2$

18. $9^3 - 5^2 + 6^2$

19. $8^3 \times 5^3 \div 5^2$

20. $10^3 \div 8^2 \times 4^2$

21 $7^3 - 10^2 \div 2^2$

22 $3^3 + 4^3 \times 6^2$

Solve.

23   Given that $41^2 = 1{,}681$, find the square of 410.

24   Given that $14^3 = 2{,}744$, find the cube of 140.

25   Evaluate $13^2 + 20^3 - 18^3$.

26   Find three consecutive numbers whose cubes have a sum 2,241.

27 A class wants to make a giant square banner to hang in the school gym. The banner will have sides that are each 28 feet long. It will be made from smaller paper squares that are each 4 feet long. How many paper squares will the class need to make the giant banner?

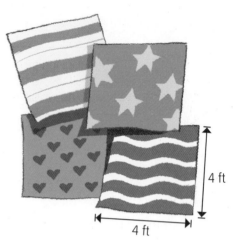

4 ft

4 ft

28 This week, customers at a carpet store pay $3 for a square foot of carpet. Next week, the store will have a sale. During the sale, each square foot of carpet will cost only $2. Diego wants to carpet two square rooms in his house. The floor in one room is 10 feet by 10 feet. The floor in the other room is 14 feet by 14 feet. How much money will Diego save if he waits to buy carpet during the sale?

29 A cubic crate holds cubic wooden boxes. Each of the crate's inside edges is 16 feet long. Each wooden box has outside edges that are each 4 feet long. How many wooden boxes can fit inside the cubic crate?

16 ft

Name: _____ Date: _____

Mathematical Habit 6 **Use precise mathematical language**

1 Show two methods to write 70 as a product of its prime factors.
   Which method do you prefer? Why?

2 Write two statements to relate any two of the numbers.

   70   4,900   343,000

> Since $13 \times 13 = 169$, you can say that the square of 13 is equal to 169. What statement relates 11 to 1,331?

Problem Solving with Heuristics

Mathematical Habit **1** **Persevere in solving problems**

1 Mr. Williams wants to create a rectangular patio in his back yard using square tiles. He does not want to cut any tiles. His patio measures 144 inches by 108 inches. Find the fewest square tiles he can use. (Hint: First, find the largest size tile he can use.)

2 There are 168 balloons and 336 fruit tarts at a party. Each child at the party receives the same number of balloons and fruit tarts. What is the maximum number of children who can share the balloons and fruit tarts?

3 A container holds two cubes of different sizes. The total volume of the two cubes is 3,718 cubic inches. What is the length of an edge of each cube?

> ? How do you express a whole number as a product of its factors?

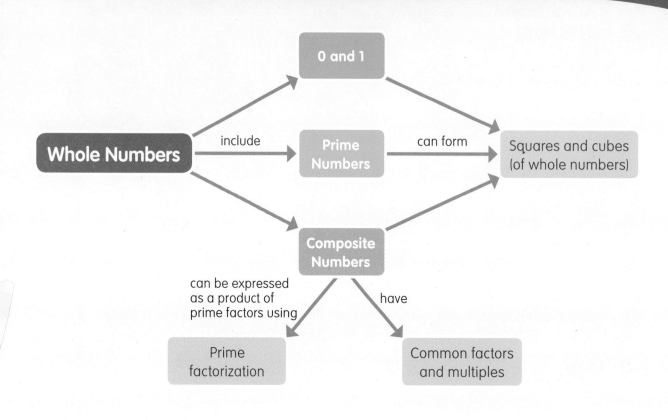

KEY CONCEPTS

- A composite number has more than two factors. Examples of composite numbers are 4, 6, 15, and 24.

- A prime number has only two factors, 1 and the number itself. Examples of prime numbers are 2, 5, 17, and 31.

- We can write a composite number as a product of its prime factors.

- The greatest common factor of two or more whole numbers is the greatest factor among all the common factors of the numbers.

- The least common multiple of two or more numbers is the least multiple among all the common multiples of the numbers.

- The square of a whole number is the number multiplied by itself. For example, the square of the number 15 is 15 × 15.

- The cube of a whole number is the number multiplied by itself, and multiplied by itself again. For example, the cube of the number 16 is 16 × 16 × 16.

© 2020 Marshall Cavendish Education Pte Ltd

Name: _____ Date: _____

Express each number as a product of its prime factors.

1 42

2 150

Find the common factors of each pair of numbers.

3 21 and 63

4 35 and 70

Find the greatest common factor of each pair of numbers.

5 8 and 12

6 42 and 32

Find the first three common multiples of each pair of numbers.

7 4 and 5

8 8 and 12

Find the least common multiple of each pair of numbers.

9 6 and 15

10 8 and 11

Find the square of each number.

11 14

12 30

Find the cube of each number.

13 15

14 20

Find the value of each expression.

15 $4^3 + 6^2$

16 $8^3 - 5^2$

17 $5^3 \times 4^3 - 13^2$

18 $8^2 + 10^3 \div 5^2$

Solve.

19 Given that $63^2 = 3{,}969$, find the square of 630.

20 Given that $16^3 = 4{,}096$, find the cube of 160.

21 Find two consecutive numbers whose squares differ by 25.

22 Matthew is packing 120 pencils and 108 notebooks equally into as many boxes as possible.

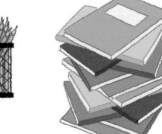

a Find the greatest number of boxes that Matthew can pack the items into.

b Find the number of pencils and notebooks in each box.

23 Ana and Ella are driving go-carts around a track. Ana takes 10 minutes and Ella takes 6 minutes to drive one lap. Suppose the two of them start together at a point. After how many minutes would the two meet again at the start point?

24 How many squares with sides that are each 6 inches long are needed to cover a square with sides that are each 30 inches long, without overlapping?

25 A large cubic box holds small wooden cubes. The large cubic box has inside edges that are each 18 inches long. Each small wooden cube has edges that are each 3 inches long. How many small wooden cubes can fit inside the box?

Assessment Prep
Answer each question.

26 A freight plane leaves the airport every 6 days, and a passenger plane leaves the airport every 11 days. Both planes leave the airport on March 21. On which day will both planes next leave the airport on the same day?

Ⓐ May 24

Ⓑ May 25

Ⓒ May 26

Ⓓ May 27

27 Pedro wants to use 4-inch square tiles to cover a 16-inch square tray. How many square tiles does Pedro need to cover the square tray completely without overlapping? Write your answer and your work or explanation in the space below.

28 A metal rod with a volume of 4,394 cubic inches is cut into two equal halves. One of the halves is melted and cast into a cube. How long is each edge of the cube? Write your answer and your workings or explanation in the space below.

A Collage of Photographs

Rachel is planning a party. She wants to make a collage of photographs taken by her guests. The dimensions of the collage are shown below. She needs to choose the size of the photographs to use in the collage.

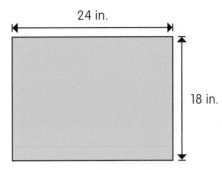

1 Rachel is thinking of using 4-inch square photographs to make the collage. By doing so, no photographs will have to be cut. Is this correct? Explain your answer.

2 a Find the greatest possible length of square photographs that Rachel can use to make the rectangular collage, so that no photographs will have to be cut.

b Find the number of photographs that she can use.

3 Rachel's brother suggests using 3-inch square photographs. How many of these photographs would fill the collage?

4 Each photograph will go inside a frame. The frames come in two colors. Orange frames come in packs of 9 and yellow frames come in packs of 12. Rachel wants to use an equal number of each color. Suppose that she uses all the frames in the packs. What is the least possible number of packs of each colored frame she will need to buy? Explain your answer.

Rubric

Point(s)	Level	My Performance
7–8	4	• Most of my answers are correct. • I showed complete understanding of the concepts. • I used effective and efficient strategies to solve the problems. • I explained my answers and mathematical thinking clearly and completely.
5–6.5	3	• Some of my answers are correct. • I showed adequate understanding of the concepts. • I used effective strategies to solve the problems. • I explained my answers and mathematical thinking clearly.
3–4.5	2	• A few of my answers are correct. • I showed some understanding of the concepts. • I used some effective strategies to solve the problems. • I explained some of my answers and mathematical thinking clearly.
0–2.5	1	• A few of my answers are correct. • I showed little understanding of the concepts. • I used limited effective strategies to solve the problems. • I did not explain my answers and mathematical thinking clearly.

Teacher's Comments

STEAM

Cartesian Diver

The numbers you read and write belong to the decimal number system. This system expresses every number in base 10, meaning each place in a number is occupied by a numeral from 0 to 9. The decimal number system includes negative numbers.

Task

Work in small groups.

The Cartesian diver activity models the principle of buoyancy. It also models changes in vertical distances, as you act on a bottle of water to cause a "diver" to move up or down.

1. The internet offers numerous variations of the Cartesian diver activity. Search several possibilities and select the activity that interests you most.

2. Gather the required materials, which will include an empty 2-liter plastic soda bottle. Use a pen to mark vertical distances, in inches, on the outside of the bottle. Mark the top of the bottle, where its surface is vertical, as zero. Use this vertical number line to observe changes in your diver's position.

3. As you will discover, squeezing and then releasing the water-filled bottle changes the diver's buoyancy. This causes the diver to move down and up. Use negative numbers to represent the diver's positions.

4. Add an extra challenge. Bend the arms of brass fasteners to make small loops. Drop the loops in the bottle, where they will sink to the bottom. Attach paper clips to the diver. Then, squeeze and release to help your diver pick up the fasteners.

Number Lines and Negative Numbers

How cold is an iceberg?

How cold must ocean water be before an iceberg forms? Freshwater freezes at 0°C, but salt water has a lower freezing point. So, icebergs form when the temperature is below 0°C. The temperature in Antarctica, where many icebergs form, is usually below 0°C. Have you experienced temperatures below 0°C? How do you express the temperatures?

In this chapter, you will learn to use negative numbers to represent temperatures below 0°C. You will also learn how to use negative numbers to solve a variety of problems.

? How do you express and compare numbers less than 0?

Comparing numbers to 1,000,000

a Which is greater, 135,000 or 153,000?

Hundred Thousands	Ten Thousands	Thousands	Hundreds	Tens	Ones
1	3	5	0	0	0
1	5	3	0	0	0

The hundred thousands are the same.

Compare the ten thousands.
5 ten thousands are greater than 3 ten thousands.

So, 153,000 is greater than 135,000.
153,000 > 135,000

b Which is less, 261,000 or 264,000?

Hundred Thousands	Ten Thousands	Thousands	Hundreds	Tens	Ones
2	6	1	0	0	0
2	6	4	0	0	0

The hundred thousands and ten thousands are the same.

Compare the thousands.
1 thousand is less than 4 thousands.

So, 261,000 is less than 264,000.
261,000 < 264,000

▶ **Quick Check**

Compare each pair of numbers using > or <.
Use a place-value chart to help you.

1 33,260   34,649

2 51,707   51,077

3 480,000   408,999

4 600,123   605,321

The Number Line

Learning Objectives:
• Represent whole numbers, fractions, and decimals on a number line.
• Interpret and write statements of inequality for two given positive numbers using the symbols > and <.

New Vocabulary
positive number
inequality

THINK

Show 1.625, $1\frac{7}{8}$ and $1\frac{11}{16}$ on a number line. Explain how you can use the number line to find the greatest difference between any of the two numbers. Can you use the same strategy to find the least difference between any two numbers? Why or why not?

ENGAGE

a   Think of two whole numbers which have a difference between 10 and 20. Draw a number line with these two numbers as the end points. Compare the two numbers you have chosen. Which is greater? How does this relate to their positions on the number line? Explain if this is always the case.

b   If the number line is divided into equal intervals such that the marked points between intervals are whole numbers, what is the maximum number of intervals? Explain your answer.

LEARN   Represent whole numbers on a number line and, compare two numbers using > or <

①   The set of whole numbers (0, 1, 2, 3, 4, …) can be represented on a number line. The marked points at equal intervals on the number line represent whole numbers.

A number line can be either horizontal or vertical.
On a horizontal number line, the numbers increase from left to right.
On a vertical number line, the numbers increase from bottom to top.

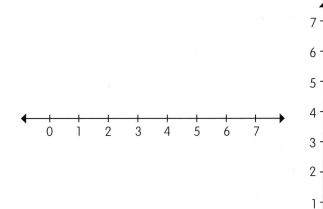

Positive numbers are all the numbers greater than 0. On a horizontal number line, they are to the right of 0. On a vertical number line, they are above 0.

The set of positive numbers also includes positive fractions and decimals.

2 Draw a horizontal number line to represent the whole numbers between 5 and 12.

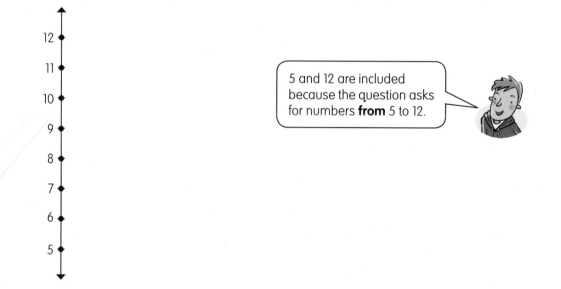

Then, compare 6 and 11 using > or <.
On the number line, 11 is to the right of 6.
So, 11 > 6. This is called a statement of inequality .

5 and 12 are not included because the question asks for numbers **between** 5 and 12.

3 Draw a vertical number line to represent the whole numbers from 5 to 12.

5 and 12 are included because the question asks for numbers **from** 5 to 12.

Then, compare 5 and 12 using > or <.
On the number line, 5 is below 12.
So, 5 < 12.

TRY **Practice representing whole numbers on a number line, and comparing two numbers using > or <**

Draw a horizontal number line to represent each set of whole numbers.

1 Positive whole numbers less than 5

2 Whole numbers greater than 9 but less than 14

Draw a vertical number line to represent each set of whole numbers.

3 Odd numbers between 1 and 10

4 Positive odd numbers < 15

Compare each pair of numbers using > or <. Draw a number line to help you.

5 23 ⬤ 45

6 318 ⬤ 183

7 1,405 ⬤ 541

8 9,909 ⬤ 9,990

Draw a number line with endpoints labeled 0 and 1. What are two ways to divide the number line into equal intervals? Label the numbers on the number line in two ways. Explain your thinking.

LEARN Represent fractions, mixed numbers, and decimals on a number line

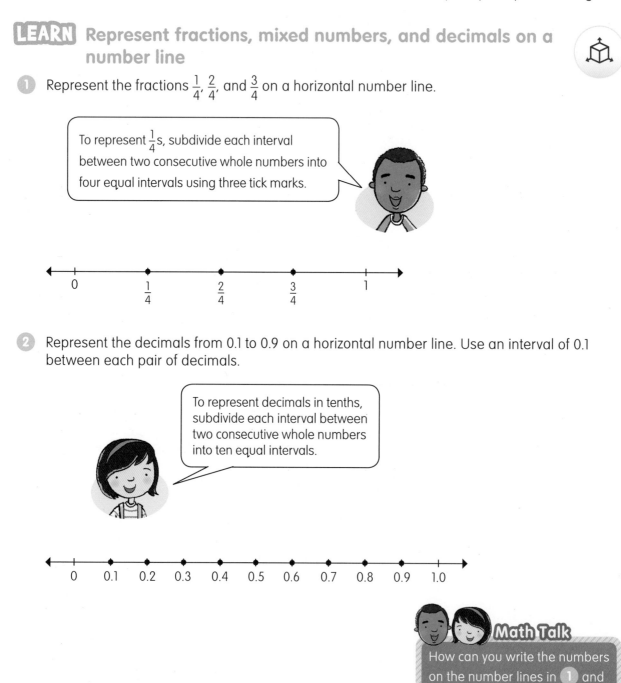

1 Represent the fractions $\frac{1}{4}$, $\frac{2}{4}$, and $\frac{3}{4}$ on a horizontal number line.

> To represent $\frac{1}{4}$s, subdivide each interval between two consecutive whole numbers into four equal intervals using three tick marks.

2 Represent the decimals from 0.1 to 0.9 on a horizontal number line. Use an interval of 0.1 between each pair of decimals.

> To represent decimals in tenths, subdivide each interval between two consecutive whole numbers into ten equal intervals.

Math Talk

How can you write the numbers on the number lines in 1 and 2 in another way? Discuss.

3 Represent the fractions $\frac{1}{5}$, $\frac{2}{5}$, $\frac{3}{5}$, and $\frac{4}{5}$ on a vertical number line.

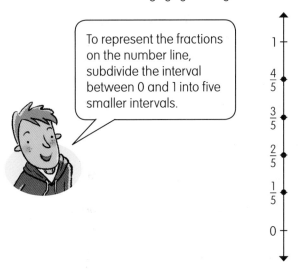

To represent the fractions on the number line, subdivide the interval between 0 and 1 into five smaller intervals.

1

$\frac{4}{5}$

$\frac{3}{5}$

$\frac{2}{5}$

$\frac{1}{5}$

0

4 Represent the decimals 2.0, 2.2, 2.4, 2.6, …, and 4.0 on a vertical number line.

To represent the decimals, subdivide the interval from 2.0 to 4.0 into ten equal intervals of 0.2.

4.0
3.8
3.6
3.4
3.2
3.0
2.8
2.6
2.4
2.2
2.0

To decide how many tick marks to show on the number line, I can count on by 0.2s, marking them as I go:
2.0, 2.2, 2.4, 2.6, 2.8, 3.0, 3.2, 3.4, 3.6, 3.8, and 4.0.

Math Talk
How can you write the numbers on the number lines in 3 and 4 in another way? Discuss.

TRY Practice representing fractions, mixed numbers, and decimals on a number line

Draw a horizontal number line to represent each set of numbers.

1. Fractions and mixed numbers greater than 0 but less than 2, with an interval of $\frac{1}{3}$ between each pair of numbers

2. Decimals between 0 and 1, with an interval of 0.25 between each pair of decimals

3. Decimals greater than 8.0 but less than 12.0, with an interval of 0.8 between each pair of decimals

Draw a vertical number line to represent each set of numbers.

4. Mixed numbers greater than 6 but less than 7, with an interval of $\frac{1}{6}$ between each pair of mixed numbers

5. Positive fractions less than 1, with an interval of $\frac{1}{12}$ between each pair of fractions

6. Decimals greater than 7.2 but less than 9.6, with an interval of 0.3 between each pair of decimals

a   Draw a number line with endpoints labeled 0 and 1. Ask your partner to call out two fractions or decimals between 0 and 1. Mark them on the number line. Which is greater? Explain your answer.

b   Kathy has a set of numbers greater than 2/5 but less than 0.75. Find 3 possible numbers in fractions or in decimals.

LEARN Use > or < to write statements of inequality involving fractions and decimals

1   You can draw a number line to compare two fractions.

Compare $\frac{2}{3}$ and $\frac{5}{6}$. Draw a number line to help you.

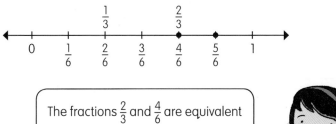

The fractions $\frac{2}{3}$ and $\frac{4}{6}$ are equivalent and are represented by the same point on a number line.

The fraction $\frac{5}{6}$ lies to the right of $\frac{2}{3}$. This means that $\frac{5}{6}$ is greater than $\frac{2}{3}$.

You can write $\frac{5}{6} > \frac{2}{3}$.

2   You can draw a number line to compare two decimals.

Compare 1.3 and 1.15. Draw a number line to help you.

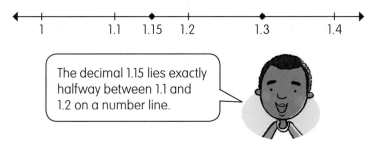

The decimal 1.15 lies exactly halfway between 1.1 and 1.2 on a number line.

The decimal 1.15 lies to the left of 1.3. This means that 1.15 is less than 1.3.
You can write 1.15 < 1.3.

3 You can draw a number line to compare a fraction and a decimal.

Compare 0.62 and $\frac{3}{5}$. Draw a number line to help you.

$\frac{3}{5} = 0.6$

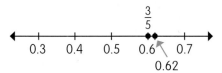

0.6 lies to the left of 0.62.

So, $\frac{3}{5} < 0.62$.

TRY Practice using > or < to write statements of inequality involving fractions and decimals

Fill in the missing decimals on the number line. Then, compare each pair of decimals using > or <.

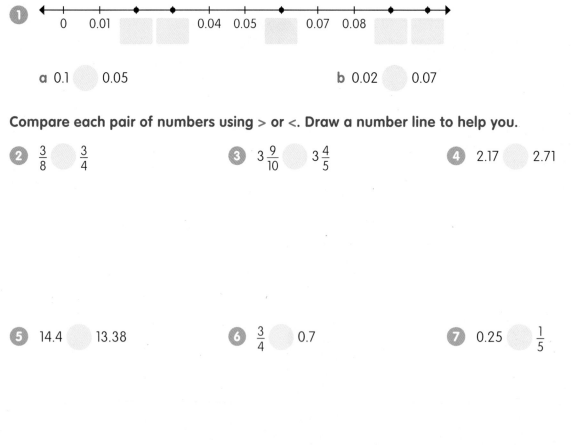

1

0   0.01   0.04 0.05   0.07 0.08

a 0.1 ◯ 0.05   b 0.02 ◯ 0.07

Compare each pair of numbers using > or <. Draw a number line to help you.

2 $\frac{3}{8}$ ◯ $\frac{3}{4}$ **3** $3\frac{9}{10}$ ◯ $3\frac{4}{5}$ **4** 2.17 ◯ 2.71

5 14.4 ◯ 13.38   **6** $\frac{3}{4}$ ◯ 0.7   **7** 0.25 ◯ $\frac{1}{5}$

INDEPENDENT PRACTICE

Complete each number line by filling in the missing values.

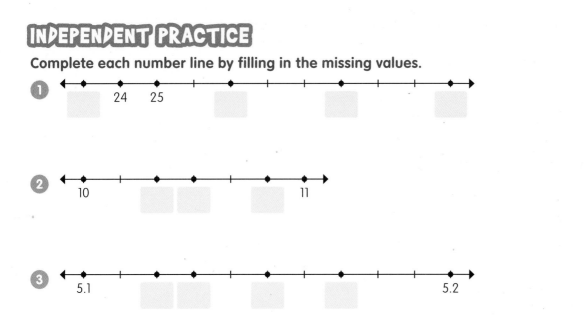

1 [   ]   24   25   [   ]   [   ]   [   ]

2 10   [   ]   [   ]   [   ]   11

3 5.1   [   ]   [   ]   [   ]   [   ]   5.2

Draw a horizontal number line to represent each set of numbers.

4 Odd numbers from 11 to 21

5 Positive whole numbers less than 9

6 Whole numbers greater than 12 but less than 18

7 Mixed numbers between 0 and 2, with an interval of $\frac{1}{3}$ between each pair of numbers

8 Decimals from 7.0 to 8.4, with an interval of 0.2 between each pair of decimals

© 2020 Marshall Cavendish Education Pte Ltd

1 The Number Line   **53**

Draw a vertical number line to represent each set of numbers.

9 Even numbers between 20 and 32

10 Positive whole numbers less than 13

11 Whole numbers greater than 6 but less than 16

12 Positive fractions less than 1, with an interval of $\frac{1}{8}$ between each pair of fractions

13 Decimals between 10 and 15, with an interval of 0.75 between each pair of decimals

Compare each pair of numbers using > or <. Draw a number line to help you.

⑭ $2\frac{3}{7}$ ◯ $\frac{9}{7}$

⑮ $\frac{17}{25}$ ◯ $1\frac{7}{25}$

⑯ $1\frac{4}{5}$ ◯ $1\frac{2}{3}$

⑰ 33.61 ◯ 36.13

⑱ 59.05 ◯ 59.5

⑲ 98.072 ◯ 98.027

Draw a horizontal number line from 2 to 3 to represent each set of numbers.

⑳ $2\frac{4}{5}, 2\frac{3}{20}, 2\frac{1}{2}, 2\frac{11}{20}, 2\frac{9}{20}$

㉑ 2.5, 2.125, 2.375, 2.875

Draw a horizontal number line from 0 to 1 to represent each set of numbers.

㉒ $\frac{1}{3}, \frac{1}{4}, \frac{3}{8}, \frac{3}{4}, \frac{7}{8}, \frac{5}{6}$

㉓ 0.1, 0.25, 0.05, 0.8, 0.75, 0.95

Compare each pair of numbers using > or <. Draw a number line to help you.

24. $0.8 \bigcirc \dfrac{1}{10}$

25. $\dfrac{1}{5} \bigcirc 0.25$

26. $\dfrac{3}{5} \bigcirc 0.3$

27. $0.14 \bigcirc \dfrac{1}{4}$

28. $\dfrac{2}{5} \bigcirc 0.3$

29. $0.64 \bigcirc \dfrac{9}{10}$

30. $0.2 \bigcirc \dfrac{1}{6}$

31. $\dfrac{7}{8} \bigcirc 0.87$

Solve.

32. The wingspan of one butterfly is $1\dfrac{9}{16}$ inches. The wingspan of another butterfly is $1\dfrac{5}{8}$ inches. Write an inequality comparing the two wingspans.

33. For a class project, Jacob made a model of the Empire State Building that was 23.7 centimeters tall. His friend Daniel made a model that was $23\dfrac{3}{5}$ centimeters tall. Whose model was taller? How much taller was it?

Name: _____ Date: _____

Negative Numbers

Learning Objectives:
- Recognize and use negative numbers to represent quantities in real-world situations.
- Represent, compare, and order positive and negative numbers on a number line.

New Vocabulary
negative number
opposite

THINK

Think of a positive number and a negative number and represent them on a number line. Using the number line, write

a a statement about the distance between the two numbers you have chosen,

b an inequality comparing the two numbers.

Next represent their opposites on another number line and repeat the two steps for this new number line.

Compare the statements and the inequalities you have written. What can you observe? Do you think your observations will hold true for other pairs of numbers? Explain.

ENGAGE

Draw a horizontal number line with 10 equal intervals and label the endpoints 0 and 10. Locate the numbers "3" and "4" on your number line, then complete the following statement.

_____ is _____ less than _____.

Now, extend the number line to the left of 0 by 1 interval. What can you say about the number represented by this interval? Give a real-world situation where you might need to make use of this number.

LEARN Recognize and use negative numbers in real-world situations

① Positive and negative numbers can be used to represent real-world quantities.

You can use them to represent temperature readings that are above or below zero, as shown in the table. Notice that you use a negative sign "−" to show negative numbers. You do not need a plus sign "+" to show that a number is positive.

Time	12 A.M.	4 A.M.	8 A.M.	12 P.M.	4 P.M.	8 P.M.
Temperature (°F)	−5	−12	−8	4	10	2

② You can use positive and negative numbers to represent gains or losses. For example, in the game of football, −15 can be used to represent a loss of 15 yards, and 30 can be used to represent a gain of 30 yards.

③ You can use positive and negative numbers to represent values that are above and below a certain value, such as elevations above or depressions below sea level.

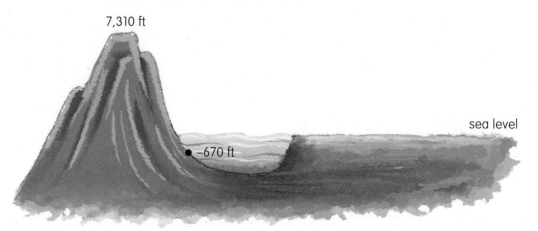

7,310 ft

sea level

−670 ft

For example, a depression that is 670 feet below sea level can be represented by −670 feet, and a mountain peak that is 7,310 feet above sea level can be represented by 7,310 feet.

④ You can use positive and negative numbers to represent debits and credits. A debit is an amount someone owes. A credit is an amount owed to someone. For example, −$180 means a debit of $180, and $79 means a credit of $79.

TRY Practice using negative numbers in real-world situations

Write a positive or negative number to represent each situation.

① 36°F below zero

② A debit of $10,540

③ 29,035 feet below sea level

④ A gain of 45 yards

Fill in each blank.

5 The table shows the elevations of four locations compared to sea level.

Location	New Orleans	Death Valley	Mount Davidson	Pilot Mountain
Elevation (ft)	−8	−282	928	2,421

a New Orleans is 8 feet _____ sea level.

b Mount Davidson is _____ feet above sea level.

c The deepest location among the four locations is _____.

d The highest location among the four locations is _____.

e The location nearest to sea level is _____.

ENGAGE

On a number line, locate 3, 5, and 6. Discuss with your partner how you would represent −3, −5, and −6 on the same number line. How many strategies can you think of?

LEARN Represent negative numbers on a number line

1 Like positive numbers, negative numbers can also be represented on a number line.

On a horizontal number line, the negative numbers are placed to the left of zero. The lesser number always lies to the left of the greater number.

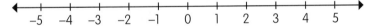

−5 −4 −3 −2 −1 0 1 2 3 4 5

negative numbers

> On a horizontal number line, the numbers become greater as you move to the right, and less as you move to the left.
>
> 4 is greater than 1.
> −4 is less than −1.

On a vertical number line, the negative numbers are placed below zero. The lesser number always lies below the greater number.

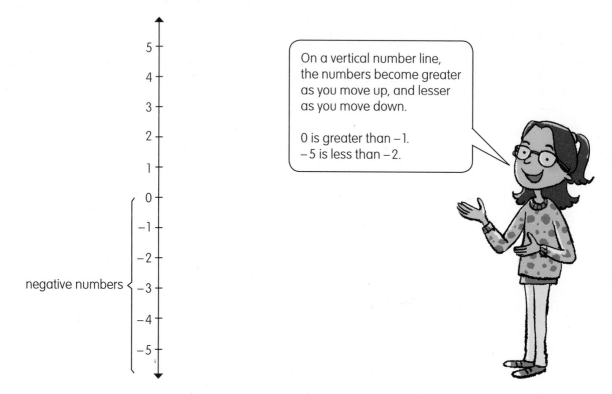

> On a vertical number line, the numbers become greater as you move up, and lesser as you move down.
>
> 0 is greater than −1.
> −5 is less than −2.

Notice that for every positive number, there is a corresponding negative number. For example, for the positive number 3, its corresponding negative number is −3.

On a number line, both 3 and −3 are the same distance from 0, but are on opposite sides of 0. You say that 3 is the opposite of −3 and −3 is the opposite of 3.

> Zero is neither positive nor negative. Zero is its own opposite.

2 Draw a horizontal number line to represent the numbers from 0 to 6 and their opposites.

$$\overleftarrow{\bullet\underset{-6}{\,}\;\bullet\underset{-5}{\,}\;\bullet\underset{-4}{\,}\;\bullet\underset{-3}{\,}\;\bullet\underset{-2}{\,}\;\bullet\underset{-1}{\,}\;\bullet\underset{0}{\,}\;\bullet\underset{1}{\,}\;\bullet\underset{2}{\,}\;\bullet\underset{3}{\,}\;\bullet\underset{4}{\,}\;\bullet\underset{5}{\,}\;\bullet\underset{6}{\,}\;}\overrightarrow{\,}$$

Math Note

Every positive or negative number has an opposite that is the same distance from 0. The opposite of 0 is 0 itself.

© 2020 Marshall Cavendish Education Pte ltd

3 Draw a vertical number line to represent the following set of numbers:
$-26, -29, -30, -32,$ and -34.

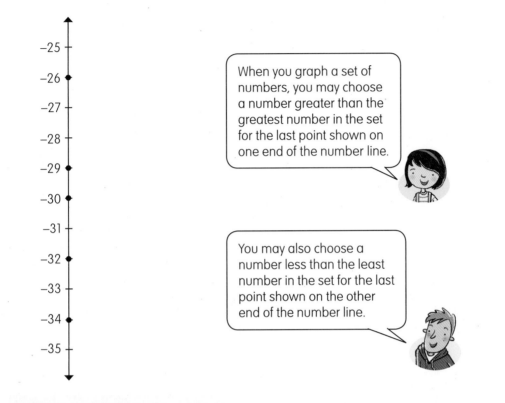

When you graph a set of numbers, you may choose a number greater than the greatest number in the set for the last point shown on one end of the number line.

You may also choose a number less than the least number in the set for the last point shown on the other end of the number line.

TRY **Practice representing negative numbers on a number line**

Draw a horizontal number line to represent each set of numbers.

1 $-13, -11, -9, -6$

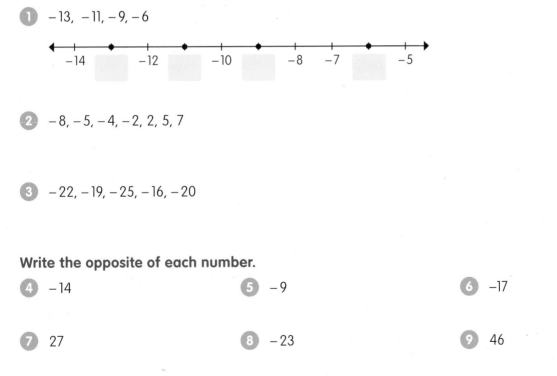

2 $-8, -5, -4, -2, 2, 5, 7$

3 $-22, -19, -25, -16, -20$

Write the opposite of each number.

4 -14

5 -9

6 -17

7 27

8 -23

9 46

ENGAGE

Which number is greater, 24 or 43? How can you use a number line to show this? Discuss with your partner how you can use this information to compare −24 and −43. Then, think of three more negative numbers. Discuss how you would compare these three numbers.

LEARN Use > or < to write statements of inequality involving negative numbers

1 Use the number line to compare each pair of numbers using > or <.

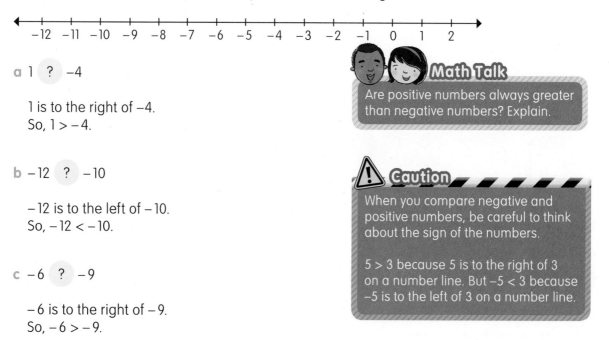

a 1 ? −4

1 is to the right of −4.
So, 1 > −4.

b −12 ? −10

−12 is to the left of −10.
So, −12 < −10.

c −6 ? −9

−6 is to the right of −9.
So, −6 > −9.

Math Talk

Are positive numbers always greater than negative numbers? Explain.

⚠️ **Caution**

When you compare negative and positive numbers, be careful to think about the sign of the numbers.

5 > 3 because 5 is to the right of 3 on a number line. But −5 < 3 because −5 is to the left of 3 on a number line.

Activity Representing negative numbers on a number line and, comparing two numbers using > or <

Work in pairs.

Your teacher will give you and your partner a set of number cards with these numbers on them:

© 2020 Marshall Cavendish Education Pte Ltd

① Draw a number line and divide it into ten equal intervals. Label the endpoints as −100 and 0. Shuffle the cards and place them face down on your table.

② Choose one card each and turn them over. Locate and write the numbers shown on the cards on the number line you drew in ①.

③ Write a statement of inequality for the two numbers you represented on the number line. Check each other's answers.

④ Repeat ② and ③ using other number cards a few more times.

TRY Practice using > or < to write statements of inequality involving negative numbers

Compare each inequality using > or <. Draw a number line to help you.

① −15 ◯ −6

② −20 ◯ −23

③ −30 ◯ −3

④ −19 ◯ 0

⑤ 12 ◯ −31

⑥ −75 ◯ 46

ENGAGE

Nitrogen freezes at −210°C and oxygen freezes at −218.8°C. Which element freezes at a higher temperature? Write an inequality regarding these two temperatures.

LEARN Interpret and explain statements of order involving negative numbers in real-world situations

1. The table shows the lowest recorded temperature in Alaska for each month from July through December.

Month	Jul.	Aug.	Sep.	Oct.	Nov.	Dec.
Temperature (°F)	16	8	−13	−48	−61	−72

September's lowest recorded temperature of −13°F is lower than August's lowest recorded temperature of 8°F.
To compare these two temperatures using an inequality, you can write −13°F < 8°F.

2. The table shows the elevations of some natural features.

Natural Feature	Elevation (From Sea Level)
Death Valley	−282 feet
Lake Assal	−509 feet
Driskill Mountain	535 feet

The elevation of Death Valley, which is −282 feet, is greater than the elevation of Lake Assal, which is −509 feet.
To compare the two elevations using an inequality, you can write −282 ft > −509 ft.

The elevation of Lake Assal, which is −509 feet, is less than the elevation of Driskill Mountain, which has an elevation of 535 feet.
To compare the two elevations using an inequality, you can write −509 ft < 535 ft.

TRY Practice interpreting and explaining statements of order involving negative numbers in real-world situations

Write an inequality for each statement using > or <.

1. 0°C is warmer than −5°C.

2. The elevation of the Valdes Peninsula, which is −131 feet, is less than the elevation of the Caspian Sea, which is −92 feet.

Write a statement to describe each inequality.

3. −61°F < 47°F

4. −520 ft > −893 ft

© 2020 Marshall Cavendish Education Pte Ltd

INDEPENDENT PRACTICE

Write a positive or negative number to represent each situation.

1. 438°C above zero

2. 164°F below zero

3. 8,327 feet below sea level

4. 12,316 feet above sea level

5. A loss of 20 yards

6. A credit of $3,401

Complete each number line by filling in the missing values.

7.

| | | | | −6 | | | | −2 |

8.

| | | | | −30 | | −27 | |

Write the opposite of each number.

9. 8

10. −5

11. 21

12. −29

13. 24

14. −106

Draw a horizontal number line to represent each set of numbers.

15. Negative even numbers from −24 to −10

16. The opposites of the whole numbers from 35 to 45

Draw a vertical number line to represent each set of numbers.

17 Negative odd numbers between −91 and −103

18 Positive and negative even numbers greater than −6 but less than 12

Use the number line to compare each pair of numbers using > or <.

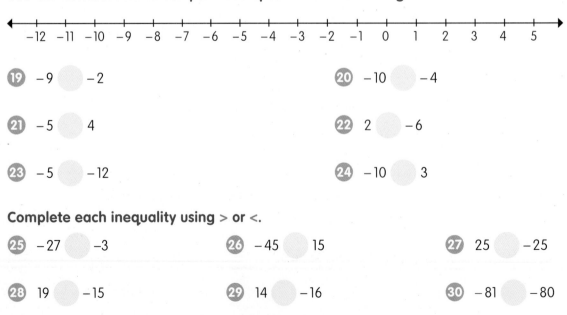

19 −9 ◯ −2

20 −10 ◯ −4

21 −5 ◯ 4

22 2 ◯ −6

23 −5 ◯ −12

24 −10 ◯ 3

Complete each inequality using > or <.

25 −27 ◯ −3

26 −45 ◯ 15

27 25 ◯ −25

28 19 ◯ −15

29 14 ◯ −16

30 −81 ◯ −80

Order the numbers in each set from least to greatest.

31 3, 7, −2, −9, 0, −5

32 −10, 8, 34, −13, 10, −17

Order the numbers in each set from greatest to least.

33 −14, 43, −20, −57, 19, 31

34 98, −101, −76, 125, −92, 113

Answer each question.

35 Name two numbers that are each 2 units away from −7. Give the opposites of these two numbers.

36 **Mathematical Habit 2** Use mathematical reasoning
Is the opposite of a number always negative? Explain your answer.

37 Write an inequality using > or < for the following statement: −22°C is colder than −4°C.

38 | Mathematical Habit 3 | Construct viable arguments

Your friend says that the statement $0 < -15$ is correct. Explain why the statement is incorrect.

39 The elevation of the deepest part of the Pacific Ocean is $-36,200$ feet. The elevation of the deepest part of the Indian Ocean is $-24,442$ feet. Write an inequality to compare the elevations. In which of the two oceans is the deepest part farther from sea level?

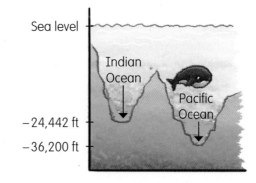

40 The temperature at which a substance boils is called its boiling point. The boiling points of two elements are shown in the table.

Element	Boiling Point (°C)
Oxygen	-183
Nitrogen	-196

Write an inequality to compare the two boiling points. Which element has the greater boiling point?

Write a statement to describe each inequality.

41 -45 ft > -80 ft

42 $-436°F < -271°F$

3 Absolute Value

Learning Objectives:
- Recognize the absolute value of a number as its distance from 0 on the number line.
- Interpret absolute value as magnitude for a positive or negative quantity in a real-world situation.

New Vocabulary
absolute value

THINK

a Tank A and tank B originally had 14 fish each. After one month, tank A had an increase of 4 fish and tank B had an increase of −5 fish. Which tank had a greater change in the number of fish?

b Tank C also originally had 14 fish. After one month, it had a change of 6 fish. What is the possible number of fish in tank C after one month? How would you represent this change on a number line?

ENGAGE

a The current temperature is 18°C. It has dropped by 18°C. What is the new temperature?

b In an experiment, the temperature reading at the start was unknown. The temperature first rose to 18°C, before dropping to −18°C. If the temperature dropped three-quarters as much as it rose, what was the temperature reading at the start?

LEARN Write the absolute value of a number

① The given number line shows the distance of −5 and 5 from 0.

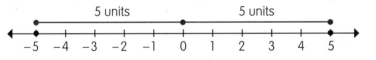

Notice that even though −5 is negative, its distance from 0 is still 5 units.

> The absolute value of a number is the distance of that number from 0 on a number line.
>
> Since distances are always positive, the absolute value of a positive or negative number is always positive.
>
> Absolute value bars are used to show the absolute value of a number.

The absolute value of −5 is 5. You can write $|-5| = 5$.
The absolute value of 5 is 5. You can write $|5| = 5$.

2 Use the number line to find the absolute value of each of the following numbers.

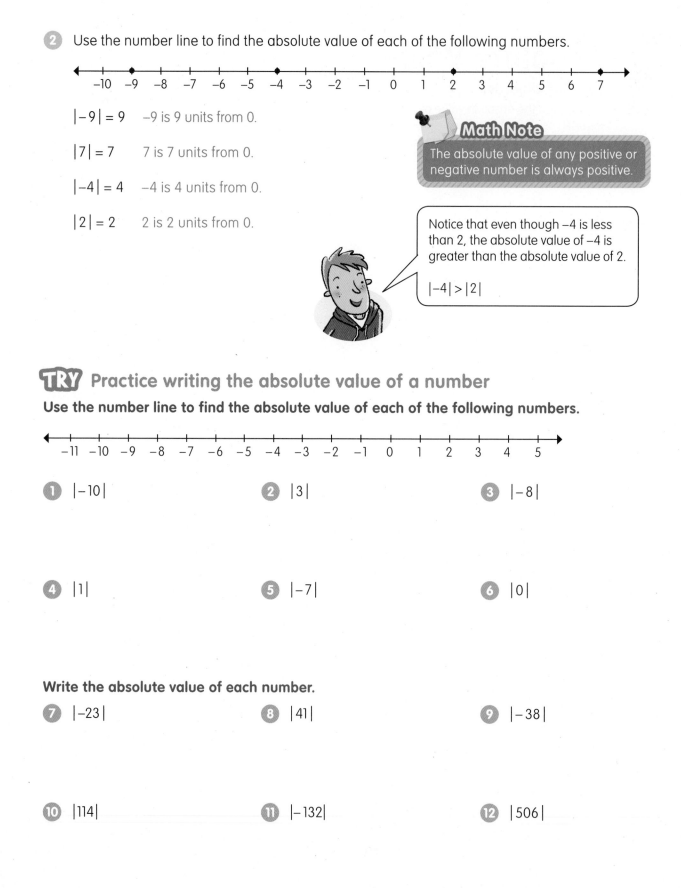

$|-9| = 9$ −9 is 9 units from 0.

$|7| = 7$ 7 is 7 units from 0.

$|-4| = 4$ −4 is 4 units from 0.

$|2| = 2$ 2 is 2 units from 0.

Math Note

The absolute value of any positive or negative number is always positive.

Notice that even though −4 is less than 2, the absolute value of −4 is greater than the absolute value of 2.

$|-4| > |2|$

TRY Practice writing the absolute value of a number

Use the number line to find the absolute value of each of the following numbers.

1 $|-10|$

2 $|3|$

3 $|-8|$

4 $|1|$

5 $|-7|$

6 $|0|$

Write the absolute value of each number.

7 $|-23|$

8 $|41|$

9 $|-38|$

10 $|114|$

11 $|-132|$

12 $|506|$

1 At the end of a game, Team A had – 5 points and Team B had – 8 points. Use absolute values to explain which team ended the game with fewer points.

2 Ben's account balance shows – $216.75. Will's account balance shows $180. Who has more money in the bank? How much more? How do you know?

LEARN Use absolute values to interpret real-world situations

1 The figure shows a section from Mr. Carter's bank account statement.

Date	Deposit	Withdrawal	Balance
May 31			$280
June 15	$40		$320
June 24		$490	– $170

As of May 31, Mr. Carter had $280 in his bank account. On June 24, after he withdrew $490, he had –$170 in his bank account.

$$|-170| = 170$$

This means that Mr. Carter had overdrawn $170.

2 A dog is sitting on a cliff, 35 feet above sea level. A dolphin is swimming 6 feet below sea level. An octopus is moving along the seabed, 40 feet below sea level.

You can use positive and negative numbers to show the elevation of the animals relative to sea level.

Dog's elevation = 35 ft
Dolphin's elevation = – 6 ft
Octopus's elevation = – 40 ft

To decide which animal is farthest from sea level, you do not need to think about whether the animals are above or below sea level. You can use absolute values to compare distances.

Distance of dog from sea level = $|35|$
$= 35$ ft

Distance of dolphin from sea level = $|-6|$
$= 6$ ft

Distance of octopus from sea level = $|-40|$
$= 40$ ft

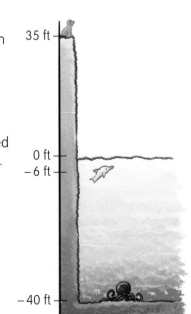

The octopus is the farthest from sea level.

Answer each question.

1. Ms. Parker withdrew $20 from her bank account on Monday, and she withdrew $40 on Wednesday. On Saturday, she deposited $150 in the bank account. Ms. Parker wrote −20 to represent the amount she withdrew on Monday. What numbers should she use to represent the other amounts given above?

2. Mr. Cooper had −$200, Mr. Perez had $180, and Ms. Wilson had −$190 in their bank accounts. Who has the most money in the bank account?

3. At a parking garage, you can park underground or above ground. The lowest part of the underground parking is 40 feet below ground level. The highest part of the parking garage is 20 feet above ground level. The limousine parking area is 23 feet below ground level.

   a Use positive and negative numbers to represent the locations of the three different parts of the parking garage with respect to ground level.

   b Which part of the parking garage is closest to ground level?

INDEPENDENT PRACTICE

Use the number line to find the absolute value of each of the following numbers.

1 $|-11|$

2 $|4|$

3 $|-6|$

Write the absolute value of each number.

4 $|35|$

5 $|-46|$

6 $|-77|$

Complete each inequality using > or <.

7 $|-26|$ _____ $|30|$

8 $|-92|$ _____ $|-114|$

9 $|511|$ _____ $|-500|$

10 $|-707|$ _____ $|-628|$

Answer each question.

11 Two numbers have an absolute value of 16. Which of the two numbers is greater than 12?

12 **Mathematical Habit 6** Use precise mathematical language
Amy graphed a point to represent the absolute value of a number on a number line. If the original number is less than -10, describe all the possible values for the point Amy graphed on the number line. Explain your thinking.

13 The table shows a monthly bank account statement for the period March to July.

Month	Mar.	Apr.	May	Jun.	Jul.
Balance	−$450	−$180	$200	$10	−$240

a For which months was the account overdrawn?

b How much was shown in the bank account in March?

c In which month was the account overdrawn by the greatest amount?

d In which month was the account overdrawn by the least amount?

14 The table shows some locations with their elevations.

Location	Salton City	Desert Shores	Laguna Salada	Bombay Beach
Elevation (ft)	−124.7	−196.9	−32.8	−223.1

a Which location is the closest to sea level?

b Which locations are within 200 feet of sea level?

c How much farther from sea level is Desert Shores than Salton City?

d Write the locations in order from the location that is farthest from sea level to the location that is closest to sea level.

15 The table shows the average surface temperature of some planets.

Planet	Earth	Saturn	Uranus	Mars
Average Surface Temperature (°C)	14	−178	−216	−63

a Which planet has the highest average surface temperature?

b Which planet has the lowest average surface temperature?

c On Earth, the boiling temperature of water at sea level is 100°C. Which planet has an average surface temperature that is closest to this temperature?

d Order the temperatures from lowest to highest.

Mathematical Habit 6 Use precise mathematical language

What is the relationship between whole numbers and negative numbers? Explain your answer.

Problem Solving with Heuristics

Mathematical Habit 4 Using mathematical models

1 You can interpret a negative sign in front of a number as meaning "the opposite of." So, − 3 means the opposite of 3.

   a What number is −(− 3) the opposite of?

   b What number is −(− 3) equal to?

   Draw a number line to explain your answers.

2 On a certain day, the maximum recorded temperature was 15°C and the minimum recorded temperature was − 8°C. How many degrees Celsius is the difference between the recorded maximum and recorded minimum temperatures? Draw a number line to explain your answer.

CHAPTER WRAP-UP

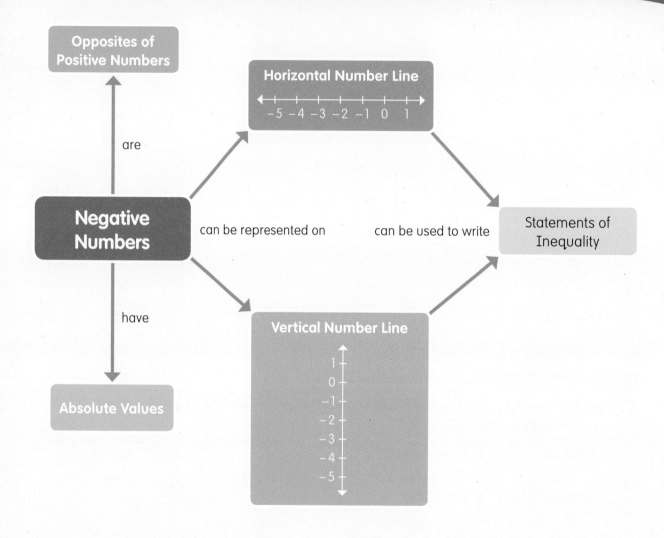

KEY CONCEPTS

- A negative number is the opposite of its corresponding positive number. For example, 6 and −6 are opposites.
- On a horizontal number line, the numbers increase from left to right.
- On a vertical number line, the numbers increase from bottom to top.
- The absolute value of a number is its distance from 0 on a number line.
- The absolute value of a positive or a negative number is a positive value. The absolute value of 0 is 0.
- As the values of negative numbers decrease, their corresponding absolute values increase.

Name: _____ Date: _____

Draw a horizontal number line to represent each set of numbers.

1 Positive whole numbers less than 8

2 Whole numbers greater than 25 but less than 33

3 Mixed numbers from 4 to 6, with an interval of $\frac{1}{4}$ between each pair of numbers

4 Decimals between 3.0 and 3.8, with an interval of 0.2 between each pair of decimals

Write the opposite of each number.

5 -47

6 56

7 69

8 -78

Draw a horizontal number line to represent each set of numbers.

9 −41, −37, −34, −30, −28, −25, −22

10 −133, −129, −126, −122, −119

Draw a vertical number line to represent each set of numbers.

11 −8, −6, −2, 1, 3, 4

12 Negative odd numbers greater than −40 but less than −28

Write a positive or negative number to represent each situation.

13 A deposit of $94

14 181°F below zero

15 The plane's altitude is 23,920 feet

16 The elevation of a sunken ship that is 11 meters beneath the ocean's surface

17 A gain of 35 yards

Complete each inequality using > or <.

18 -14 ⬤ -18

19 17 ⬤ -11

20 -34 ⬤ 23

21 -157 ⬤ -145

Order the numbers in each set.

22 Order the numbers from greatest to least:
15, -14, 7, 2, -5, -6, and -9.

23 Order the numbers from least to greatest:
112, -140, -50, 51, -122, 175, and -182.

Write an inequality for each statement using > or <.

24 −112°C is warmer than −143°C.

25 The lowest recorded temperature yesterday was −4°F, which is colder than today's lowest recorded temperature of 4°F.

Write the absolute value of each number.

26 |79|

27 |−88|

28 |−102|

29 |256|

Complete each inequality using > or <.

30 |−65| ⬤ |−57|

31 |111| ⬤ |−124|

32 |−153| ⬤ |135|

33 |−209| ⬤ |−278|

Answer each question.

34 The Afar Depression is a land formation in Africa. At one location in the Afar Depression, the elevation is −75 meters. At another location, the elevation is −125 meters. Write an inequality to compare the elevations. Which elevation is farther from sea level?

35 The table shows temperature readings taken at the same location at three different times.

Time	12:30 A.M.	4:30 A.M.	8:30 A.M.
Temperature (°C)	−20	−4	12

a At what time was the location the coldest?

b Between 12:30 A.M. and 8:30 A.M., the temperature was always rising. Between which two times shown in the table did the temperature reach 0°C?

36 Company A owes Company B $2,400, and Company C $1,660. Company X owes Company A $2,750, and Company Y owes Company A $1,500.

a Company A writes the number −2,400 to represent the amount the company owes Company B. What numbers should Company A use to represent the other amounts given above?

b Which company owes the most money?

c Which is greater, the amount of money Company A owes, or the amount of money that other companies owe Company A?

Assessment Prep
Answer each question.

37 The picture shows part of a thermometer measuring temperature in degrees Fahrenheit. What is the temperature, in degrees Fahrenheit, shown on the thermometer to the nearest integer? Write your answer in the answer grid.

38 Three values on a number line are labeled x, y, and z.
$x = -z$, $y = -y$, and $z = -7$.
Which number line correctly shows the values of x, y, and z?

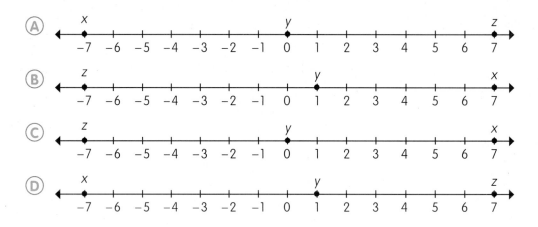

39 Sea level is located at an elevation of 0 meters. Here are elevations of some locations near a valley.

Golf course: −60 m	Hotel: 185 m
Visitor center: 56 m	Tourist attraction: −98 m

Determine whether each location has an elevation above sea level or below sea level. Write each location correctly in the table below.

Locations Above Sea Level	Locations Below Sea Level

© 2020 Marshall Cavendish Education Pte Ltd

Name: _____   Date: _____

Average High Temperatures of Antarctica

The average high temperatures of Antarctica for six months of a certain year are shown in the table below. Use the information to answer the following problems.

Month	Jan.	Mar.	May	Jul.	Sep.	Nov.
Average High Temperature (°F)	−18	−65	−70	−68	−69	−36

1 Place each temperature on the number line below.

$$\xleftarrow{\hspace{1cm}}\!\!|\!\!-\!\!|\!\!-\!\!|\!\!-\!\!|\!\!-\!\!|\!\!-\!\!|\!\!-\!\!|\!\!-\!\!|\!\!-\!\!|\!\!\xrightarrow{\hspace{1cm}}$$

0°F

2 Which month has the lowest average high temperature?

3 Temperatures above 0°F are represented by positive numbers. Temperatures below 0°F are represented by negative numbers. What does 0 represent on this scale?

4 **a** How far from 0°F is May's average high temperature?

b What is the absolute value of May's average high temperature?

5 Use the number line in **1** to explain why May's average high temperature is lower than July's average high temperature. Does this mean it was colder in May than in July? Explain your answer.

6 How many degrees Fahrenheit is the difference between May's average high temperature and November's average high temperature?

Rubric

Point(s)	Level	My Performance
7–8	4	• Most of my answers are correct. • I showed complete understanding of the concepts. • I used effective and efficient strategies to solve the problems. • I explained my answers and mathematical thinking clearly and completely.
5–6.5	3	• Some of my answers are correct. • I showed adequate understanding of the concepts. • I used effective strategies to solve the problems. • I explained my answers and mathematical thinking clearly.
3–4.5	2	• A few of my answers are correct. • I showed some understanding of the concepts. • I used some effective strategies to solve the problems. • I explained some of my answers and mathematical thinking clearly.
0–2.5	1	• A few of my answers are correct. • I showed little understanding of the concepts. • I used limited effective strategies to solve the problems. • I did not explain my answers and mathematical thinking clearly.

Teacher's Comments

Chapter 3

Fractions and Decimals

What do architects do?

Architects design buildings, and they have a lot to think about. They must choose all of the materials they need to build a structure from the ground up. They calculate quantities of every item, from the smallest nail to the largest sheet of steel.

Many buildings have wooden skeletons. The vertical bones in the skeleton are called studs. Architects figure out how many studs they need and how far apart they should stand. They must be the right size and in the right quantity to support a building. Calculations often include fractions and decimals.

In this chapter, you will work with fractions and decimals, and learn skills that you will find useful in solving many real-world problems.

How do you add, subtract, multiply, or divide fractions and decimals?

Name: _____ Date: _____

Adding and subtracting decimals

a
```
    3 . 8
  + 2 . 1
  -------
    5 . 9
```

b
```
    1   1
    7 . 8 6
  + 4 . 7 5
  ---------
  1 2 . 6 1
```

c
```
    8 . 2 6
  - 7 . 0 3
  ---------
    1 . 2 3
```

d
```
    5  10 10
    6 . 1 0
  - 2 . 3 4
  ---------
    3 . 7 6
```

▶ **Quick Check**
Add or subtract.

1 5.3 + 6.49

2 6.51 − 2.03

3 9.62 + 7.08

4 8.4 − 7.52

Expressing improper fractions as mixed numbers

$\frac{16}{5} = \frac{15}{5} + \frac{1}{5}$ Rewrite as a sum.

$= 3 + \frac{1}{5}$ Write the improper fraction as a whole number.

$= 3\frac{1}{5}$ Write the sum as a mixed number.

▶ **Quick Check**
Express each improper fraction as a mixed number in simplest form.

5 $\frac{19}{3}$

6 $\frac{26}{4}$

7 $\frac{30}{7}$

8 $\frac{38}{5}$

9 $\frac{50}{8}$

10 $\frac{69}{9}$

Expressing mixed numbers as improper fractions

$2\frac{5}{6} = 2 + \frac{5}{6}$ Rewrite as a sum.

$= \frac{12}{6} + \frac{5}{6}$ Write the whole number as a fraction.

$= \frac{17}{6}$ Write the sum as an improper fraction.

▶ Quick Check
Express each mixed number as an improper fraction.

⑪ $3\frac{1}{4}$

⑫ $4\frac{3}{7}$

⑬ $8\frac{5}{9}$

Multiplying fractions by fractions

▶ Method 1

$\frac{3}{4} \times \frac{2}{9} = \frac{3 \times 2}{4 \times 9}$ Multiply the numerators.
Multiply the denominators.

$= \frac{6}{36}$ Simplify the products.

$= \frac{1}{6}$ Write the fraction in simplest form.

▶ Method 2

$\frac{3}{4} \times \frac{2}{9} = \frac{\overset{1}{3}}{\underset{2}{4}} \times \frac{\overset{1}{2}}{\underset{3}{9}}$ Divide 3 and 9 by their common factor, 3
Divide 2 and 4 by their common factor, 2.

$= \frac{1 \times 1}{2 \times 3}$ Multiply the numerators.
Multiply the denominators.

$= \frac{1}{6}$ Simplify the products.

▶ Quick Check
Multiply. Write each product in simplest form.

⑭ $\frac{2}{5} \times \frac{7}{8}$

⑮ $\frac{5}{9} \times \frac{6}{7}$

16. $\dfrac{10}{11} \times \dfrac{33}{5}$

17. $\dfrac{8}{7} \times \dfrac{35}{12}$

Dividing fractions by a whole number

▶ **Method 1**

$\dfrac{2}{3} \div 4 = \dfrac{1}{\underset{2}{4}} \times \dfrac{\overset{1}{2}}{3}$ Write as a multiplication expression.
Divide 2 and 4 by their common factor, 2.

$= \dfrac{1}{6}$ Multiply.

▶ **Method 2**

$\dfrac{2}{3} \div 4 = \dfrac{\overset{1}{2}}{3} \times \dfrac{1}{\underset{2}{4}}$ Write as a multiplication expression.
Divide 2 and 4 by their common factor, 2.

$= \dfrac{1}{6}$ Multiply.

▶ **Quick Check**

Divide. Write each quotient in simplest form.

18. $\dfrac{3}{4} \div 6$

19. $\dfrac{4}{5} \div 10$

Dividing whole numbers by a unit fraction

$2 \div \dfrac{1}{4} = 2 \times 4$ Write as a multiplication expression.

$= 8$ Multiply.

▶ **Quick Check**

Divide. Write each quotient in simplest form.

20. $5 \div \dfrac{1}{3}$

21. $8 \div \dfrac{1}{8}$

1 Dividing Fractions

Learning Objective:
• Divide a fraction, whole number, or mixed number by a fraction or a mixed number.

💡 THINK

Lily has $\frac{3}{4}$ of a rectangular paper strip. She cuts it into two parts. One part is $\frac{3}{20}$ of the whole paper strip. How many pieces must she cut the other part so that each piece is $\frac{3}{20}$ of the whole paper strip?

ENGAGE

Show how you find the number of two-fifths in 2 wholes using . Draw a picture to record your thinking. How does your answer help you to predict the number of two-fifths in 4 wholes? What about the number of two-fifths in 5 wholes? Explain your thinking.

LEARN Divide a whole number by a proper fraction

1 Some children shared 4 granola bars. Each child had $\frac{2}{3}$ of a bar.
How many children were there?

Number of children = $4 \div \frac{2}{3}$

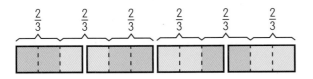

> How many two-thirds are in 4 wholes?

Number of two-thirds in 2 wholes = 3

Number of two-thirds in 1 whole = $3 \div 2$
$$= \frac{3}{2}$$

Number of two-thirds in 4 wholes = $4 \times \frac{3}{2}$

$4 \div \frac{2}{3} = 4 \times \frac{3}{2}$
$$= \frac{12}{2}$$
$$= 6$$

There were 6 children.

> $\frac{2}{3}$ and $\frac{3}{2}$ are reciprocals. Dividing by a fraction is the same as multiplying by its reciprocal. So, dividing by $\frac{2}{3}$ is the same as multiplying by $\frac{3}{2}$.

2 What is $5 \div \frac{2}{3}$?

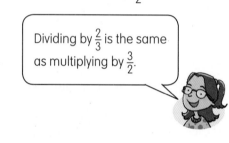

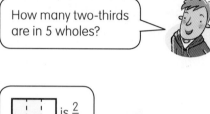
How many two-thirds are in 5 wholes?

Number of two-thirds in 2 wholes = 3

Number of two-thirds in 1 whole = 3 ÷ 2

$$= \frac{3}{2}$$

Number of two-thirds in 5 wholes = $5 \times \frac{3}{2}$

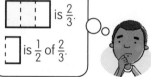

$5 \div \frac{2}{3} = 5 \times \frac{3}{2}$

$$= \frac{15}{2}$$

$$= 7\frac{1}{2}$$

Dividing by $\frac{2}{3}$ is the same as multiplying by $\frac{3}{2}$.

Activity Dividing a whole number by a proper fraction

Work in pairs.

Activity 1

① Use 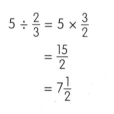 to find how many three-quarters there are in 3 wholes.

Then, find $3 \div \frac{3}{4}$.

Example:

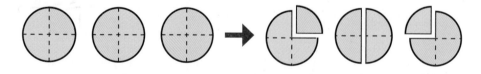

② Ask your partner to find $3 \times \frac{4}{3}$.

③ Compare your answers in ① and ②. What do you notice?

④ Trade places. Repeat ① to ③ to find how many two-fifths there are in 2 wholes.

Activity 2

1. Use 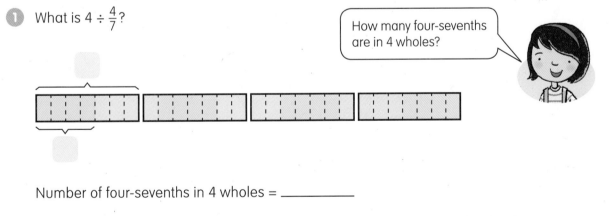 to find how many three-quarters there are in 4 wholes.
   Then, find $4 \div \frac{3}{4}$.

2. Ask your partner to find $4 \times \frac{4}{3}$.

3. Compare your answers in ① and ②. What do you notice?

4. Trade places. Repeat ① to ③ to find how many two-fifths there are in 3 wholes.

TRY **Practice dividing a whole number by a proper fraction**

Fill in each blank.

1. What is $4 \div \frac{4}{7}$?

> How many four-sevenths are in 4 wholes?

Number of four-sevenths in 4 wholes = _____

$4 \div \frac{4}{7}$ = _____

2 What is $7 \div \frac{3}{4}$?

How many three-quarters are in 7 wholes?

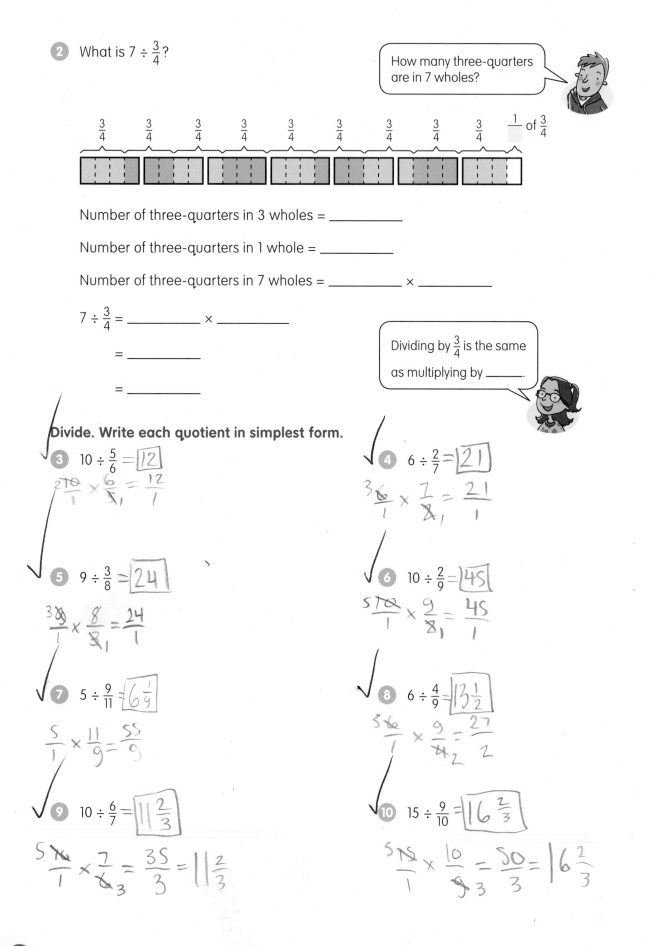

$\frac{3}{4}$ $\frac{3}{4}$ $\frac{3}{4}$ $\frac{3}{4}$ $\frac{3}{4}$ $\frac{3}{4}$ $\frac{3}{4}$ $\frac{3}{4}$ $\frac{3}{4}$ $\frac{1}{}$ of $\frac{3}{4}$

Number of three-quarters in 3 wholes = _____

Number of three-quarters in 1 whole = _____

Number of three-quarters in 7 wholes = _____ × _____

$7 \div \frac{3}{4}$ = _____ × _____

= _____

= _____

Dividing by $\frac{3}{4}$ is the same

as multiplying by _____.

Divide. Write each quotient in simplest form.

3 $10 \div \frac{5}{6} = \boxed{12}$

$\frac{\overset{2}{\cancel{10}}}{1} \times \frac{6}{\cancel{5}_1} = \frac{12}{1}$

4 $6 \div \frac{2}{7} = \boxed{21}$

$\frac{\overset{3}{\cancel{6}}}{1} \times \frac{7}{\cancel{2}_1} = \frac{21}{1}$

5 $9 \div \frac{3}{8} = \boxed{24}$

$\frac{\overset{3}{\cancel{9}}}{1} \times \frac{8}{\cancel{3}_1} = \frac{24}{1}$

6 $10 \div \frac{2}{9} = \boxed{45}$

$\frac{\overset{5}{\cancel{10}}}{1} \times \frac{9}{\cancel{2}_1} = \frac{45}{1}$

7 $5 \div \frac{9}{11} = \boxed{6\frac{1}{9}}$

$\frac{5}{1} \times \frac{11}{9} = \frac{55}{9}$

8 $6 \div \frac{4}{9} = \boxed{13\frac{1}{2}}$

$\frac{\overset{3}{\cancel{6}}}{1} \times \frac{9}{\cancel{4}_2} = \frac{27}{2}$

9 $10 \div \frac{6}{7} = \boxed{11\frac{2}{3}}$

$\frac{\overset{5}{\cancel{10}}}{1} \times \frac{7}{\cancel{6}_3} = \frac{35}{3} = 11\frac{2}{3}$

10 $15 \div \frac{9}{10} = \boxed{16\frac{2}{3}}$

$\frac{\overset{5}{\cancel{15}}}{1} \times \frac{10}{\cancel{9}_3} = \frac{50}{3} = 16\frac{2}{3}$

Show how you find the number of eighths in $\frac{3}{4}$ using manipulatives or a picture. Now, find the number of thirds in $\frac{5}{6}$. Draw a picture to explain your thinking.

Divide a proper fraction by a unit fraction

1 Vijay had $\frac{2}{3}$ of a pizza. He cut it into equal slices. Each slice was $\frac{1}{6}$ of the whole pizza. How many equal slices did Vijay cut?

How many sixths are in $\frac{2}{3}$?

$$\frac{2}{3} \div \frac{1}{6} = 4$$

Vijay cut the pizza into 4 equal pieces.

2 How many quarters are in $\frac{5}{8}$?

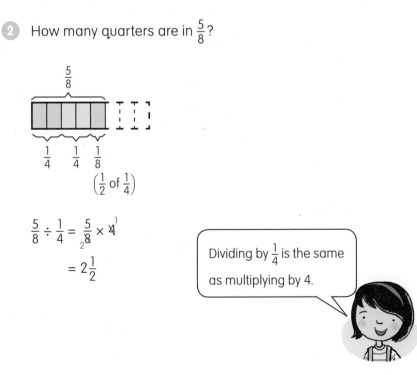

$$\frac{5}{8} \div \frac{1}{4} = \frac{5}{\underset{2}{8}} \times \overset{1}{4}$$
$$= 2\frac{1}{2}$$

Dividing by $\frac{1}{4}$ is the same as multiplying by 4.

Activity Dividing a proper fraction by a unit fraction

Work in pairs.

Activity 1

① Fold a rectangular strip of paper into quarters. Use your model to find how many quarters there are in $\frac{1}{2}$. Then, find $\frac{1}{2} \div \frac{1}{4}$.

Example:

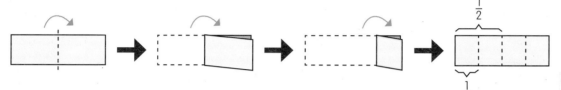

② Ask your partner to find $\frac{1}{2} \times 4$.

③ Compare your answers in ① and ②. What do you notice?

④ Trade places. Repeat ① to ③ to find how many eighths there are in $\frac{1}{2}$.

Activity 2

① Fold a rectangular strip of paper into quarters. Use your model to find how many halves there are in $\frac{3}{4}$. Then, find $\frac{3}{4} \div \frac{1}{2}$.

② Ask your partner to find $\frac{3}{4} \times 2$.

③ Compare your answers in ① and ②. What do you notice?

④ Trade places. Repeat ① to ③ to find how many thirds there are in $\frac{5}{6}$.

TRY Practice dividing a proper fraction by a unit fraction

Fill in each blank.

1 Jack's neighbor gave him $\frac{1}{3}$ of a pie. Jack cut the pie into small slices. Each slice is $\frac{1}{6}$ of the original pie. How many small slices did Jack cut?

How many sixths are in $\frac{1}{3}$?

_____ ÷ _____ = _____

Jack cut the pie into _____ small slices.

2 How many thirds are in $\frac{1}{2}$?

$$\frac{1}{2}$$

$$\frac{1}{3} \quad \frac{1}{6}$$

$$\left(\frac{1}{2} \text{ of } \frac{1}{3}\right)$$

_____ ÷ _____ = _____ × _____

= _____

Dividing by $\frac{1}{3}$ is the same as multiplying by _____.

Divide. Write each quotient in simplest form.

3 $\frac{2}{3} \div \frac{1}{9} = \boxed{6}$

$\frac{2}{\cancel{3}} \times \frac{\cancel{9}^{3}}{1} = \frac{6}{1}$

4 $\frac{3}{4} \div \frac{1}{12} = \boxed{9}$

$\frac{3}{\cancel{4}^{1}} \times \frac{\cancel{12}^{3}}{1} = \frac{9}{1}$

5 $\frac{4}{9} \div \frac{1}{7} = \boxed{3\frac{1}{9}}$

$\frac{4}{9} \times \frac{7}{1} = \frac{28}{9} = 3\frac{1}{9}$

6 $\frac{6}{7} \div \frac{1}{5} = \boxed{4\frac{2}{7}}$

$\frac{6}{7} \times \frac{5}{1} = \frac{30}{7} = 4\frac{2}{7}$

Look at the two expressions:

$$\frac{2}{3} \div \frac{2}{9}$$

$$\frac{4}{5} \div \frac{3}{5}$$

Use manipulatives or visualization to find the answers.
What is the same about their solutions? What is different? Explain your reasoning.

LEARN Divide a proper fraction by a proper fraction

1. Alexa had $\frac{3}{4}$ of a waffle. She cut it into equal pieces. Each piece was $\frac{3}{8}$ of the waffle.

How many equal pieces did Alexa cut?

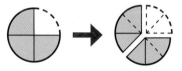

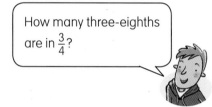

How many three-eighths are in $\frac{3}{4}$?

The model shows that there are 2 three-eighths in $\frac{3}{4}$.

Another way to divide is to multiply by the reciprocal of the divisor.

$$\frac{3}{4} \div \frac{3}{8} = \frac{3}{4} \times \frac{8}{3}$$

$$= \frac{\overset{1}{\cancel{3}}}{\underset{1}{\cancel{4}}} \times \frac{\overset{2}{\cancel{8}}}{\underset{1}{\cancel{3}}}$$

$$= 2$$

Dividing by $\frac{3}{8}$ is the same as multiplying by $\frac{8}{3}$.

Alexa cut the waffle into 2 equal pieces.

2. How many two-sevenths are in $\frac{5}{7}$?

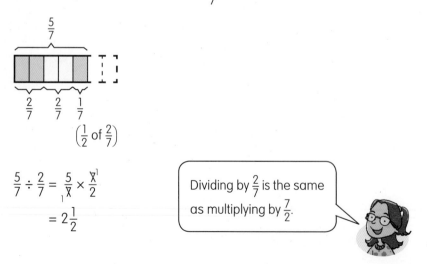

$$\left(\frac{1}{2} \text{ of } \frac{2}{7}\right)$$

$$\frac{5}{7} \div \frac{2}{7} = \frac{5}{\underset{1}{\cancel{7}}} \times \frac{\overset{1}{\cancel{7}}}{2}$$

$$= 2\frac{1}{2}$$

Dividing by $\frac{2}{7}$ is the same as multiplying by $\frac{7}{2}$.

Work in pairs.

① Find each quotient.

a $4 \div \frac{2}{5}$ and $\frac{2}{5} \div 4$

b $\frac{1}{4} \div \frac{2}{3}$ and $\frac{2}{3} \div \frac{1}{4}$

c $\frac{4}{5} \div \frac{3}{10}$ and $\frac{3}{10} \div \frac{4}{5}$

d $\frac{5}{8} \div \frac{3}{4}$ and $\frac{3}{4} \div \frac{5}{8}$

② What do you observe about the product of each pair of quotients?

③ Given that $\frac{6}{7} \div 9 = \frac{2}{21}$ and $\frac{10}{11} \div \frac{5}{6} = \frac{12}{11}$, find each of the following quotients mentally.

a $9 \div \frac{6}{7}$

b $\frac{5}{6} \div \frac{10}{11}$

④ **Mathematical Habit 6** **Use precise mathematical language**
Explain the meaning of each division statement in words.

a $4 \div \frac{2}{5}$ and $\frac{2}{5} \div 4$

b $\frac{1}{4} \div \frac{2}{3}$ and $\frac{2}{3} \div \frac{1}{4}$

TRY Practice dividing a proper fraction by a proper fraction

Fill in each blank.

1   David had $\frac{8}{9}$ of a fruit tart and some plates. He put $\frac{2}{9}$ of the fruit tart on each plate.

How many plates did he have?

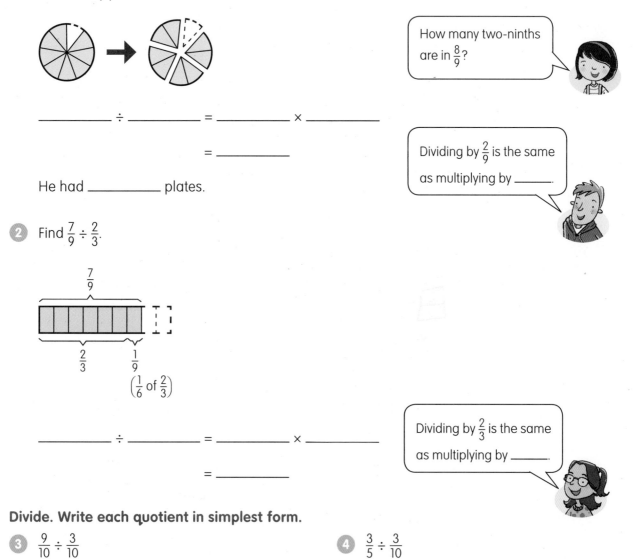

How many two-ninths are in $\frac{8}{9}$?

_____ ÷ _____ = _____ × _____

= _____

He had _____ plates.

Dividing by $\frac{2}{9}$ is the same as multiplying by _____.

2   Find $\frac{7}{9} \div \frac{2}{3}$.

$\frac{7}{9}$

$\frac{2}{3}$ $\frac{1}{9}$

$\left(\frac{1}{6} \text{ of } \frac{2}{3}\right)$

Dividing by $\frac{2}{3}$ is the same as multiplying by _____.

_____ ÷ _____ = _____ × _____

= _____

Divide. Write each quotient in simplest form.

3   $\frac{9}{10} \div \frac{3}{10}$

4   $\frac{3}{5} \div \frac{3}{10}$

Real-World Problems: Fractions

Learning Objective:
• Solve real-world problems involving fractions.

THINK

Ashley, Bryan, and Caleb share a bag of tokens. Ashley and Bryan receive $\frac{2}{5}$ of the bag of tokens. Bryan and Caleb receive $\frac{7}{10}$ of the bag of tokens. Caleb receives twice as many tokens as Ashley. How many times as many tokens as Bryan does Caleb receive?

ENGAGE

Finish the story:
Julian baked 9 apple pies. He cut the pies and gave each child an equal amount. Each child received $\boxed{?}$ of an apple pie.

Draw a bar model to show the number of children who received a slice of pie. Exchange your bar model with a partner and identify the division expression represented by the bar model.

LEARN Divide a whole number by a proper fraction to solve real-world problems

1. A chef cooks 12 pounds of pasta each day. She uses $\frac{3}{16}$ pound of pasta for each serving she prepares. How many servings of pasta does she prepare each day?

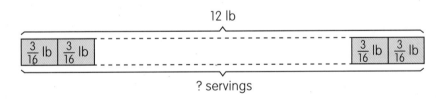

12 lb

$\frac{3}{16}$ lb $\frac{3}{16}$ lb ... $\frac{3}{16}$ lb $\frac{3}{16}$ lb

? servings

$12 \div \frac{3}{16} = 12 \times \frac{16}{3}$ Rewrite using the reciprocal of the divisor.

       $= 64$ Multiply.

She prepares 64 servings of pasta each day.

Check
$64 \times \frac{3}{16} = 12$. The answer is correct.

TRY Practice dividing a whole number by a proper fraction to solve real-world problems

Solve.

1 Ms. Martin bought 6 loaves of bread. She cut each loaf into an equal number of slices for a group of children. Each slice was $\frac{3}{10}$ of a loaf of bread, and each child received one slice. How many children were in the group?

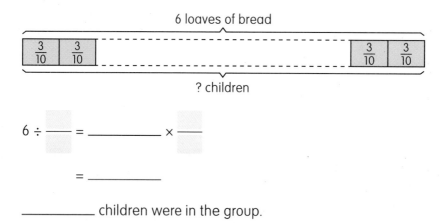

6 loaves of bread

? children

$$6 \div \underline{\hspace{1cm}} = \underline{\hspace{2cm}} \times \underline{\hspace{1cm}}$$

$$= \underline{\hspace{2cm}}$$

_____ children were in the group.

ENGAGE

Create a story about this bar model. Use proper fractions and/or unit fractions in your story.

Write the expression represented by the bar model. Share your story and expression with your partner.

LEARN Divide a proper fraction by a unit fraction to solve real-world problems

1 A plank is $\frac{4}{5}$ meter in length. A worker cuts it into some pieces, each $\frac{1}{10}$ meter long. How many pieces did he cut the plank into?

$\frac{4}{5}$ m

? pieces

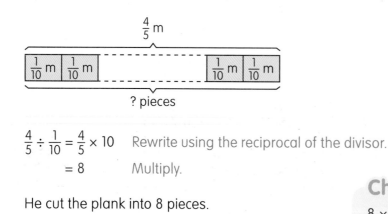

$\frac{4}{5} \div \frac{1}{10} = \frac{4}{5} \times 10$ Rewrite using the reciprocal of the divisor.

$\quad\quad\quad = 8$ Multiply.

He cut the plank into 8 pieces.

Check

$8 \times \frac{1}{10} = \frac{4}{5}$ m. The answer is correct.

TRY Practice dividing a proper fraction by a unit fraction to solve real-world problems

Solve.

1 Shanti had $\frac{2}{3}$ liter of water. She used the water to fill a few glasses completely. The capacity of each glass is $\frac{1}{9}$ liter. How many glasses of water did Shanti fill?

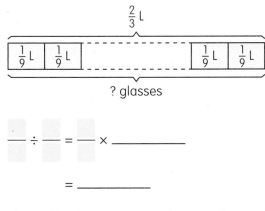

$$\frac{}{} \div \frac{}{} = \frac{}{} \times \underline{\hspace{2cm}}$$

$$= \underline{\hspace{2cm}}$$

Shanti filled _____ glasses of water.

ENGAGE

Dylan has a piece of paper. He colors $\frac{1}{2}$ of the paper red and $\frac{2}{3}$ of the remaining paper blue. Next, Dylan divides the last part into 2 equal pieces. He colors one piece yellow and the other piece green. On a piece of paper, recreate Dylan's model. What questions could you ask about the colored pieces? Trade your questions with a partner and answer their questions.

LEARN Divide a fraction by a whole number to solve multi-step real-world problems

1 Each month, Mr. Lee spends $\frac{1}{3}$ of his salary, saves $\frac{3}{8}$ of the remainder, and divides the rest equally into college savings programs for his 3 children.

a What fraction of Mr. Lee's salary goes into each college savings program?

b Mr. Lee's salary is $5,400. How much money goes into each college savings program each month?

STEP 1 Understand the problem.

> What fraction of Mr. Lee's salary does he spend each month? What fraction of his salary is left? What fraction of the remainder does he save? What fraction of the remainder goes into each college savings program? What do I need to find?

STEP 2 Think of a plan.
I can draw a bar model.

STEP 3 Carry out the plan.

▶ **Method 1**

spending   savings   3 college savings programs

a $\frac{5}{12} \div 3 = \frac{5}{12} \times \frac{1}{3}$

$= \frac{5}{36}$

$\frac{5}{36}$ of Mr. Lee's salary goes into each college savings program.

b Mr. Lee's salary = $5,400

$\frac{1}{36}$ of Mr. Lee's salary = $5,400 \div 36$

$= \$150$

$\frac{5}{36}$ of Mr. Lee's salary = $\$150 \times 5$

$= \$750$

$750 goes into each college savings program each month.

▶ **Method 2**

a $\frac{{}^1\cancel{3}}{\cancel{8}_4} \times \frac{\cancel{8}^1}{\cancel{3}_1} = \frac{1}{4}$

Mr. Lee saves $\frac{1}{4}$ of his salary.

$1 - \frac{1}{3} - \frac{1}{4} = 1 - \frac{4}{12} - \frac{3}{12}$

$= \frac{5}{12}$

$\frac{5}{12}$ of Mr. Lee's salary goes into 3 college savings program.

$\frac{5}{12} \div 3 = \frac{5}{12} \times \frac{1}{3}$

$= \frac{5}{36}$

$\frac{5}{36}$ of Mr. Lee's salary goes into each college savings program.

b $\frac{5}{36} \times \$5,400 = \$750$

$750 goes into each college savings program each month.

Check the answer.
I can work backwards to check my answer.

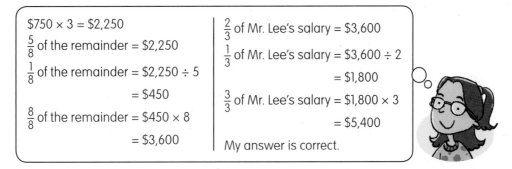

$750 \times 3 = $2,250$

$\frac{5}{8}$ of the remainder = $2,250

$\frac{1}{8}$ of the remainder = $2,250 ÷ 5

$= 450

$\frac{8}{8}$ of the remainder = $450 × 8

$= $3,600$

$\frac{2}{3}$ of Mr. Lee's salary = $3,600

$\frac{1}{3}$ of Mr. Lee's salary = $3,600 ÷ 2

$= $1,800$

$\frac{3}{3}$ of Mr. Lee's salary = $1,800 × 3

$= $5,400$

My answer is correct.

TRY Practice dividing a fraction by a whole number to solve multi-step real-world problems

Solve.

1. Taylor buys 1 kilogram of beans and gives away $\frac{1}{4}$ kilogram. $\frac{1}{6}$ of the remaining beans are green and the rest are red. Taylor packs the red beans equally into 10 packs.

a What is the mass of red beans in each pack? Express your answer as a fraction in simplest form.

▶ **Method 1**

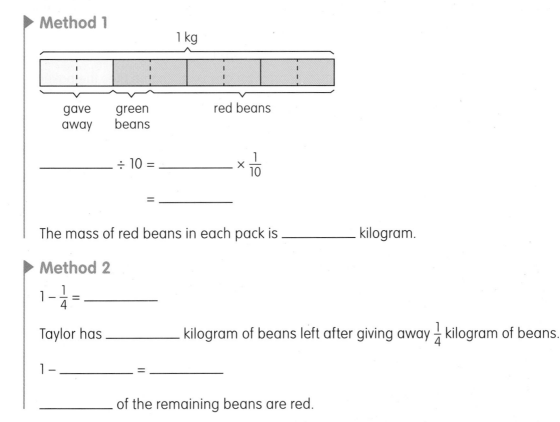

1 kg

gave away   green beans   red beans

_____ ÷ 10 = _____ × $\frac{1}{10}$

= _____

The mass of red beans in each pack is _____ kilogram.

▶ **Method 2**

$1 - \frac{1}{4} =$ _____

Taylor has _____ kilogram of beans left after giving away $\frac{1}{4}$ kilogram of beans.

$1 -$ _____ = _____

_____ of the remaining beans are red.

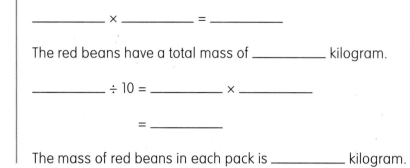

_____ × _____ = _____

The red beans have a total mass of _____ kilogram.

_____ ÷ 10 = _____ × _____

= _____

The mass of red beans in each pack is _____ kilogram.

b Taylor wants to sell 2 kilograms of red beans. How many of packs of red beans does she need?

_____ ÷ _____ = _____ × _____

= _____

She needs _____ packs of red beans.

ENGAGE

a A baker bought 20 sticks of butter. She used $\frac{3}{5}$ of the butter on Saturday. On Sunday, she baked 12 pies using the remaining butter. Draw a model to show all the information. Explain how you can use your model to find the amount of butter used for each pie.

b Discuss with your partner how you would find how many of the same pies the baker could bake with 18 sticks of butter.

LEARN Divide a whole number by a fraction to solve multi-step real-world problems

① A school district buys 96 packages of highlighters. $\frac{3}{8}$ of the packages go to the English department, and the rest go to the Math department. The Math department gives $\frac{2}{3}$ of each package to each Math teacher working in the school district.

96 packages

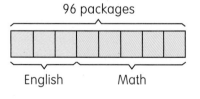

English   Math

a How many packages go to the Math department?

▶ **Method 1**

8 units = 96

1 unit = 96 ÷ 8

= 12

5 units = 12 × 5

= 60

▶ **Method 2**

$1 - \frac{3}{8} = \frac{5}{8}$

$\frac{5}{8}$ of the packages go to the Math department.

$\frac{5}{\overset{}{8}_1} \times \overset{12}{\cancel{96}} = 60$

60 packages go to the Math department.

b How many Math teachers will receive highlighters?

$60 \div \frac{2}{3} = \overset{30}{\cancel{60}} \times \frac{3}{\cancel{2}_1}$

$= 90$

90 Math teachers will receive highlighters.

2 Kaylee has 9 sticks of modeling clay. She cuts the sticks into thirds and shares the pieces equally with some children. Each child receives $\frac{2}{3}$ of a stick.

a How many children are there altogether?

$9 \div \frac{2}{3} = 9 \times \frac{3}{2}$

$= \frac{27}{2}$

$= 13\frac{1}{2}$

There are 13 children altogether.

When you divide 9 by $\frac{2}{3}$, you get $13\frac{1}{2}$. Why is $13\frac{1}{2}$ not the answer to the question, "How many children are there altogether?"

b What fraction of a stick of clay is left?

$13 \times \frac{2}{3} = \frac{26}{3}$

$= 8\frac{2}{3}$

$9 - 8\frac{2}{3} = \frac{1}{3}$

$\frac{1}{3}$ of a stick of clay is left.

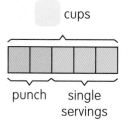 **Practice dividing a whole number by a fraction to solve multi-step real-world problems**

Solve.

1 Amelia buys 75 cups of juice for a party. She uses $\frac{2}{5}$ of the juice to make punch. She then uses the remaining juice to pour single servings that are $\frac{5}{6}$-cup each.

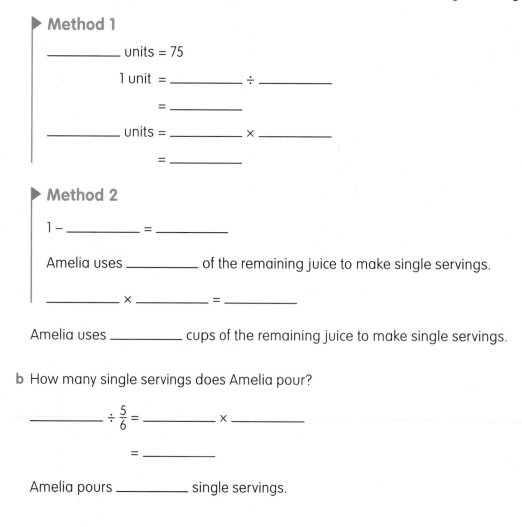

☐ cups

punch   single servings

a How many cups of the remaining juice does Amelia use to make single servings?

▶ **Method 1**

_____ units = 75

1 unit = _____ ÷ _____

= _____

_____ units = _____ × _____

= _____

▶ **Method 2**

1 – _____ = _____

Amelia uses _____ of the remaining juice to make single servings.

_____ × _____ = _____

Amelia uses _____ cups of the remaining juice to make single servings.

b How many single servings does Amelia pour?

_____ ÷ $\frac{5}{6}$ = _____ × _____

= _____

Amelia pours _____ single servings.

2 Sydney bakes 5 pumpkin pies. She cuts the pies into quarters and distributes the slices equally among her neighbors. Each neighbor receives $\frac{3}{4}$ of a pie.

a How many neighbors receive pie?

_____ $\div \frac{3}{4}$ = _____ $\times$ _____

= _____

_____ neighbors receive pie.

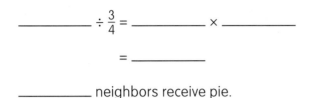

Math Talk

When you divide 5 by $\frac{3}{4}$, you get a mixed number. Can the number of neigbors Sydney has be a mixed number? Why?

b What fraction of a pie is left?

_____ $\times \frac{3}{4}$ = _____

5 – _____ = _____

_____ of a pie is left.

3 Some bottles, each containing $\frac{2}{5}$ gallon of water, are used to fill a 7-gallon container.

a How many full bottles of water are needed to fill the container to its brim?

b How much water is left after filling the 7-gallon container to its brim?

ENGAGE

1 A farmer uses $\frac{1}{8}$ of a field to build a ticketing booth. Of the remaining field, he divides it into several small plots for carnival rides. Each small plot is $\frac{1}{16}$ of the whole field. Draw a model to show the different plots indicating the number of small plots there are in the field.

2 Write a story about the expression: $\frac{1}{4} \div \frac{1}{3}$.

LEARN Divide a fraction by a fraction to solve real-world problems

1 Sebastian uses $\frac{2}{3}$ of his back yard to plant tomatoes and another $\frac{1}{9}$ of it to plant lettuce. He then divides the rest of his back yard into several small plots of land. Each small plot of land is $\frac{1}{18}$ of his entire back yard.

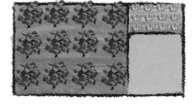

a How many small plots of land are there?

b The area of Sebastian's back yard is 90 square yards. What is the area of each small plot of land?

▶ **Method 1**

$\frac{2}{3} = \frac{6}{9}$

Sebastian uses $\frac{6}{9}$ of his back yard to plant tomatoes.

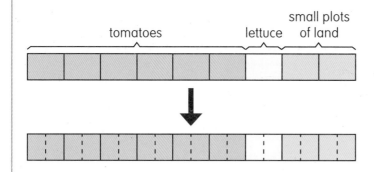

a From the bar model, there are 4 small plots of land.

b 18 units = 90
    1 unit = 90 ÷ 18
          = 5

The area of each small plot of land is 5 square yards.

▶ **Method 2**

a $\frac{2}{3} + \frac{1}{9} = \frac{6}{9} + \frac{1}{9}$

$\qquad\quad = \frac{7}{9}$

$\frac{7}{9}$ of Sebastian's back yard is used for tomatoes and lettuce.

$1 - \frac{7}{9} = \frac{2}{9}$

$\frac{2}{9}$ of Sebastian's back yard is divided into several small plots of land.

$\frac{2}{9} \div \frac{1}{18} = \frac{2}{\cancel{9}_1} \times \cancel{18}^2$

$\qquad\quad = 4$

There are 4 small plots of land.

b $\frac{1}{\cancel{18}_1} \times \cancel{90}^5 = 5$

The area of each small plot of land is 5 square yards.

> The area of each small plot is $\frac{1}{18}$ of 90 square yards.

Activity Solving real-world problems involving fractions

Work in pairs.

① Read the real-world problem. Draw a bar model for the problem.

> Ian had 2 kilograms of dried beans. He gave $\frac{2}{5}$ of the beans away and cooked $\frac{1}{4}$ of the remaining beans. He then packed the rest into small bags. Each bag held $\frac{1}{5}$ kilogram of beans.
>
> a How many bags of beans could he pack?
>
> b What was the mass of beans left unpacked?

2. Use the bar model to solve the problem. Use a calculator to check each other's answer.

3. Repeat the activity to solve each of the following real-world problems.

   a Jennifer had a bag of rice. She cooked an equal amount of rice each day. After 2 days, she was left with $\frac{4}{5}$ of the bag of rice. After another 5 days, she was left with 6 kilograms of rice. How much rice was there in the bag at first?

   b Robert bought $1\frac{1}{4}$ kilograms of meat on Monday and another $1\frac{1}{8}$ kilograms of meat on Tuesday. He cooked $1\frac{5}{8}$ kilograms of the meat he bought and divided the rest into $\frac{1}{8}$-kilogram portions. How many $\frac{1}{8}$-kilogram portions were there?

   c Alex and Chloe shared a 1-meter long ribbon. The piece of ribbon that Alex received was $\frac{1}{4}$ meter longer than the piece that Chloe received. What was the length of the ribbon, in meters, that Chloe received?

TRY Practice dividing a fraction by a fraction to solve real-world problems

Solve.

1. $\frac{3}{4}$ of the beads in a jar were orange and the rest were yellow. Hailey packed the yellow beads equally into bags. The number of yellow beads in each bag was $\frac{1}{12}$ of the total number of beads.

   a How many bags of yellow beads did Hailey pack?

   b There were 72 orange beads. How many yellow beads were there in each bag?

▶ **Method 1**

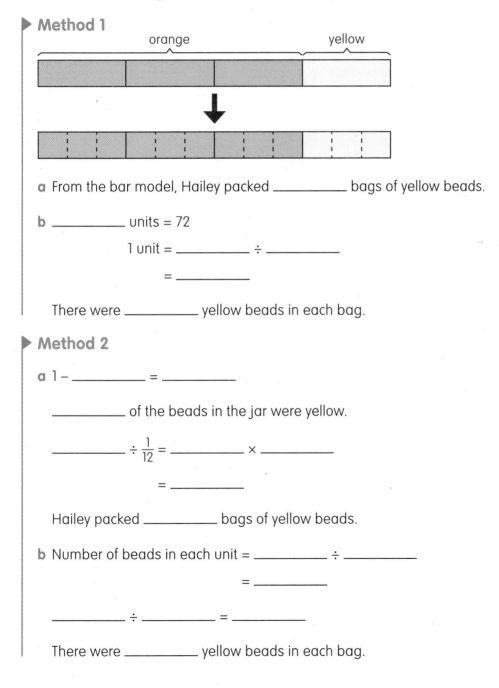

   a From the bar model, Hailey packed _____ bags of yellow beads.

   b _____ units = 72

   1 unit = _____ ÷ _____

   = _____

   There were _____ yellow beads in each bag.

▶ **Method 2**

   a 1 – _____ = _____

   _____ of the beads in the jar were yellow.

   _____ ÷ $\frac{1}{12}$ = _____ × _____

   = _____

   Hailey packed _____ bags of yellow beads.

   b Number of beads in each unit = _____ ÷ _____

   = _____

   _____ ÷ _____ = _____

   There were _____ yellow beads in each bag.

2 $\frac{3}{5}$ of the beads in a box were blue and the rest were red. Lauren divided the blue beads equally into small packs so that each pack of blue beads held $\frac{1}{10}$ of the number of beads in the box. She then divided the red beads equally into small packs. Each pack of red beads held $\frac{1}{5}$ of the number of beads that were originally in the box.

a Find the number of packs of blue beads and the number of packs of red beads.

Number of packs of blue beads = $\frac{3}{5}$ ÷ _____

= _____ × _____

= _____

Number of packs of red beads = _____ ÷ _____

= _____ × _____

= _____

There were _____ packs of blue beads and _____ packs of red beads.

b There were 16 red beads in the box. How many blue beads were there in each pack?

$\frac{2}{5}$ of the box = 16 beads

$\frac{1}{5}$ of the box = _____ ÷ _____

= _____ beads

$\frac{3}{5}$ of the box = _____ × _____

= _____ beads

_____ ÷ 6 = _____

There were _____ blue beads in each pack.

Name: _____   Date: _____

Solve.

1 A group of children shared 6 fruit tarts equally. Each child received $\frac{2}{9}$ of a tart. How many children were in the group?

2 A rectangle has an area of 15 square meters. It is divided into parts, each with an area of $\frac{3}{8}$ square meter. How many parts are there?

3 24 pints of apple juice are poured into $\frac{3}{4}$-pint bottles. How many bottles are there?

4 40 pounds of sugar are repackaged into packets, each holding $\frac{5}{16}$ pound of sugar. How many packets of sugar are there?

5 $\frac{6}{7}$ of a rectangle is colored red. Timothy cuts this red part into a number of pieces so that each piece is $\frac{2}{7}$ of the whole rectangle. How many red pieces does Timothy have?

6 Karen used $\frac{5}{8}$ yard of ribbon to make weights to add on to the tail of her kite. She cut the length of ribbon into equal pieces that were each $\frac{1}{12}$ yard long. How many $\frac{1}{12}$-yard pieces did Karen cut?

$\frac{1}{12}$ yard

7 A rectangular plot of land has an area of $\frac{3}{4}$ square mile. Its width is $\frac{3}{20}$ mile. What is the length of the plot of land?

8 How many $\frac{3}{8}$-cup servings are in a pitcher containing $6\frac{3}{4}$ cups of orange juice?

9 Dae buys $8\frac{1}{3}$ pounds of meat to make meat patties. He uses $\frac{5}{9}$ pound of meat for each meat patty. How many meat patties can Dae make?

10 A carpenter has a 6-foot long board. He wants to cut the board into pieces that are each $\frac{4}{5}$-foot long.

a How many $\frac{4}{5}$-foot long pieces can the carpenter cut from the board?

b What length of the original board will be left after the carpenter has cut all the pieces that are $\frac{4}{5}$-foot long?

11 A candle maker has $4\frac{1}{2}$ pounds of wax. She wants to cut the wax into pieces that are $\frac{2}{3}$ pound each.

a How many $\frac{2}{3}$-pound pieces can she divide the wax into?

$\frac{2}{3}$ lb

b How much wax is left over?

12 Makayla read $\frac{1}{6}$ of a book on Monday and another $\frac{1}{3}$ of the book on Tuesday. She took another 4 days to finish reading the book. She read the same number of pages on each of the 4 days.

a What fraction of the book did Makayla read on each of the 4 days?

b If she read 40 pages on each of these 4 days, find the number of pages in the book.

13 A costume designer has 40 yards of red fabric for making costumes for a musical. In the musical, 8 performers will wear red dresses, and 14 performers will wear red scarves. The costume designer uses $3\frac{1}{2}$ yards for each dress and $\frac{3}{4}$ yards for a scarf.

    a After making the dresses and scarves, the costume designer wants to use the leftover fabric to make some sashes for the dresses. If each sash uses $\frac{1}{4}$ yards of fabric, how many sashes can the costume designer make?

    b The costume designer decides to make each sash smaller, so that each of the 8 dresses can have a sash. What fraction of a yard of fabric should the costume designer use to make each sash?

14 The capacity of a large milk carton is $2\frac{3}{4}$ liters. The milk from one dozen large milk cartons is poured into a machine. The machine pumps the milk into bottles that each holds $\frac{2}{5}$ liter. How many bottles of milk can be filled?

15 Mr. Nelson used $\frac{3}{8}$ of his money to buy some pens and $\frac{2}{5}$ of the remainder to buy 2 notebooks. A notebook costs 3 times as much as a pen. How many pens did he buy?

3 Adding and Subtracting Decimals Fluently

Learning Objective:
• Add and subtract multi-digit decimals fluently.

THINK

Find each missing digit.

a

```
    1 ? . ? 0 6
  +  ? 9 . 8 7 ?
  ─────────────────
    4 3 . 0 8 1
```

b

```
    3 ? . 0 6 4
  - 1 5 . 9 ? ?
  ─────────────────
      ? 1 . 1 3 6
```

ENGAGE

Recall and discuss what you learned about place value and decimal addition. Show how you find the sum of 4.25 and 5.798. Share your method.

LEARN Add multi-digit decimals

① Add 6.528 and 8.965.

6.528 + 8.965 = ?

Step 1
Add the thousandths and regroup.

```
        1
    6 . 5 2 8
  + 8 . 9 6 5
  ─────────────
          .   3
```

8 thousandths + 5 thousandths
= 13 thousandths
= 1 hundredth 3 thousandths

Step 2
Add the hundredths.

```
        1
    6 . 5 2 8
  + 8 . 9 6 5
  ─────────────
          . 9 3
```

1 hundredth + 2 hundredths + 6 hundredths
= 9 hundredths

Step 3
Add the tenths and regroup.

```
    ¹   ¹
   6 . 5 2 8
+  8 . 9 6 5
   _____
     . 4 9 3
```

5 tenths + 9 tenths
= 14 tenths
= 1 one 4 tenths

6.528 + 8.965 = 15.493

Step 4
Add the ones and regroup.

```
   ¹   ¹
   6 . 5 2 8
+  8 . 9 6 5
   _____
 1 5 . 4 9 3
```

1 one + 6 ones + 8 ones
= 15 ones
= 1 ten 5 ones

> 6.528 is close to 7.
> 8.965 is close to 9.
> 7 + 9 = 16
> 15.493 is close to 16.
> So, the answer is reasonable.

TRY Practice adding multi-digit decimals

Estimate. Then, add.

1.
```
   5 . 6 0 8
+  7 . 7 6 5
```

2.
```
   1 . 8 0 9
+  6 . 4 7 6
```

3.
```
   7 . 3 9
+  8 . 4 9 9
```

4.
```
   4 . 7 6 3
+  2 . 0 7
```

5.
```
    8 . 3 9 3
+ 1 5 . 0 7 9
```

6.
```
  3 8 . 0 8 1
+    6 . 7 8 9
```

Write in vertical form. Then, add.

7. 23.59 + 4.675

8. 47.418 + 54.692

Discuss with your classmates whether your answers are reasonable.

ENGAGE

Recall what you learned about place value and decimal subtraction. Show how you find the difference between 5.152 and 2.38 using vertical subtraction. Share your method.

LEARN Subtract multi-digit decimals

1 Subtract 2.383 from 5.152.

5.152 – 2.383 = ?

Step 1
Regroup.
5 hundredths 2 thousandths
= 4 hundredths 12 thousandths

Subtract the thousandths.

```
          4  12
  5 . 1   5̶  2̶
- 2 . 3   8  3
  .           9
```

12 thousandths – 3 thousandths
= 9 thousandths

Step 2
Regroup.
1 tenth 4 hundredths
= 14 hundredths

Subtract the hundredths.

```
       0  14  12
  5 . 1̶   5̶   2̶
- 2 . 3   8   3
  .       6   9
```

14 thousandths – 8 thousandths
= 6 thousandths

Step 3
Regroup.
5 ones = 4 ones 10 tenths

Subtract the tenths.

```
  4   10  14  12
  5̶ . 1̶   5̶   2̶
- 2 . 3   8   3
  .   7   6   9
```

10 tenths – 3 tenths = 7 tenths

5.152 – 2.383 = 2.769

Step 4
Subtract the ones.

```
  4   10  14  12
  5̶ . 1̶   5̶   2̶
- 2 . 3   8   3
  2 . 7   6   9
```

4 ones – 2 ones = 2 ones

> 5.152 is close to 5.
> 2.383 is close to 2.
> 5 – 2 = 3
> 2.769 is close to 3.
> So, the answer is reasonable.

TRY Practice subtracting multi-digit decimals

Estimate. Then, subtract.

1
```
   5 . 6 3 1
 - 3 . 8 0 7
```

2
```
   4 . 0 8 4
 - 2 . 8 7 5
```

3
```
   7 . 3 0 9
 - 1 . 6 4
```

4
```
   6 . 3 8 5
 - 4 . 3 8 7
```

5
```
  1 8 . 3 5
 -  5 . 7 3 4
```

6
```
  3 2 . 0 0 8
 -  7 . 6 1 7
```

Write in vertical form. Then, subtract.

7 23.27 − 6.198

8 40.005 − 13.65

Math Talk

Discuss with your classmates whether your answers are reasonable.

INDEPENDENT PRACTICE

Estimate. Then, add.

1
```
    3 . 6 5 7
+   2 . 9 0 8
_____
```

2
```
    2 . 5 6 9
+   9 . 7 2 3
_____
```

3
```
    1 . 8 5
+   8 . 3 3 6
_____
```

4
```
    4 . 9 7 8
+   6 . 7 3
_____
```

5
```
    6 . 8 5 2
+ 1 0 . 9 7 7
_____
```

6
```
  2 4 . 0 6 8
+   8 . 9 7 4
_____
```

Write in vertical form. Then, add. Check if each answer is reasonable.

7 6.376 + 37.124

8 40.704 + 9.396

9 3.587 + 57.43

10 69.732 + 84.569

Estimate. Then, subtract.

⑪
```
    5 . 9 1 9
  - 3 . 7 4 8
```

⑫
```
    8 . 5 2 5
  - 5 . 8 1 7
```

⑬
```
    9 . 3 2 4
  - 3 . 6 3
```

⑭
```
    1 6 . 7 5
  -   2 . 1 7 4
```

⑮
```
    2 5 . 0 6 8
  -   8 . 4 3 9
```

⑯
```
    4 1 . 2 5 6
  - 3 7 . 5 8
```

Write in vertical form. Then, subtract. Check if each answer is reasonable.

⑰ 32.496 – 9.51

⑱ 89.59 – 78.982

⑲ 28.235 – 19.185

⑳ 60.723 – 24.904

4 Multiplying Decimals Fluently

Learning Objectives:
• Multiply a decimal by a whole number.
• Multiply a decimal by a decimal fluently.

THINK

Find each missing digit.

a
```
    0 . 1 2 5
  ×         ?
  _____
    0 . ? 7 5
```

b
```
      3 . ?
  ×   0 . 2
  _____
    0 . ? 2
```

ENGAGE

a Choose a whole number and a decimal. Create a visual to represent the multiplication of the two numbers: ? × ? . ? . Draw a number line to show how you find the product. What other ways can you use to find the product?

b If the positions of the whole number and decimal are switched, will the answer be the same? Explain your reasoning.

LEARN Multiply a decimal by a whole number

① Multiply 0.4 by 3.

▶ **Method 1**

Draw a number line to help you to multiply.

$0.4 \times 3 = 3 \times 0.4$

3×0.4 means 3 groups of 0.4.

Math Note

Commutative Property of Multiplication:
Two numbers can be multiplied in either order.

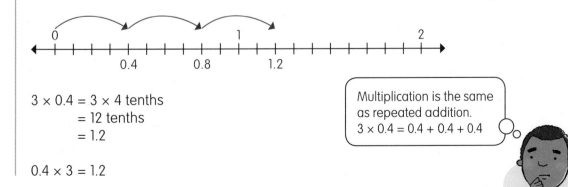

$3 \times 0.4 = 3 \times 4$ tenths
$\qquad\quad = 12$ tenths
$\qquad\quad = 1.2$

Multiplication is the same as repeated addition.
$3 \times 0.4 = 0.4 + 0.4 + 0.4$

$0.4 \times 3 = 1.2$

▶ **Method 2**

Multiply using vertical form. First, ignore the decimal points as you multiply. Then, decide where to place the decimal point in the product.

```
  1
  0 . 4   ←——— 1 decimal place
×    3
─────────
  1 . 2   ←——— 1 decimal place
```

You are multiplying 4 tenths (0.4) by 3, so you need to place the decimal point to show that the answer is 12 tenths (1.2).

$0.4 \times 3 = 1.2$

2 Alex wants to place 7 pictures of his favorite bands on a bulletin board. Each picture is 0.15 meter wide. How wide does the bulletin board need to be for all of the pictures to fit in one row?

$7 \times 0.15 = ?$

▶ **Method 1**

Draw a number line to help you to multiply.

7×0.15 means 7 groups of 0.15.

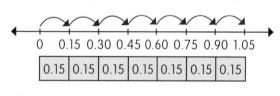

0.15 m

$7 \times 0.15 = 7 \times 15$ hundredths
$\qquad\qquad = 105$ hundredths
$\qquad\qquad = 1.05$

The bulletin board needs to be 1.05 meters wide for all of the pictures to fit in one row.

▶ **Method 2**

Multiply using vertical form. First, ignore the decimal points as you multiply. Then, decide where to place the decimal point in the product.

```
  1 3
  0 . 1 5   ←——— 2 decimal places
×      7
───────────
  1 . 0 5   ←——— 2 decimal places
```

You are multiplying 15 hundredths (0.15) by 7, so you need to place the decimal point to show that the answer is 105 hundredths (1.05).

$7 \times 0.15 = 0.15 \times 7$
$\qquad\qquad = 1.05$

The bulletin board needs to be 1.05 meters wide for all of the pictures to fit in one row.

TRY Practice multiplying a decimal by a whole number

Multiply.

1 0.9 × 4

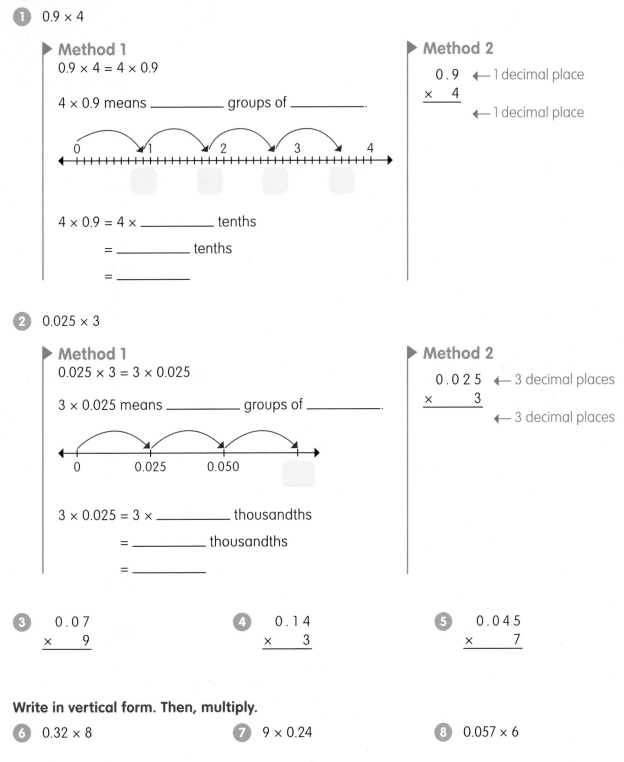

▶ **Method 1**

0.9 × 4 = 4 × 0.9

4 × 0.9 means _____ groups of _____.

4 × 0.9 = 4 × _____ tenths

      = _____ tenths

      = _____

▶ **Method 2**

  0.9 ← 1 decimal place
×   4
      ← 1 decimal place

2 0.025 × 3

▶ **Method 1**

0.025 × 3 = 3 × 0.025

3 × 0.025 means _____ groups of _____.

3 × 0.025 = 3 × _____ thousandths

      = _____ thousandths

      = _____

▶ **Method 2**

  0.025 ← 3 decimal places
×   3
       ← 3 decimal places

3
  0.07
×   9

4
  0.14
×   3

5
  0.045
×   7

Write in vertical form. Then, multiply.

6 0.32 × 8

7 9 × 0.24

8 0.057 × 6

ENGAGE

Recall and discuss what you learned about multiplying two fractions with 10 in the denominator and multiplying a whole number by a fraction with 10 in the denominator. Show two methods to find the product of 0.2 and 0.5. Share your methods.

LEARN Multiply tenths by tenths

1 Find the value of 0.4 × 0.5.

▶ **Method 1**
Express the decimals as fractions, then multiply.

$$0.4 \times 0.5 = \frac{4}{10} \times \frac{5}{10}$$ Express the decimals as fractions.

$$= \frac{20}{100}$$ Multiply.

$$= 0.20$$ Express as a decimal.

$$= 0.2$$

> When you multiply the denominators, you get a denominator of 100. So, the product is 20 hundredths, which can be written as 2 tenths.

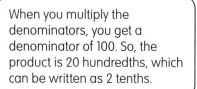

▶ **Method 2**
Multiply using vertical form. First, ignore the decimal points as you multiply. Then, decide where to place the decimal point in the product.

```
      2
   0 . 4  ←——— 1 decimal place
 × 0 . 5  ←——— + 1 decimal place
 ─────────
   0 . 2  0  ←——— 2 decimal places
```

$$0.4 \times 0.5 = 0.20$$
$$= 0.2$$

> You are multiplying 4 tenths (0.4) by 5 tenths (0.5), so you need to place the decimal point to show that the answer is 20 hundredths (0.20).

TRY Practice multiplying tenths by tenths

Multiply.

1 0.3 × 0.6

▶ **Method 1**

$$0.3 \times 0.6 = \frac{3}{} \times \frac{}{}$$

$$= \frac{}{}$$

$$= \underline{}$$

▶ **Method 2**

```
   0 . 3  ←——— 1 decimal place
 × 0 . 6  ←——— + 1 decimal place
 ─────────
          ←——— 2 decimal places
```

ENGAGE

1. Express 0.8 × 0.3 as product of fractions with 10 in the denominator. Then find the product.

2. Show and discuss another method to find the product of two decimals with one decimal place.

LEARN Multiply two decimals with one decimal place

1. Find the value of 2.8 × 0.3.

Multiply using vertical form. First, ignore the decimal points as you multiply. Then, decide where to place the decimal point in the product.

```
        2
     2 . 8  ◄——— 1 decimal place
  ×  0 . 3  ◄——— + 1 decimal place
  ─────────
     0 . 8  4  ◄——— 2 decimal places
```

You are multiplying 28 tenths (2.8) by 3 tenths (0.3), so you need to place the decimal point to show that the answer is 84 hundredths (0.84).

2.8 × 0.3 = 0.84

Check

$2.8 \times 0.3 = \frac{28}{10} \times \frac{3}{10}$. 10 × 10 = 100, so the product is a fraction with a *hundred* in the denominator. So, 2.8 × 0.3 = 84 *hundredths*.

2. Find the value of 3.6 × 1.2.

```
     3 . 6  ◄——— 1 decimal place
  ×  1 . 2  ◄——— + 1 decimal place
  ─────────
     7   2
  3  6   0
  ─────────
  4 . 3  2  ◄——— 2 decimal places
```

You are multiplying 36 tenths (3.6) by 12 tenths (1.2), so you need to place the decimal point to show that the answer is 432 hundredths (4.32).

3.6 × 1.2 = 4.32

Check

$3.6 \times 1.2 = \frac{36}{10} \times \frac{12}{10}$. 10 × 10 = 100, so the product is a fraction with a *hundred* in the denominator. So, 3.6 × 1.2 = 432 *hundredths*.

TRY Practice multiplying two decimals with one decimal place

Write in vertical form. Then, multiply.

1. 3.2 × 0.6

2. 4.3 × 5.7

ENGAGE

Choose a decimal with one decimal place. Now, choose another decimal with two decimal places. Use what your know about multiplying fractions or decimals to find the product of the two decimals. Explain your thinking.

LEARN Multiply decimals with one or more decimal places

1 Find the value of 0.56 × 1.2.

```
    0 . 5   6  ←——— 2 decimal places
  ×       1 . 2  ←——— + 1 decimal place
    ─────────────
        1   1   2
    0   5   6   0
    ─────────────
    0 . 6   7   2  ←——— 3 decimal places
```

You are multiplying 56 hundredths (0.56) by 12 tenths (1.2), so you need to place the decimal point to show that the answer is 672 thousandths (0.672).

0.56 × 1.2 = 0.672

Check

$0.56 \times 1.2 = \frac{56}{100} \times \frac{12}{10}$. 100 × 10 = 1,000, so the product is a fraction with a *thousand* in the denominator. So, 0.56 × 1.2 = 672 *thousandths*.

TRY Practice multiplying decimals with one or more decimal places

Write in vertical form. Then, multiply.

1 0.89 × 0.4

2 0.43 × 1.5

MATH SHARING

Mathematical Habit 7 Make use of structure

The model on the right shows 0.2 × 0.6 = 0.12.

1 Find two other decimals that give a product of 0.12.

2 Find two decimals that give a product of 0.36.

Share with your classmates how you found the decimals.

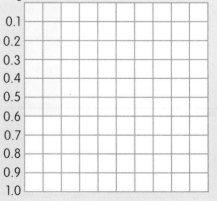

© 2020 Marshall Cavendish Education Pte Ltd

INDEPENDENT PRACTICE

Write in vertical form. Then, multiply.

1 0.9×12

2 0.47×5

3 0.063×9

4 0.85×11

5 0.1×0.2

6 0.2×0.3

7 0.4×0.4

8 0.6×0.7

9 0.7×0.9

Multiply mentally.

10 0.7×8

11 0.9×9

12 0.9×11

13 0.7×0.4

14 0.8×0.6

15 0.3×0.9

16 0.7×0.7

17 0.5×0.9

18 0.8×0.9

19 0.15×6

20 0.22×4

21 0.25×3

22 0.032×5

23 0.041×8

24 0.055×9

Write in vertical form. Then, multiply.

25 1.2×0.6

26 0.89×1.2

27 2.3×1.5

28 3.4×6.7

29 4.9×6.3

30 5.8×7.8

31 0.46×1.3

32 0.52×2.9

33 1.7×0.96

34 0.705×0.5

35 0.8×0.985

36 0.597×0.21

Answer the question.

37 **Mathematical Habit 6** Use precise mathematical language

Your friend knows how to find the product $\frac{57}{100} \times \frac{3}{10}$. However, your friend does not know how to find the product 0.57×0.3. Write an explanation that will help your friend understand how to multiply the two decimals.

5 Dividing Decimals Fluently

Learning Objectives:
- Divide a whole number by a decimal.
- Divide a decimal by a decimal fluently.

THINK

How do you interpret 6 ÷ 0.3 and 0.45 ÷ 0.5? Show two methods to find each quotient.

ENGAGE

Choose a whole number and a decimal. Draw a bar model to represent dividing the whole number by the decimal. Trade your bar model with your partner and find the division expression represented. Discuss your answers.

LEARN Divide a whole number by a decimal

1 Eric and his friend live 1 mile apart on the same street. Each block on this street is 0.2 mile long. How many blocks apart do the two friends live?

1 ÷ 0.2 = ?

▶ **Method 1**

Draw a bar model to help you to divide.

The division expression 1 ÷ 0.2 means "How many 0.2s are in 1 whole?"

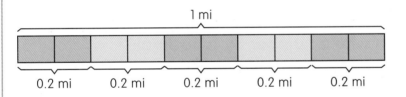

The bar model shows the division of 1 mile into five equal parts of 0.2 mile.

The bar model shows that:

1 ÷ 0.2 = 5

The two friends live 5 blocks apart.

▶ **Method 2**

Express the decimal as a fraction, then divide.

$1 \div 0.2 = 1 \div \frac{2}{10}$ Express the decimal as a fraction.

$ = 1 \times \frac{10}{2}$ Rewrite using the reciprocal of the divisor.

$ = 5$ Simplify.

2 Find the value of 16 ÷ 0.4.

The division expression 16 ÷ 0.4 means " How many 0.4s are in 16?"

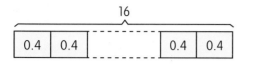

Division is the inverse of multiplication. Use the reciprocal of the divisor to find the answer.

$16 \div 0.4 = 16 \div \frac{4}{10}$ Express the decimal as a fraction.

$= \overset{4}{\cancel{16}} \times \frac{10}{\underset{1}{\cancel{4}}}$ Rewrite using the reciprocal of the divisor.
                Divide 16 and 4 by their common factor, 4.

$= 40$ Simplify.

3 Find the value of 96 ÷ 0.12.

The division expression 96 ÷ 0.12 means " How many 0.12s are in 96?"

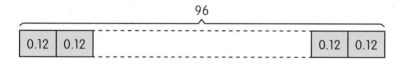

$96 \div 0.12 = 96 \div \frac{12}{100}$ Express the decimal as a fraction.

$= \overset{8}{\cancel{96}} \times \frac{100}{\underset{1}{\cancel{12}}}$ Rewrite using the reciprocal of the divisor.
                Divide 96 and 12 by their common factor, 12.

$= 800$ Simplify.

TRY **Practice dividing a whole number by a decimal**

Divide.

1 1 ÷ 0.5

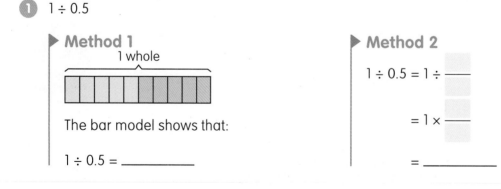

▶ **Method 1**

1 whole

The bar model shows that:

1 ÷ 0.5 = _____

▶ **Method 2**

$1 \div 0.5 = 1 \div \dfrac{}{}$

$= 1 \times \dfrac{}{}$

$=$ _____

2 $48 \div 0.3$

$48 \div 0.3 = 48 \div \dfrac{}{}$

$= 48 \times \dfrac{}{}$

$= \underline{}$

3 $75 \div 0.15$

$75 \div 0.15 = 75 \div \dfrac{}{}$

$= 75 \times \dfrac{}{}$

$= \underline{}$

ENGAGE

Divide 0.6 by 0.2. Now, divide 6 by 2. Discuss the meaning of dividing decimals by comparing the two divisions. Then, complete the following: $0.6 \div 0.2$ means there are how many _____ in _____. Draw a number line to show the meaning of dividing 0.6 by 0.2. Explore two other different methods to divide 0.6 by 0.2.

LEARN Divide tenths by tenths

1 Find the value of $0.8 \div 0.2$.

▶ **Method 1**

Draw a number line to help you to divide.

The division expression $0.8 \div 0.2$ means "How many 0.2s are in 0.8?"

Each small interval represents 0.2. There are 4 intervals.

The number line shows that: $0.8 \div 0.2 = 4$

▶ **Method 2**

Express the decimals as fractions, then divide.

$0.8 \div 0.2 = \dfrac{8}{10} \div \dfrac{2}{10}$ Express the decimals as fractions.

$= \dfrac{\overset{4}{\cancel{8}}}{\underset{1}{\cancel{10}}} \times \dfrac{\overset{1}{\cancel{10}}}{\underset{1}{\cancel{2}}}$ Rewrite using the reciprocal of the divisor.
Divide the numerators and denominators by their common factors.

$= 4$ Simplify.

▶ **Method 3**

Express the quotient as a fraction, then divide.

$0.8 \div 0.2 = \dfrac{0.8}{0.2}$ Express the quotient as a fraction.

$= \dfrac{8}{2}$ Multiply both the numerator and denominator by 10 to make the divisor a whole number.

$= 4$ Simplify.

TRY **Practice dividing tenths by tenths**

Divide.

1 $0.9 \div 0.3$

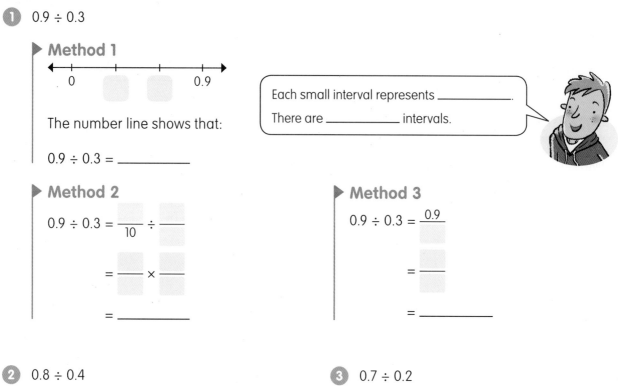

▶ **Method 1**

The number line shows that:

$0.9 \div 0.3 =$ _____

Each small interval represents _____.
There are _____ intervals.

▶ **Method 2**

$0.9 \div 0.3 = \dfrac{}{10} \div \dfrac{}{}$

$= \dfrac{}{} \times \dfrac{}{}$

$=$ _____

▶ **Method 3**

$0.9 \div 0.3 = \dfrac{0.9}{}$

$= \dfrac{}{}$

$=$ _____

2 $0.8 \div 0.4$

3 $0.7 \div 0.2$

ENGAGE

Divide 0.36 by 0.03. Discuss how dividing 36 hundredths by 3 hundredths is similar to dividing 36 by 3. Then, complete the following: $0.36 \div 0.03$ means how many _____ are there in _____. Draw a number line to show the meaning of dividing 0.36 by 0.03. Explore two other different methods to divide 0.36 by 0.03.

LEARN **Divide hundredths by hundredths**

1 Find the value of $0.56 \div 0.04$.

The division expression $0.56 \div 0.04$ means "How many 0.04s are in 0.56?"

There will be many intervals if you try to show this on a number line.

```
◄──┬────┬────┬────┬──────┬──►
   0   0.04 0.08 0.12  ...  0.56
```

Instead of using a number line, you can use the other methods to find the answer.

Method 1

Express the decimals as fractions, then divide.

$$0.56 \div 0.04 = \frac{56}{100} \div \frac{4}{100}$$ Express the decimals as fractions.

$$= \frac{\overset{14}{\cancel{56}}}{\underset{1}{\cancel{100}}} \times \frac{\overset{1}{\cancel{100}}}{\underset{1}{\cancel{4}}}$$ Rewrite using the reciprocal of the divisor.
Divide the numerators and denominators by their common factors.

$$= 14$$ Simplify.

Method 2

Express the quotient as a fraction, then divide.

$$0.56 \div 0.04 = \frac{0.56}{0.04}$$ Express the quotient as a fraction.

$$= \frac{56}{4}$$ Multiply both the numerator and denominator by 100 to make the divisor a whole number.

$$= 14$$ Simplify.

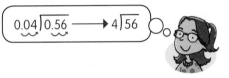

 Practice dividing hundredths by hundredths

Divide.

1 $0.72 \div 0.03$

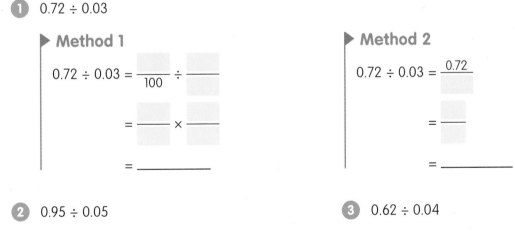

▶ **Method 1**

$$0.72 \div 0.03 = \frac{\boxed{}}{100} \div \frac{\boxed{}}{\boxed{}}$$

$$= \frac{\boxed{}}{\boxed{}} \times \frac{\boxed{}}{\boxed{}}$$

$$= \underline{}$$

▶ **Method 2**

$$0.72 \div 0.03 = \frac{0.72}{\boxed{}}$$

$$= \frac{\boxed{}}{\boxed{}}$$

$$= \underline{}$$

2 $0.95 \div 0.05$

3 $0.62 \div 0.04$

ENGAGE

Explore and discuss various ways to divide 1.84 by 0.2 using one or more of the following strategies: number line, fraction and multiplication method. Share the methods with your partner.

LEARN Divide decimals with one or more decimal places

1 Find the value of 1.96 ÷ 0.4.

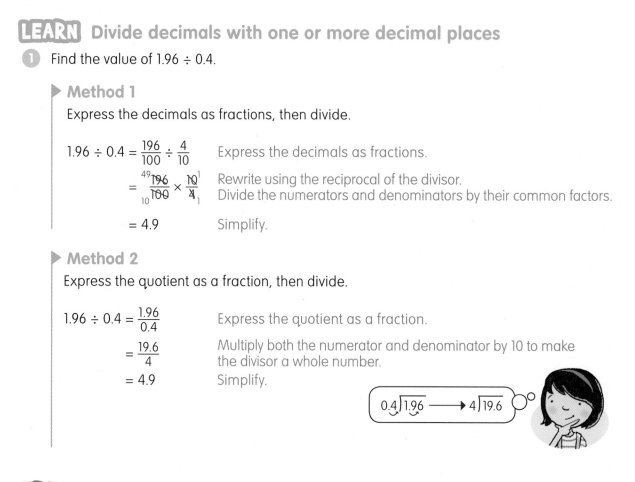

▶ Method 1

Express the decimals as fractions, then divide.

$1.96 ÷ 0.4 = \frac{196}{100} ÷ \frac{4}{10}$ Express the decimals as fractions.

$= \frac{\overset{49}{\cancel{196}}}{\underset{10}{\cancel{100}}} × \frac{\overset{1}{\cancel{10}}}{\underset{1}{\cancel{4}}}$ Rewrite using the reciprocal of the divisor.
Divide the numerators and denominators by their common factors.

$= 4.9$ Simplify.

▶ Method 2

Express the quotient as a fraction, then divide.

$1.96 ÷ 0.4 = \frac{1.96}{0.4}$ Express the quotient as a fraction.

$= \frac{19.6}{4}$ Multiply both the numerator and denominator by 10 to make the divisor a whole number.

$= 4.9$ Simplify.

$0.4\overline{)1.96} \longrightarrow 4\overline{)19.6}$

TRY Practice decimals with one or more decimal places

Divide.

1 1.68 ÷ 0.6

▶ Method 1

$1.68 ÷ 0.6 = \frac{\boxed{}}{100} ÷ \frac{\boxed{}}{\boxed{}}$

$= \frac{\boxed{}}{\boxed{}} × \frac{\boxed{}}{\boxed{}}$

$= \underline{}$

▶ Method 2

$1.68 ÷ 0.6 = \frac{1.68}{\boxed{}}$

$= \frac{\boxed{}}{\boxed{}}$

$= \underline{}$

2 2.88 ÷ 0.8

3 6.54 ÷ 1.2

INDEPENDENT PRACTICE

Divide.

1 4 ÷ 0.5

2 5 ÷ 0.2

3 7 ÷ 0.4

4 42 ÷ 0.7

5 86 ÷ 0.5

6 93 ÷ 0.4

7 1 ÷ 0.02

8 8 ÷ 0.32

9 9 ÷ 0.72

10 36 ÷ 0.36

11 56 ÷ 0.28

12 81 ÷ 0.54

13 749 ÷ 0.7

14 972 ÷ 0.8

15 545 ÷ 0.25

16 0.6 ÷ 0.3

17 0.9 ÷ 0.4

18 0.64 ÷ 0.04

19 0.81 ÷ 0.06

20 0.85 ÷ 0.5

21 0.025 ÷ 0.5

22 0.816 ÷ 0.34

23 4.5 ÷ 0.2

24 8.82 ÷ 0.6

25 9.03 ÷ 1.4

26 26.1 ÷ 1.8

27 35.1 ÷ 32.5

Answer the question.

28 **Mathematical Habit 3** **Construct viable arguments**
David says that since 12 ÷ 3 = 4, 1.2 ÷ 0.3 = 0.4. Is he correct? Explain your answer.

6 Real-World Problems: Decimals

Learning Objective:
• Solve real-world problems involving decimals.

THINK

Nelson has a plot of land. He wants to divide the land into three rectangles and a square as shown. Rectangle A requires 2.8 mi of fencing, and its width is $\frac{3}{4}$ of its length. The area of rectangle C is 0.24 square miles. Find two possible areas of rectangle B.

ENGAGE

Julie mixed up her car key in a box of keys of different lengths. She only knows the total length of her car key and the door key is 5.2 centimeters and the door key is 0.6 centimeter longer than the car key. Discuss with your partner how she can determine the length of her car key.

LEARN Add or subtract decimals to solve real-world problems

1 Megan jogged 3.125 kilometers on Saturday. She jogged 4.75 kilometers on Sunday.

   a How many kilometers did Megan jog on both days?

   b What was the difference between the distances she jogged on both days?

   STEP 1 Understand the problem.

   How many kilometers did Megan jog on Saturday?
   How many kilometers did she jog on Sunday?
   What do I need to find?

   STEP 2 Think of a plan.
   I can draw a bar model.

STEP 3 Carry out the plan.

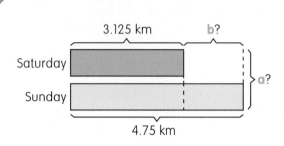

a 3.125 + 4.75 = 7.875

Megan jogged 7.875 kilometers
on both days.

b 4.75 − 3.125 = 1.625

The difference between the distances
she jogged on both days was
1.625 kilometers.

STEP 4 Check the answer.
I can use estimation to check
if my answers are reasonable.

3.125 is close to 3.
4.75 is close to 5.
3 + 5 = 8 and 7.875 is close to 8.
5 − 3 = 2 and 1.625 is close to 2.
So, my answers are reasonable.

TRY Practice adding or subtracting decimals to solve real-world problems

Solve.

1 On the first day of a camp, Luis drank 3.155 liters of water. On the same day, Mary drank
2.65 liters of water.

a How many liters of water did Luis and Mary drink in all?

_____ ◯ _____ = _____

Luis and Mary drank _____ liters of water in all.

b What was the difference between the amounts of water Luis and Mary drank?

_____ ◯ _____ = _____

The difference between the amounts of water Luis and Mary drank was _____ liter.

ENGAGE

Kyle bought an 8.5 ounce container of yogurt. If an ounce of yogurt costs $0.35, will the total cost be more or less than $3.00? How do you know? Discuss.

LEARN Multiply decimals to solve real-world problems

1 At a supermarket, a pound of almonds costs $3.90. Aisha wants to buy 4.5 pounds of almonds. How much does she have to pay?

4.5 × $3.90 = $17.55

Aisha has to pay $17.55 for the almonds.

> 4.5 × 3.90 is the same as 4.5 × 3.9.

Check

Estimate the value of 4.5 × 3.9. 4.5 is close to 5 and 3.9 is close to 4. 5 × 4 = 20 and 17.55 is close to 20. The estimate shows the answer is reasonable.

TRY Practice multiplying decimals to solve real-world problems

Solve.

1 The cost of carpeting a square yard is $8.60. How much does it cost to carpet 9.7 square yards?

9.7 ⬤ $_____ = $_____

> 9.7 × _____ is the same as 9.7 × _____.

It costs $_____ to carpet 9.7 square yards.

ENGAGE

Madison has $5.70. She wants to buy bottled water for her teammates. Each bottle of water costs $0.50. Share how you find the number of bottles she can buy. If Madison has $6.70, how can you find the greatest number of bottles that she can buy? Justify your reasoning.

LEARN Divide decimals to solve real-world problems

1. A caterer sliced 6.5 ounces of cheese into pieces that weighed 0.5 ounce each. How many pieces of cheese did the caterer slice?

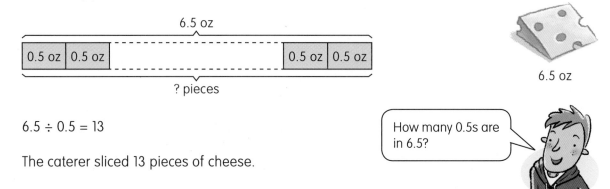

$6.5 \div 0.5 = 13$

How many 0.5s are in 6.5?

The caterer sliced 13 pieces of cheese.

TRY Practice dividing decimals to solve real-world problems

Solve.

1. A roll of cloth 12 meters long is cut into small pieces of the same size. Each piece is 0.75 meter long. How many small pieces of cloth can be cut from the 12-meter roll?

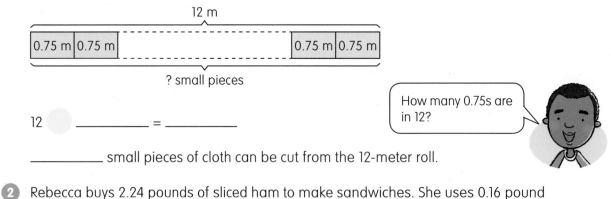

How many 0.75s are in 12?

12 ◯ _____ = _____

_____ small pieces of cloth can be cut from the 12-meter roll.

2. Rebecca buys 2.24 pounds of sliced ham to make sandwiches. She uses 0.16 pound for a sandwich. How many sandwiches can Rebecca make?

_____ ◯ _____ = _____

Rebecca can make _____ sandwiches.

INDEPENDENT PRACTICE

Solve.

1 Antonio ran 21.097 kilometers on a Sunday to prepare for a race.
The following Sunday, he ran 28.968 kilometers.

a What was the total distance Antonio ran on the two Sundays?

b What was the difference between the distances Antonio ran on the two Sundays?

2 A box has 12 bottles of jelly. Each bottle has a mass of 0.45 kilogram.
What is the total mass of the 12 bottles of jelly?

0.45 kg

3 An ounce of pine nuts costs $1.40. Brooke buys 2.5 ounces of pine nuts.
How much does she have to pay?

4 The length of a copper pipe is 6 meters. A plumber cuts the pipe into pieces, each of length 0.75 meter. How many pieces does he cut the pipe into?

6 m

5 Maya buys 6.93 pounds of raisins to make some loaves of raisin bread. Each loaf requires 0.33 pound of raisins. How many loaves of bread can she make?

6 A pail has a mass of 2.49 kilograms when it is filled with water. It has a mass of 1.445 kilograms when half of the water is removed. What is the mass of the empty pail?

1.445 kg

7 Zachary has 9.075 pounds of flour. He buys another 1.725 pounds of flour. He stores the flour in small packs. If each pack contains 0.4 pound of flour, how many packs does he use?

8 A roll of ribbon was 9 meters long. Olivia cut 8 pieces of ribbon, each of length 0.8 meter, to tie some gifts. She then cut the remaining ribbon into some pieces, each of length 0.4 meter.

a How many pieces of ribbon, each 0.4 meter in length, did Olivia have?

b What was the length of ribbon left over?

9 At a school carnival, Steven bought an equal number of bread rolls and muffins at a cost of $14.25. The cost of each muffin is twice the cost of each bread roll. Each bread roll cost $0.95. How many bread rolls did Steven buy?

10 The school librarian has $100 to spend on some books for the school. She wants to order many copies of the same book so an entire class can read the book. Each copy costs $3.95. Shipping for the books will be $6.95.

    a How many copies can the librarian order?

    b **Mathematical Habit 6** **Use precise mathematical language**
    Describe how you can use estimation to decide if your answer to **a** is reasonable.

11 A sign in an elevator says the elevator can lift up to 450 kilograms. Juan has 10 boxes that weigh 13.75 kilograms each, and a number of additional boxes that weigh 15.5 kilograms each. If he puts the 10 boxes in the elevator, how many of the additional boxes can be lifted in the same load?

Name: _____   Date: _____

Mathematical Habit 6 **Use precise mathematical language**

What are the similarities between the division of decimals and the division of whole numbers? Give an example to illustrate the similarities.

Problem Solving with Heuristics

Mathematical Habit 1 **Persevere in solving problems**

1. Aidan, Grace, and Julia raised a sum of money for a charity. Aidan raised 0.7 of the sum of money. Grace and Julia raised the rest of the money. If Grace raised $\frac{5}{12}$ of the money raised by both her and Julia, and Julia raised $847, how much money did Aidan raise?

2. A transport company delivered 900 glass fish bowls for Mr. Kim. It charged $0.60 for every fish bowl delivered safely. It had to pay Mr. Kim $6.40 for every fish bowl broken. If upon delivery of the fish bowls Mr. Kim paid a total of $519, how many fish bowls were broken?

CHAPTER WRAP-UP

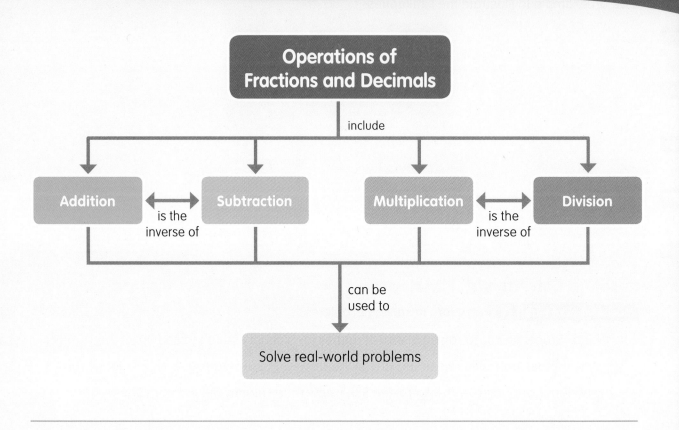

KEY CONCEPTS

• To divide any number by a fraction, multiply the number by the reciprocal of the fraction.

• When multiplying decimals, the product of
  – tenths and tenths results in hundredths or a decimal with 2 decimal places.
    Example: $0.2 \times 0.3 = \frac{2}{10} \times \frac{3}{10} = \frac{6}{100} = 0.06$ (or 6 hundredths)
  – tenths and hundredths results in thousandths or a decimal with 3 decimal places.
    Example: $0.4 \times 0.07 = \frac{4}{10} \times \frac{7}{100} = \frac{28}{1,000} = 0.028$ (or 28 thousandths)

• When dividing by a decimal, rewrite the division expression to make the divisor a whole number. Then, divide to find the quotient.

Name: _____   Date: _____

Divide. Write each quotient in simplest form.

① $16 \div \frac{2}{3}$

② $24 \div \frac{5}{6}$

③ $\frac{3}{8} \div \frac{3}{4}$

④ $\frac{7}{12} \div \frac{1}{3}$

⑤ $\frac{4}{5} \div \frac{12}{7}$

⑥ $\frac{8}{9} \div 2\frac{2}{3}$

Add.

⑦ $2.738 + 6.656$

⑧ $16.02 + 36.484$

⑨ $22.669 + 45.759$

⑩ $56.236 + 74.539$

Subtract.

⑪ $7.443 - 4.261$

⑫ $15.733 - 3.679$

⑬ $34.296 - 27.457$

⑭ $69.36 - 21.789$

Multiply.

15 0.3×8

16 16×0.7

17 0.28×6

18 7×0.068

19 0.4×0.6

20 0.5×0.8

21 5.7×0.4

22 9.3×0.89

Divide.

23 $6 \div 0.6$

24 $88 \div 0.2$

25 $5 \div 0.25$

26 $96 \div 0.16$

27 $396 \div 0.36$

28 $0.87 \div 0.03$

29 $2.66 \div 0.7$

30 $23.1 \div 15.4$

Solve.

31 In January, Victoria volunteered at a hospital for a total of 12 hours. She spent $\frac{4}{5}$ hour at the hospital every time she volunteered. How many times did Victoria volunteer in January?

32 Nathaniel is making loaves of raisin bread to sell at a fundraising event. The recipe calls for $\frac{1}{3}$ cup of raisins for each loaf, and Nathaniel has $3\frac{1}{4}$ cups of raisins.

    a How many loaves can Nathaniel make?

    b How many cups of raisins will he have left over?

33 There are some goats, cows, and sheep on a farm. $\frac{2}{5}$ of the animals were goats. There were 3 times as many sheep as cows. If there were 45 more goats than cows, how many animals were there on the farm?

34 Mr. Thompson spent $1,600 of his savings on a television set and $\frac{2}{5}$ of the remainder on a refrigerator. He had $\frac{1}{3}$ of the original amount of savings left.

a What was Mr. Thompson's original savings?

b What was the cost of the refrigerator?

35 Hana uses 8.125 pounds of ground beef to make meat loaves. She uses 7.25 pounds of ground beef to make pies.

    a How many pounds of ground beef does Hana use in all?

    b What is the difference between the amount of ground beef she uses to make meat loaves and pies?

36 It takes 76 bottles of water to fill up a tank. Each bottle is completely filled with 0.135 gallon of water. What is the capacity of the tank?

37 A flower bed has the shape of a rectangle. Its length is 2.5 meters and its width is 0.8 meter. Find the area of the flower bed.

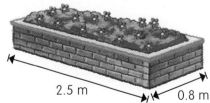

2.5 m   0.8 m

38 Luke makes 115.5 ounces of yogurt. He packs 10.5 ounces of yogurt in each container. How many containers does he need?

39 Maria buys 8.5 pounds of chicken to make tacos. She uses 0.3 pound of chicken for each taco.

a How many tacos can Maria make?

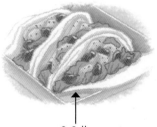

0.3 lb

b How many pounds of chicken are left over?

40 Ryan paid $21.75 for a number of packs of rice crackers. 3 packs of rice crackers cost $1.45.

a How many packs of rice crackers did Ryan buy?

3 packs for $1.45

b Mathematical Habit 2 Use mathematical reasoning
If Ryan were to buy 60 packs of the same rice crackers, would $30 be enough to pay for them? Explain your answer.

41 | Mathematical Habit 2 | Use mathematical reasoning

Leah offered to bring 2 gallons of freshly squeezed orange juice to a party. A store nearby sold a bag of 15 oranges for $5.99. For every 2 oranges she squeezed, she got 4.5 fluid ounces of juice.

a Find the minimum number of bags of oranges Leah needed to buy to make at least 2 gallons of freshly squeezed orange juice. Show your work or explanation.

b How much did Leah have to pay for the oranges?

Assessment Prep
Answer each question.

42 The area of a rectangle is $4\frac{3}{8}$ square feet, and its length is $1\frac{1}{4}$ feet. What is the rectangle's width, in feet?

Ⓐ $\frac{2}{7}$

Ⓑ $3\frac{1}{2}$

Ⓒ $3\frac{1}{8}$

Ⓓ $5\frac{5}{8}$

43 Find the value of 41.52 ÷ 0.96. Write your answer in the answer grid.

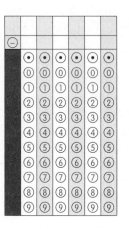

44 Jordan mixed 2.36 pounds of almonds with 3.69 pounds of cashew nuts, and formed packs of mixed nuts that each weighed 0.45 pound. What is the greatest number of 0.45-pound packs of mixed nuts he can make? Write your answer and your work or explanation in the space below.

45 Tanks are used to deliver liquid fuel to a factory.
- Each tank holds 22.5 cubic yards of fuel.
- The weight of 1 cubic yard of fuel is 0.74 tons.
- The fuel will be stored in containers that each holds 7.4 tons of fuel.

How many containers of this size are needed to hold all the fuel from 12 tanks?
Write your answer and your work or explanation in the space below.

Name: _____ Date: _____

Build a Wooden Sandbox

A carpenter wants to build a wooden sandbox for children to play in at a charity event.

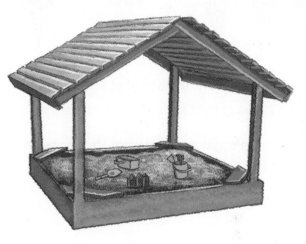

1. The carpenter wants to lay wooden planks on each of the two sides of the roof. The width of each side of the roof is $45\frac{1}{2}$ inches and the width of each wooden plank is $3\frac{1}{4}$ inches. How many wooden planks does he need for each side of the roof?

2. The sandbox has the shape of a square. Each side of the sandbox is 2.4 yards. The carpenter decides to make a cover in the same shape for the sandbox. What is the area of the cover?

3 The carpenter spent $\frac{7}{8}$ of his money on bags of sand for the sandbox. He spent $\frac{1}{2}$ of the rest of his money on some packs of bunting flags to decorate the sandbox and had $19.90 left.

a How much money did the carpenter start with? Draw a bar model to show your work.

b If each pack of bunting flags cost $1.99, how many packs did the carpenter buy?

c Each bag of sand weighs 50 pounds and costs $3.98. The carpenter needs 3,475 pounds of sand. He thinks he has bought enough sand. Do you agree or disagree? Show and explain your work.

Rubric

Point(s)	Level	My Performance
7–8	4	• Most of my answers are correct. • I showed complete understanding of the concepts. • I used effective and efficient strategies to solve the problems. • I explained my answers and mathematical thinking clearly and completely.
5–6.5	3	• Some of my answers are correct. • I showed adequate understanding of the concepts. • I used effective strategies to solve the problems. • I explained my answers and mathematical thinking clearly.
3–4.5	2	• A few of my answers are correct. • I showed some understanding of the concepts. • I used some effective strategies to solve the problems. • I explained some of my answers and mathematical thinking clearly.
0–2.5	1	• A few of my answers are correct. • I showed little understanding of the concepts. • I used limited effective strategies to solve the problems. • I did not explain my answers and mathematical thinking clearly.

Teacher's Comments

Ratio

What is the math in cooking?

When was the last time you read a new recipe? Perhaps you wanted to make a loaf of bread. The recipe you found tells you how much of each type of ingredient to use. You needed 1 cup of buttermilk and 3 cups of flour to make a loaf of bread. The ratio 1 to 3 describes the relationship between the number of cups of buttermilk and the number of cups of flour in the bread.

Now, suppose you want to make 5 loaves of bread. You need to increase the number of cups of buttermilk and the number of cups of flour you use. How many cups of buttermilk will you need? How many cups of flour will you need?

In this chapter, you will learn how to use ratios to solve problems like "scaling up" the ingredients you need in a recipe.

How does the use of ratio help you compare quantities?

Name: _____ Date: _____

Expressing fractions as equivalent fractions by multiplication

$\frac{5}{7} = \frac{5 \times 2}{7 \times 2} = \frac{10}{14}$ Multiply both the numerator and denominator by the same number, 2.

$\frac{5}{7} = \frac{5 \times 3}{7 \times 3} = \frac{15}{21}$ Multiply both the numerator and denominator by the same number, 3.

$\frac{5}{7} = \frac{10}{14} = \frac{15}{21}$

So, $\frac{5}{7}$, $\frac{10}{14}$, and $\frac{15}{21}$ are equivalent fractions.

▶ **Quick Check**

Express each fraction as two equivalent fractions using multiplication.

① $\frac{3}{4} \cdot \frac{2}{2} = \frac{6}{8}$ ② $\frac{7}{9}$ ③ $\frac{6}{11}$

Expressing fractions as equivalent fractions by division

$\frac{18}{36} = \frac{18 \div 3}{36 \div 3} = \frac{6}{12}$ Divide both the numerator and denominator by the common factor, 3.

$\frac{18}{36} = \frac{18 \div 6}{36 \div 6} = \frac{3}{6}$ Divide both the numerator and denominator by the common factor, 6.

$\frac{18}{36} = \frac{6}{12} = \frac{3}{6}$

So, $\frac{18}{36}$, $\frac{6}{12}$, and $\frac{3}{6}$ are equivalent fractions.

▶ **Quick Check**

Express each fraction as two equivalent fractions using division.

④ $\frac{16}{56}$ ⑤ $\frac{21}{63}$ ⑥ $\frac{35}{140}$

Writing equivalent fractions

Find the unknown numerator or denominator in each pair of equivalent fractions.

a $\frac{4}{7} = \frac{\boxed{?}}{42}$

$\frac{4}{7} = \frac{4 \times 6}{7 \times 6}$

$\quad = \frac{24}{42}$

b $\frac{5}{12} = \frac{35}{\boxed{?}}$

$\frac{5}{12} = \frac{5 \times 7}{12 \times 7}$

$\quad = \frac{35}{84}$

▶ **Quick Check**

Find the unknown numerator or denominator in each pair of equivalent fractions.

7 $\frac{3}{8} = \frac{}{56}$

8 $\frac{7}{9} = \frac{21}{27}$ $\overset{\cdot 3}{\underset{\cdot 3}{}}$

9 $\frac{}{11} = \frac{30}{55}$

10 $\frac{6}{} = \frac{42}{84}$

Writing fractions in simplest form

$\frac{12}{16} = \frac{12 \div 4}{16 \div 4}$ Divide both the numerator and denominator by the greatest common factor, 4.

$\quad = \frac{3}{4}$

▶ **Quick Check**

Express each fraction in simplest form.

11 $\frac{5}{45}$

12 $\frac{18}{63}$

13 $\frac{22}{55}$

Converting measurements given in one unit of measure to another

Find the unknown measurement.

a _____?_____ in. = 3 ft

1 ft = 12 in.
3 ft = 3 × 12
$\quad$ = 36 in.

b 5.2 km = _____?_____ m

1 km = 1,000 m
5.2 km = 1,000 × 5.2
$\quad$ = 5,200 m

▶ **Quick Check**
Find each unknown measurement.

⑭ _____ cm = 4 m

⑮ 9.8 kg = _____ g

⑯ 6 ft = _____ yd

⑰ 10 L = _____ mL

⑱ _____ yd = 72 in.

⑲ 5 lb = _____ oz

Interpreting a comparison bar model

Find the values of A and B.

a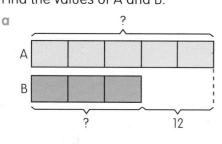

b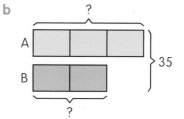

2 units = 12
  1 unit = 12 ÷ 2
       = 6

Value of A:
5 units = 6 × 5
       = 30

Value of B:
3 units = 6 × 3
       = 18

5 units = 35
  1 unit = 35 ÷ 5
       = 7

Value of A:
3 units = 7 × 3
       = 21

Value of B:
2 units = 7 × 2
       = 14

▶ **Quick Check**
Find the values of P and Q.

⑳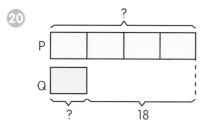

㉑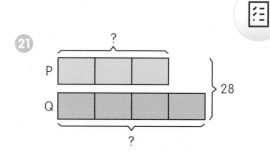

1 Comparing Two Quantities

Learning Objectives:
- Write ratios to compare two quantities.
- Interpret ratios given in fraction form.
- Use a ratio to find what fraction one quantity is of another or how many times as great one is to the other.

THINK

Aaron has $\frac{2}{5}$ as many marbles as Brandon. If both of them have 84 marbles in all, how many more marbles does Brandon have than Aaron?

ENGAGE

a Use some yellow cubes to represent one number and some green cubes to represent another number. Write three sentences to compare the two sets of cubes. Share your ideas.

b If the number of yellow cubes is 7 more than the number of green cubes, using the comparison sentences in **a**, find the least possible number of green cubes.

LEARN Write ratios to compare two quantities with the same unit

1 You can compare two numbers or quantities using a ratio.

The ratio of the number of orange cubes to the number of green cubes is 7 : 4.
The ratio shows that 7 is greater than 4.

The numbers or quantities you are comparing form the terms of a ratio.
7 and 4 are the terms of the ratio 7 : 4.

Suppose there are 7 bags of orange cubes and 4 bags of green cubes.
Each bag has an equal number of cubes.

bags with orange cubes							

bags with green cubes				

The ratio of the number of bags of orange cubes to the number of bags of green cubes is 7 : 4.

> The ratio does not give the actual number of cubes. Since each bag has an equal number of cubes, the ratio 7 : 4 also means that there are 7 orange cubes for every 4 green cubes.

2 When two quantities, such as the lengths of two rods, have the same units, you can write a ratio without units to compare the quantities.

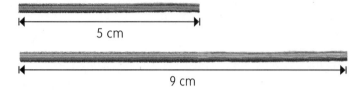

5 cm

9 cm

5 centimeters and 9 centimeters have the same unit.
So, the ratio of the length of the red rod to the length of the blue rod is 5 cm : 9 cm, or 5 : 9.
The ratio shows that 5 centimeters is shorter than 9 centimeters.

TRY **Practice writing ratios to compare two quantities with the same unit**

Write the ratio. Use greater than or less than to compare the quantities.

1 The ratio of the number of DVDs to the number of DVD sleeves is _____ : _____.

The number of DVDs is _____ the number of DVD sleeves.

2 Ms. Clark buys 4 bags of apples and 7 bags of oranges.
Each bag has an equal number of fruit.

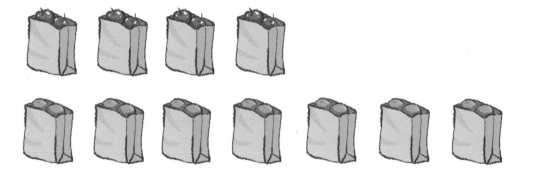

The ratio of the number of apples to the number of oranges is _____ : _____.

The number of apples is _____ the number of oranges.

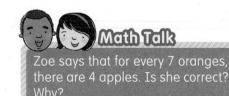

Math Talk
Zoe says that for every 7 oranges, there are 4 apples. Is she correct? Why?

③ Alexis has a cat that weighs 12 pounds and a dog that weighs 25 pounds.

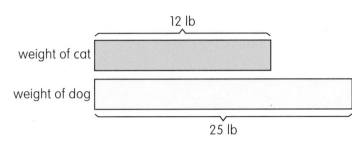

12 lb

weight of cat

weight of dog

25 lb

The ratio of the weight of the dog to the weight of the cat is _____ : _____.

The weight of the dog is _____ the weight of the cat.

ENGAGE

a   Express 2 meters and 5 centimeters in the same units. Then, express the measures as ratio.

b   Maria write the ratio as follows: 2 meters : 5 centimeters = 2 : 5. Is Maria's ratio correct? Explain.

LEARN Write ratios to compare two quantities with different units

① If you want to use a ratio to compare two quantities that have different units, such as meters and centimeters, you must first express the quantities using the same unit.

7 cm : 3 m = 7 cm : 300 cm   Express as the same unit.
          = 7 : 300   Simplify.

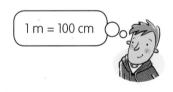

1 m = 100 cm

The ratio shows that 300 is greater than 7.

So, 3 meters is longer than 7 centimeters.

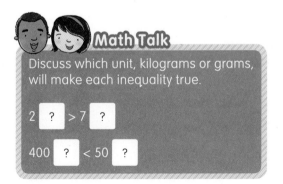

Math Talk

Discuss which unit, kilograms or grams, will make each inequality true.

2 [?] > 7 [?]

400 [?] < 50 [?]

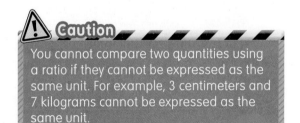

Caution

You cannot compare two quantities using a ratio if they cannot be expressed as the same unit. For example, 3 centimeters and 7 kilograms cannot be expressed as the same unit.

TRY Practice writing ratios to compare two quantities with different units

State whether each of the following can be expressed as a ratio.

1 6 kg and 84 kg

2 72 ft and 2 yd

3 3 oz and 30 in.

Fill in each blank.

4 13 cm : 2 m = 13 cm : _____ cm

 = _____ : _____

Think: 1 m = 100 cm, so 2 m = _____ cm.

5 5 kg : 13 g = _____ g : _____ g

 = _____ : _____

Think: 1 kg = 1,000 g, so 5 kg = _____ g.

6 9 mL : 7 L = _____ mL : _____ mL

 = _____ : _____

Think: 1 L = 1,000 mL, so 7 L = _____ mL.

Complete each inequality using the correct units.

7 g or kg

20 _____ > 400 _____

8 ft or yd

12 _____ < 5 _____

Math Talk

Discuss what numbers and units will make each inequality true.

?	?	<	?	?
(number)	(unit)		(number)	(unit)

?	?	>	?	?
(number)	(unit)		(number)	(unit)

ENGAGE

A box contains 28 pens and pencils in all. Draw a bar model to represent a possible ratio of the number of pens to the number of pencils. Trade your bar model with your partner. Now, write at least two ratio statements to represent your partner's bar model. Explain your thinking.

LEARN Use a part-part or a part-whole bar model to show ratios

1. There were 55 adults and 32 children at a party.

a Find the ratio of the number of adults to the number of children at the party.

Draw a part-part model.

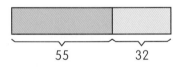

The number of adults and the number of children are parts of a whole.

The ratio of the number of adults to the number of children at the party is 55 : 32.

b Find the ratio of the number of children to the total number of people at the party.

Draw a part-whole model.

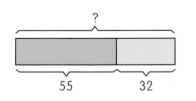

The total number of people forms the whole.

Total number of people at the party = 55 + 32
= 87

The ratio of the number of children to the total number of people at the party is 32 : 87.

Solve.

1 Miguel keeps 17 angelfish and 24 guppies.

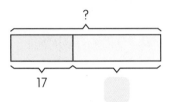

a Find the ratio of the number of angelfish to the number of guppies.

The ratio of the number of angelfish to the number of guppies is _____ : _____.

b Find the ratio of the number of guppies to the total number of fish.

Total number of fish = _____ + _____

= _____

The ratio of the number of guppies to the total number of fish is _____ : _____.

2 Logan has a string 72 centimeters long. He cuts it into two pieces. The length of the shorter piece is 31 centimeters. What is the ratio of the length of the longer piece to the total length of the string?

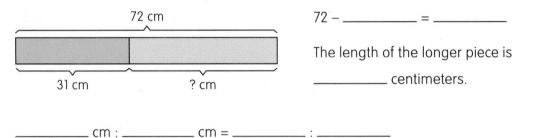

72 − _____ = _____

The length of the longer piece is

_____ centimeters.

_____ cm : _____ cm = _____ : _____

The ratio of the length of the longer piece to the total length of the string is _____ : _____.

3 The total amount of money Paige and Laila saved in a month was $45. Paige saved $13.

a Find the amount of money Laila saved.

b Find the ratio of the total amount of money Paige and Laila saved to the amount of money Laila saved.

ENGAGE

Write two fraction statements and two ratio statements to represent this bar model.

bags with orange cubes

bags with green cubes

How are the fractions and ratios the same? How are they different? Discuss.

LEARN Use a bar model to show fractions or ratios

1️⃣ You can express a fraction as a ratio.

Anna has $\frac{2}{3}$ as many hairpins as Faith.

1 unit

Anna

Faith

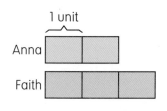

> You can draw a bar model using 2 units to represent Anna's hairpins and 3 units to represent Faith's hairpins.

The ratio of the number of hairpins Anna has to the number of hairpins Faith has is 2 : 3.

Total number of units of hairpins = 2 + 3
$$= 5$$

> Notice that $\frac{2}{3}$ does not tell you what fraction of the total number of hairpins are Anna's or Faith's. Instead, it tells you that Anna has 2 hairpins for every 3 hairpins Faith has.

The ratio of the number of hairpins Faith has to the total number of hairpins is 3 : 5.

2️⃣ You can express a ratio as a fraction.

The birds in a pet shop are parakeets and canaries.
For every 3 parakeets, there are 4 canaries.

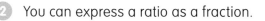

1 unit

parakeets

canaries

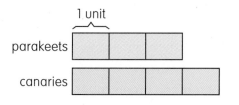

The ratio of the number of parakeets to the number of canaries is 3 : 4.

Total number of units of birds = 3 + 4
$$= 7$$

The ratio of the number of parakeets to the total number of birds is 3 : 7.

The number of parakeets is $\frac{3}{7}$ of the total number of birds.

Activity Using bar models, fractions, and ratios to compare quantities

Work in pairs.

1. Use cubes to show the statement:

   The number of blue cubes is $\frac{3}{8}$ of the number of red cubes.

2. Draw a bar model to represent the statement in 1.

3. Rewrite the statement using a ratio.

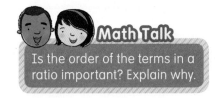

Math Talk

Is the order of the terms in a ratio important? Explain why.

4. Repeat 1 to 3 with each of the following statements.

   a The number of blue cubes is $\frac{7}{5}$ of the number of yellow cubes.

   b The number of green cubes is $\frac{9}{14}$ of the total number of red and green cubes.

TRY Practice using a bar model to show fractions or ratios

Solve.

1. The number of red parrots is $\frac{7}{8}$ of the number of green parrots.

red parrots [bar model]

green parrots [bar model]

a The ratio of the number of red parrots to the number of green parrots is _____ : _____.

b Total number of units of parrots = _____ + _____

= _____

The ratio of the number of green parrots to total number of parrots is _____ : _____.

2. For every 9 female teachers in a school, there are 5 male teachers.

a What is the ratio of the number of male teachers to the total number of teachers?

b What fraction of the teachers are females?

ENGAGE

a Isabel has $\frac{4}{7}$ as many coins as Blake. Draw a set of bar models to show the ratio.

b Isabel gives $\frac{1}{4}$ of his coins to Blake. Use your bar model to show this, and then complete the following statement: Isabel has _____ as many coins as Blake now.

LEARN Use ratios to find how many times one number or quantity is as great as another

1. The height of a giraffe and the height of a horse are represented in the bar model.

height of giraffe [bar model]

height of horse [bar model]

$$\frac{\text{Height of giraffe}}{\text{Height of horse}} = \frac{6}{3} = \frac{2}{1}$$

The height of the giraffe is 2 times the height of the horse.
The ratio of the height of the giraffe to the height of the horse is 2 : 1.

$$\frac{\text{Height of horse}}{\text{Height of giraffe}} = \frac{1}{2}$$

The height of the horse is $\frac{1}{2}$ of the height of the giraffe.

The ratio of the height of the horse to the height of the giraffe is 1 : 2.

You can use fractions and ratios to show that one quantity is a multiple of another.

TRY Practice using ratios to find how many times one number or quantity is as great as another

Solve.

1 Ali spent $12 and Jada spent $36.

a How many times the amount of money Ali spent is the amount of money Jada spent?

$$\frac{\text{Amount of money Jada spent}}{\text{Amount of money Ali spent}} = \frac{\ }{\ }$$

The amount of money Jada spent is _____ times the amount of money Ali spent.

b How many times the amount of money Jada spent is the amount of money Ali spent?

$$\frac{\text{Amount of money Ali spent}}{\text{Amount of money Jada spent}} = \frac{\ }{\ }$$

The amount of money Ali spent is _____ of the amount of money Jada spent.

MATH SHARING

Find two examples of how ratios are used in everyday life.
Discuss your examples with your classmates.

Example:
The ratio of water to cordial when making punch is 3 : 1.

INDEPENDENT PRACTICE

Write two ratios to compare the quantities.

1

2 Alyssa has 23 video game disks and Gavin has 37 video game disks.

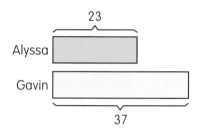

3 In a school, there are 8 classes in the sixth grade and 7 classes in the seventh grade. Each class has an equal number of students.

State whether each of the following can be expressed as a ratio.

4 6 cm and 60 g

5 54 kg and 54 m

6 12 g and 45 kg

7 87 ft and 93 yd

Solve.

8 There are 123 students in a drama club. 65 of them are in the sixth grade and the rest are in the seventh grade.

    a What is the ratio of the number of students in the seventh grade to the number of students in the sixth grade?

    b What is the ratio of the number of students in the seventh grade to the total number of students in the drama club?

9 At a music competition, the number of clarinet players is $\frac{3}{5}$ of the number of trumpet players.

    a Find the ratio of the number of clarinet players to the number of trumpet players.

    b Find the ratio of the number of trumpet players to the total number of players.

10 A fruit basket has apples and oranges. For every 4 oranges, there are 5 apples.

    a What is the ratio of the number of oranges to the total number of fruit in the basket?

    b What fraction of the fruit in the basket are apples?

11 Nicholas had $43 when he entered the museum gift shop. After spending some money, he had $18 left.

   a Find the ratio of the amount of money Nicholas spent to the amount of money he had left.

   b What fraction of his money did Nicholas spend?

12 A ribbon is cut into two pieces. The length of the longer piece is 60 inches and the length of the shorter piece is 12 inches.

60 in.

12 in.

   a How many times the length of the shorter piece is the longer piece?

   b What is the ratio of the length of the shorter piece to the original length of the ribbon?

13 Tyler's monthly allowance is $42 and Jeremiah's monthly allowance is $63. How many times Jeremiah's monthly allowance is Tyler's monthly allowance?

14 The ratio of the weight of vegetables sold to the weight of fruit sold is 45 : 144.

    a How many times the weight of vegetables sold is the weight of fruit sold?

    b What fraction of the total weight of vegetables and fruit sold is the weight of vegetables sold?

15 The ratio of the length to the width of a rectangle is 5 : 2.

    a Express the difference between the length and the width of the rectangle as a fraction of the length of the rectangle.

    b Express the width of the rectangle as a fraction of the perimeter of the rectangle.

Mathematical Habit 6 Use precise mathematical language
Describe a situation that each ratio could represent.

16 5 : 16

17 1,000 : 1

Name: _____   Date: _____

2 Equivalent Ratios

Learning Objectives:
- Write equivalent ratios.
- Write ratios in simplest form.
- Compare ratios.

THINK

At a shop, the ratio of the number of apples sold to the number of apples left is 1 : 2. The ratio of the number of oranges sold to the number of oranges left is 2 : 3. If the number of oranges and apples sold are the same, what is the ratio of the number of apples left to the number of oranges left?

ENGAGE

Draw two number lines with 0 and 1 as the endpoints. Mark the first number line with 3 equal intervals and write the fraction of each tick mark. Mark the second number line with 9 equal intervals and write the fraction of each tick mark. Circle the sets of fraction which are equal. Discuss with your partner how this can be applied to ratios.

LEARN Write equivalent ratios to show the same comparisons of numbers and quantities

1 Emma has 8 red marbles and 12 blue marbles.

The ratio of the number of red marbles to the number of blue marbles is 8 : 12.

Emma groups 2 marbles of the same color into each group.

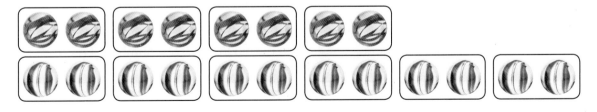

There are 4 groups of red marbles and 6 groups of blue marbles.
The ratio of the number of groups of red marbles to the number of groups of blue marbles is 4 : 6.

Next, she groups 4 marbles of the same color into each group.

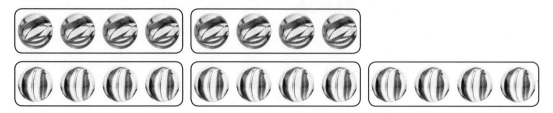

There are 2 groups of red marbles and 3 groups of blue marbles.
The ratio of the number of groups of red marbles to the number of groups of blue marbles is 2 : 3.

Notice that Emma is not changing the number of red marbles or the number of blue marbles. She is only regrouping the marbles.

8 red marbles **: 12 blue marbles**

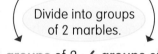

(Divide into groups of 2 marbles.)

4 groups of 2 : **6 groups** of 2

8 red marbles **: 12 blue marbles**

(Divide into groups of 4 marbles.)

2 groups of 4 : **3 groups** of 4

The ratios 8 : 12, 4 : 6, and 2 : 3 are equivalent ratios.

Activity Writing equivalent ratios to show the same comparisons of numbers and quantities

Work in pairs.

Activity 1

① Use 12 yellow cubes and 16 green cubes. Divide each set of cubes into groups of 2. Write a ratio to show the number of groups of yellow cubes to the number of groups of green cubes.

② Divide each set of cubes into groups of 4. Write a ratio to show the number of groups of yellow cubes to the number of groups of green cubes.

© 2020 Marshall Cavendish Education Pte Ltd

③ Write the two equivalent ratios of 12 : 16 you found.

Activity 2

① Use 6 yellow cubes and 18 green cubes. Divide each set of cubes into groups so that each group has the same number of cubes. Write a ratio to show the number of groups of yellow cubes to the number of groups of green cubes.

② Divide each set of cubes into groups of the same size, different from ①. Write a ratio to show the number of groups of yellow cubes to the number of groups of green cubes.

③ Divide each set of cubes into groups of the same size, different from ① and ②. Write a ratio to show the number of groups of yellow cubes to the number of groups of green cubes.

④ Write the three equivalent ratios of 6 : 18 you found.

TRY Practice writing equivalent ratios to show the same comparisons of numbers and quantities

Fill in each blank.

1

The ratio of the number of pencils to the number of erasers is _____ : _____.

2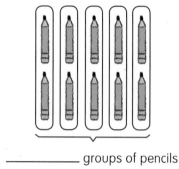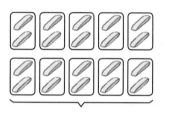

_____ groups of pencils   _____ groups of erasers

The ratio of the number of pencils to the number of erasers is _____ : _____.

3

_____ group of pencils   _____ groups of erasers

The ratio of the number of pencils to the number of erasers is _____ : _____.

4   **10 pencils : 20 erasers**   **10 pencils : 20 erasers**

   (Divide into groups of 2.)   (Divide into groups of 10.)

_____ **groups** of 2 : _____ **groups** of 2   _____ **groups** of 2 : _____ **groups** of 2

The ratios _____ : _____, _____ : _____, and _____ : _____ are equivalent ratios.

a Look at the ratio 18 : 24. Can both terms be divided by 3? Can both terms be divided by 5? Make a list of numbers that both terms can be divided by. What do you notice about the numbers in the list?

b Now, divide each term in the ratio 18 : 24 by the numbers in the list and write each result as a ratio. What can you say about the ratios?

LEARN Find equivalent ratios by division

1 A chef uses 18 cups of lentils and 54 cups of tomatoes to make lentil soup.

To use this recipe to make less soup, you use equivalent ratios to find the number of cups of lentils to the number of cups of tomatoes.

You can use division to find equivalent ratios. First, find the common factors of the terms. Then, divide the terms by the common factors.

Excluding 1, the common factors of 18 and 54 are 2, 3, 6, 9, and 18.

$\div 2$ $\left(\begin{array}{c} 18 : 54 \\ = 9 : 27 \end{array}\right)$ $\div 2$ Divide by common factor, 2.

$\div 3$ $\left(\begin{array}{c} 18 : 54 \\ = 6 : 18 \end{array}\right)$ $\div 3$ Divide by common factor, 3.

$\div 6$ $\left(\begin{array}{c} 18 : 54 \\ = 3 : 9 \end{array}\right)$ $\div 6$ Divide by common factor, 6.

$\div 9$ $\left(\begin{array}{c} 18 : 54 \\ = 2 : 6 \end{array}\right)$ $\div 9$ Divide by common factor, 9.

> Excluding 1, there are five common factors. So, you can use division to find five whole-number ratios that are equivalent to 18 : 54.

$\div 18$ $\left(\begin{array}{c} 18 : 54 \\ = 1 : 3 \end{array}\right)$ $\div 18$ Divide by common factor, 18.

18 : 54, 9 : 27, 6 : 18, 3 : 9, 2 : 6, and 1 : 3 are equivalent ratios.

1 : 3 is the simplest form because 1 and 3 do not have a common factor other than 1.

You can also write the equivalent ratios as equivalent fractions.

$$\frac{18}{54} = \frac{9}{27} = \frac{6}{18} = \frac{3}{9} = \frac{2}{6} = \frac{1}{3}$$

To use this recipe to make less soup, you can use 1 cup of lentils to 3 cups of tomatoes.

TRY Practice finding equivalent ratios by division

Use division to find all whole-number ratios equivalent to each of the following.

① 18 : 27

② 8 : 48

State whether each pair of ratios is equivalent.

③ 7 : 8 and 8 : 7

④ 1 : 3 and 5 : 15

⑤ 5 : 2 and 15 : 6

ENGAGE

Jackson has 12 apples and 18 oranges. How do you use ratio to find the greatest number of bags he needs to place an equal number of apples and an equal number of oranges in each bag? Explain your thinking.

LEARN Use the greatest common factor to write ratios in simplest form

You can write a ratio in simplest form by dividing the terms by their greatest common factor.

① Express the ratio 50 : 20 in simplest form.

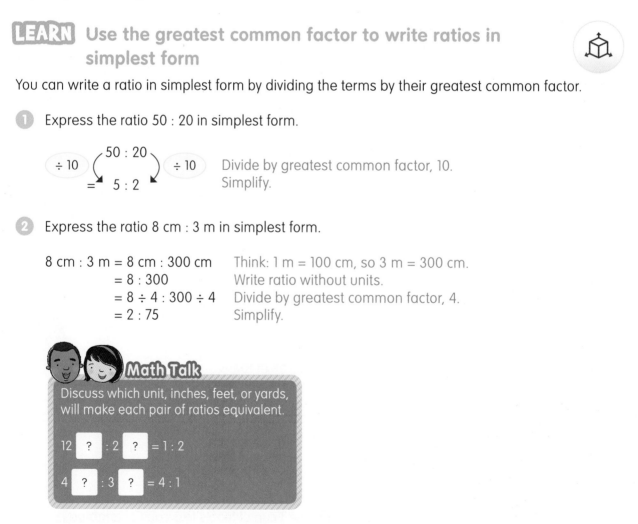

$$\div 10 \quad \overset{\displaystyle 50 : 20}{\underset{\displaystyle =\ 5 : 2}{}} \quad \div 10$$

Divide by greatest common factor, 10.
Simplify.

② Express the ratio 8 cm : 3 m in simplest form.

8 cm : 3 m = 8 cm : 300 cm   Think: 1 m = 100 cm, so 3 m = 300 cm.
        = 8 : 300   Write ratio without units.
        = 8 ÷ 4 : 300 ÷ 4   Divide by greatest common factor, 4.
        = 2 : 75   Simplify.

Math Talk

Discuss which unit, inches, feet, or yards, will make each pair of ratios equivalent.

12 [?] : 2 [?] = 1 : 2

4 [?] : 3 [?] = 4 : 1

© 2020 Marshall Cavendish Education Pte Ltd

Practice using the greatest common factor to write ratios in simplest form

Express each ratio in simplest form.

1 12 : 64

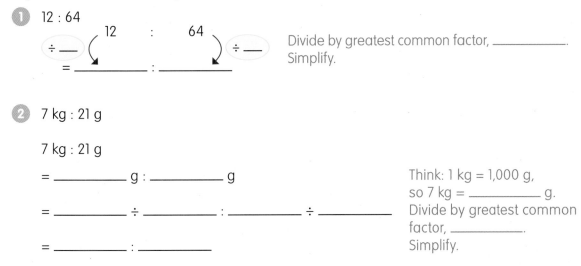

Divide by greatest common factor, _____.
Simplify.

= _____ : _____

2 7 kg : 21 g

7 kg : 21 g

= _____ g : _____ g

= _____ ÷ _____ : _____ ÷ _____

= _____ : _____

Think: 1 kg = 1,000 g,
so 7 kg = _____ g.
Divide by greatest common
factor, _____.
Simplify.

ENGAGE

Find the missing factors.

÷ ⬚   (18 : 42)   ÷ ⬚
= ◣ 3 : 7 ◢

Explain how you did it.

Next, find the missing numbers.

× 3   (⬚ : ⬚)   × 3
= 12 : 36

Explain how you did it.

Given that 3 : 2 = 12 : ⬚ , share two methods to find the missing term.

LEARN **Find the missing term in a pair of equivalent ratios**

Given three terms in a pair of equivalent ratios, you can find the missing term.

Find the missing terms in each of the following equivalent ratios.

1 4 : 5 = 12 : ⬚

▶ Method 1

× 3   (**4** : 5)   × 3
= ◣ **12** : 15 ◢

▶ Method 2

÷ 3   (**4** : 5)   ÷ 3
= **12** : 15

The missing term is 15.

2 $42 : 54 = \boxed{?} : 9$

▶ **Method 1**

$÷ 6 \Big(\begin{array}{c} 42 : \mathbf{54} \\ = \ 7 : \mathbf{9} \end{array} \Big) ÷ 6$

▶ **Method 2**

$× 6 \Big(\begin{array}{c} 42 : \mathbf{54} \\ = \ 7 : \mathbf{9} \end{array} \Big) × 6$

The missing term is 7.

TRY **Practice finding the missing term in a pair of equivalent ratios**

Find the missing term in each pair of equivalent ratios.

1 $48 : 64 = \boxed{?} : 8$

2 $4 : 9 = 36 : \boxed{?}$

3 $\boxed{?} : 35 = 7 : 5$

4 $7 : \boxed{?} = 42 : 54$

ENGAGE

Compare the corresponding values of the ratios.

$1 : 2$ $3 : 6$ $6 : 10$ $10 : 20$ $12 : 24$ $15 : 18$

What do you notice? Which of the ratios are equivalent?
Share your observations. Now, change a term in the rest of the ratios to make all the ratios equivalent.

LEARN **Work with tables of ratios**

1 The table shows the different amounts of tea and milk used to make cups of milk tea of different cup sizes.

Cup Size	A	B	C	D	E
Amount of Tea (mL)	180	270	360	450	540
Amount of Milk (mL)	60	90	120	150	180

The ratio of the amount of tea used to the amount of milk used for each cup size is as shown.

Cup Size	A	B	C	D	E
Tea : Milk	180 : 60	270 : 90	360 : 120	450 : 150	540 : 180
Tea : Milk (Simplest Form)	3 : 1	3 : 1	3 : 1	3 : 1	3 : 1

What can you say about the ratios?

The ratio of the amount of tea used to the amount of milk used is the same for each cup size.

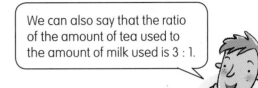

We can also say that the ratio of the amount of tea used to the amount of milk used is 3 : 1.

TRY Practice working with tables of ratios

Fill in the table.

① Mr. Smith uses the following table to prepare four mixtures of cement and sand using identical pails.

Mixture	A	B	C	D
Number of Pails of Cement	4	8	12	16
Number of Pails of Sand	3	6	9	12
Cement : Sand	4 : 3	8 : 6		
Cement : Sand (Simplest Form)	4 : 3			
$\dfrac{\text{Number of Pails of Cement}}{\text{Number of Pails of Sand}}$	$\dfrac{4}{3}$			

ENGAGE

a   Draw some circles on a piece of paper. For every 3 red cubes you put inside each circle, put 2 blue cubes. How do you find the number of red cubes and the number of blue cubes inside 5 circles? Explain your reasoning.

b   Now, consider this problem. Sabri made 4 jugs of mixed juice. To make each jug of juice, he used apples and carrots in the ratio 5 : 3. How many apples and carrots did he use in all?

LEARN Work with descriptions of ratios to find quantities

1 To make 1 portion of dough, Sophia mixes 5 cups of flour with every 3 cups of water.

a Find the ratio of the amount of flour used to the amount of water used to make 1 portion of dough.

Amount of flour : Amount of water = 5 : 3

The ratio of the amount of flour used to the amount of water used to make 1 portion of dough is 5 : 3.

b Sophia wants to make 5 portions of dough. How many cups of flour and how many cups of water does she need?

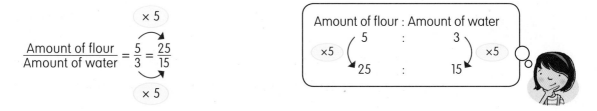

$$\frac{\text{Amount of flour}}{\text{Amount of water}} = \frac{5}{3} = \frac{25}{15}$$

(×5)

(×5)

Amount of flour : Amount of water

×5 (5 : 3) ×5

25 : 15

She needs 25 cups of flour and 15 cups of water.

c Sophia uses 21 cups of water to make the same type of dough. How many cups of flour does she need?

▶ **Method 1**

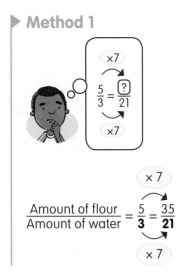

×7

$$\frac{5}{3} = \frac{?}{21}$$

×7

× 7

$$\frac{\text{Amount of flour}}{\text{Amount of water}} = \frac{5}{3} = \frac{35}{21}$$

× 7

She needs 35 cups of flour.

▶ **Method 2**

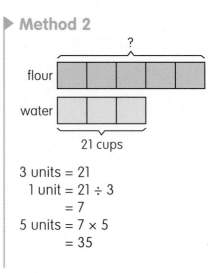

?

flour

water

21 cups

3 units = 21
1 unit = 21 ÷ 3
      = 7
5 units = 7 × 5
      = 35

Work in pairs.

① A gingerbread man recipe makes 12 cookies. Use the recipe below to find the ratio of the amount of flour needed to the amount of brown sugar needed.

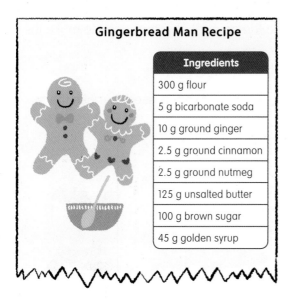

Gingerbread Man Recipe

Ingredients
300 g flour
5 g bicarbonate soda
10 g ground ginger
2.5 g ground cinnamon
2.5 g ground nutmeg
125 g unsalted butter
100 g brown sugar
45 g golden syrup

② Use the ratio in ① to find the amounts of flour and brown sugar needed to make 48 cookies. Check each other's answer.

③ Take turns to find each of the following and check the answers.

a Find the amount of ground ginger and ground cinnamon needed to make 6 cookies.

b Find the amount of flour and golden syrup needed to make 72 cookies.

TRY Practice working with descriptions of ratios to find quantities

Solve.

1. A recipe for each bowl of a yogurt and cereal mix uses 3 tablespoons of cereal for every 2 tablespoons of yogurt.

    a Find the ratio of the amount of cereal used to the amount of yogurt used to make the mix.

       Amount of cereal : Amount of yogurt = _____ : _____

       The ratio of the amount of cereal used to the amount of yogurt used to make the mix is

       _____ : _____.

    b Ms. Brown wants to make 4 bowls of the yogurt and cereal mix. How many tablespoons of cereal and how many tablespoons of yogurt does she need?

       $$\frac{\text{Amount of cereal}}{\text{Amount of yogurt}} = \frac{3}{2}$$

       $$= \frac{}{}$$

       She needs _____ tablespoons of cereal and _____ tablespoons of yogurt.

    c Mr. Gray uses 24 tablespoons of cereal. How many tablespoons of yogurt does he need?

       ▶ **Method 1**

       $$\frac{\text{Amount of cereal}}{\text{Amount of yogurt}} = \frac{3}{2} = \frac{}{}$$

       ▶ **Method 2**

       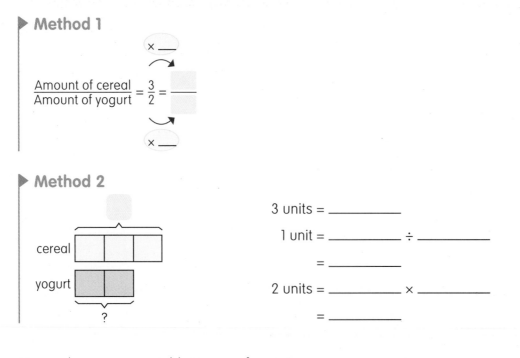

       3 units = _____

       1 unit = _____ ÷ _____

       = _____

       2 units = _____ × _____

       = _____

       He needs _____ tablespoons of yogurt.

2 A recipe uses 200 milliliters of apple juice concentrate for every 500 milliliters of water to make a drink.

a Find the ratio of the amount of apple juice concentrate used to the amount of water used to make the drink.

Amount of apple juice concentrate : Amount of water = _____ : _____

= _____ : _____

The ratio of the amount of apple juice concentrate used to the amount of water used to make the drink is _____ : _____.

b Find the missing numbers in the table.

Amount of Apple Juice Concentrate (mL)		200	600		1,400
Amount of Water (mL)	250	500		2,500	

$$\frac{2}{5} = \frac{}{250}$$

× _____

× _____

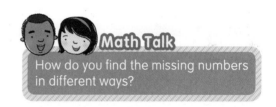

Math Talk

How do you find the missing numbers in different ways?

c Valeria uses 800 milliliters of apple juice concentrate to make the same drink. How much water does she need?

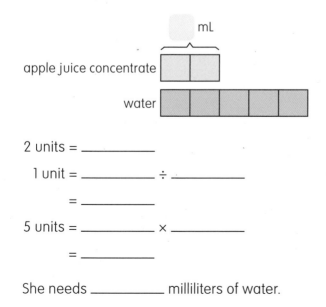

2 units = _____

1 unit = _____ ÷ _____

= _____

5 units = _____ × _____

= _____

She needs _____ milliliters of water.

ENGAGE

The ratio of the number of red cubes to the number of green cubes is 2 : 3. The ratio of the number of green cubes to the number of yellow cubes is 6 : 5. Make a list of equivalent ratios for each given ratio. What do you notice from the two lists? Share your observations.

LEARN Find equivalent ratios involving two sets of ratios

1. The ratio of the number of students from Class A to the number of students from Class B at a concert is 4 : 5. The ratio of the number of students from Class B to the number of students from Class C is 10 : 9. Find the ratio of the number of students from Class A to the number of students from Class B to the number of students from Class C at the concert.

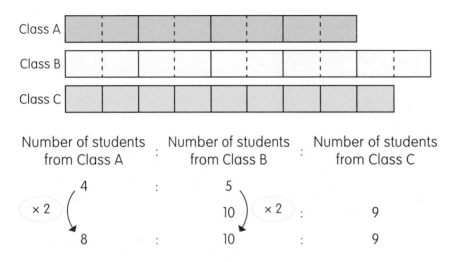

The ratio of the number of students from Class A to the number of students from Class B to the number of students from Class C at the concert is 8 : 10 : 9.

TRY Practice finding equivalent ratios involving two sets of ratios

Solve.

1. The ratio of the area of Rectangle A to the area of Rectangle B is 7 : 11. The ratio of the area of Rectangle A to the area of Rectangle C is 21 : 40. Find the ratio of the area of Rectangle A to the area of Rectangle B to the area of Rectangle C.

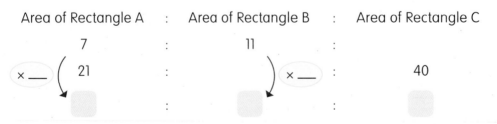

The ratio of the area of Rectangle A to the area of Rectangle B to the area of Rectangle C is

_____ : _____ : _____.

INDEPENDENT PRACTICE

Use division to find all whole-number ratios equivalent to each of the following.

1 12 : 30

2 42 : 24

State whether each pair of ratios are equivalent.

3 11 : 17 and 17 : 11

4 7 : 11 and 21 : 33

5 15 : 35 and 25 : 45

6 15 : 20 and 20 : 25

7 38 : 19 and 2 : 1

8 12 : 8 and 18 : 12

Express each ratio in simplest form.

9 13 : 39

10 16 : 40

11 25 : 15

12 56 : 21

13 30 : 54

14 72 : 48

15 26 cm : 4 m

16 9 kg : 36 g

17 35 min : 2 h

Find the missing term in each pair of equivalent ratios.

18 7 : 9 = 49 : [?]

19 12 : 5 = [?] : 60

20 4 : [?] = 48 : 180

21 [?] : 13 = 77 : 143

22 45 : 36 = [?] : 12

23 30 : 48 = 5 : [?]

24 72 : [?] = 6 : 7

25 [?] : 88 = 11 : 8

26 [?] : 12 = 63 : 108

Find the equivalent ratios.

27 Use multiplication to find three ratios equivalent to 8 : 12.

28 Use division to find all whole-number ratios equivalent to 168 : 56.

Find the missing term in each pair of equivalent ratios.

29 63 : 27 = 49 : [?]

30 81 : 18 = [?] : 8

31 24 : [?] = 5 : 20

32 [?] : 24 = 15 : 5

33 60 : 144 = [?] : 60

34 125 : 80 = 75 : [?]

35 90 : [?] = 42 : 7

36 [?] : 112 = 63 : 72

37 [?] : 45 = 96 : 108

Fill in the table.

38 Natalie used the following table to prepare five mixtures of orange paint using pails of red paint and yellow paint. The pails she used are identical.

Mixture	A	B	C	D	E
Number of Pails of Red Paint	3	6	9	12	21
Number of Pails of Yellow Paint	5	10	15	20	35
Red Paint : Yellow Paint					
Red Paint : Yellow Paint (Simplest Form)					
$\dfrac{\text{Number of Pails of Red Paint}}{\text{Number of Pails of Yellow Paint}}$					

Solve.

39 Daniel uses 5 fluid ounces of lemonade concentrate for every 9 fluid ounces of orange juice concentrate to make a serving of fruit punch.

    a Find the ratio of the number of fluid ounces of orange juice concentrate to the number of fluid ounces of lemonade concentrate he uses.

    b If Daniel wants to make 4 servings of fruit punch, how many fluid ounces of lemonade concentrate and how many fluid ounces of orange juice concentrate does he need?

    c If Daniel uses 45 fluid ounces of lemonade concentrate to make the fruit punch, how many fluid ounces of orange juice concentrate does he use?

40 A manufacturer's instruction states that for every 3 cups of cleaning agent used, 5 cups of water should be used.

a Find the ratio of the amount of cleaning agent used to the amount of water used.

b Find the missing numbers in the table.

Amount of Cleaning Agent (cups)	3	9	12		
Amount of Water (cups)	5			35	45

c A worker uses 24 cups of cleaning agent. How much water does he need?

41 The ratio of the number of stamps Brianna has to the number of stamps Aiden has is 5 : 6 and the ratio of the number of stamps Brianna has to the number of stamps Claire has is 15 : 13. Find the ratio of the number of stamps Brianna has to the number of stamps Aiden has to the number of stamps Claire has.

42 A fruit seller packs different fruit into baskets of the same size. The ratio of the weight of bananas to the weight of apples to the weight of pears is the same for all the baskets. The table shows the different weights of fruit in the baskets. Find the missing numbers in the table.

Number of Baskets	Weight of Fruit (lb)		
	Bananas	Apples	Pears
1		6	
2	8		
3	12	18	15

Name: _____   Date: _____

3 Real-World Problems: Ratios

Learning Objective:
• Solve real-world problems involving ratios.

THINK

The ratio of the ages of Layla to Bruno is 3 : 7. After some years, Bruno is twice as old as Layla. How old was Bruno 5 years ago?

ENGAGE

Isaac makes green paint by mixing blue and yellow paint in the ratio 3 : 2. The total volume of green paint is 10 fluid ounces. Find the volume of blue and yellow paint used to make the green paint. If Issac has $3\frac{1}{2}$ ounces of yellow paint, how much blue paint will he need to make green paint of the same shade?

LEARN Solve real-world problems involving ratios

1. Isabella prepares a fruit punch using apple juice and orange juice in the ratio 4 : 3. The total volume of the fruit punch is 630 milliliters. What is the volume of apple juice Isabella uses?

STEP 1 Understand the problem.

What is the ratio of the volume of apple juice to the volume of the orange juice? What is the total volume of the fruit punch? What do I need to find?

STEP 2 Think of a plan.
I can draw a model.

STEP 3 Carry out the plan.

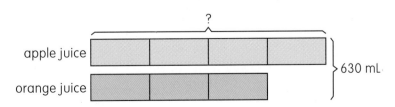

Volume of apple juice : Volume of orange juice = 4 : 3

Total volume of fruit punch = 4 + 3
= 7 units

7 units = 630
1 unit = 630 ÷ 7
= 90
4 units = 90 × 4
= 360

Isabella uses 360 milliliters of apple juice.

STEP 4 Check the answer.
I can work backwards to check my answer.

> 3 units = 90 × 3
> = 270
> Isabella uses 270 milliliters of orange juice.
>
> Volume of apple juice : Volume of orange juice
> = 360 mL : 270 mL
> = 360 : 270
> = 4 : 3
> My answer is correct.

TRY **Practice solving real-world problems involving ratios**

Solve.

1 A box contains a total of 1,380 baseball and football cards. The number of baseball cards to the number of football cards is in the ratio 5 : 1. How many baseball cards are there?

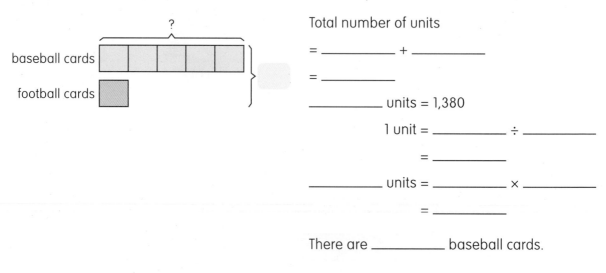

Total number of units

= _____ + _____

= _____

_____ units = 1,380

1 unit = _____ ÷ _____

= _____

_____ units = _____ × _____

= _____

There are _____ baseball cards.

ENGAGE

Adrina prepares a snack mixture consisting of almonds, cashews and raisins. The ratio of the mass of almonds to cashews to raisins is 3:1:2. The mass of the mixture is 240 grams. What is the mass of the almonds? Draw a bar model to represent these masses. Compare your bar model with your partner's.

LEARN Solve real-world problems involving ratios of three quantities

① Mason prepares a ceramic glaze mixture of feldspar, red iron oxide and silica. The ratio of the mass of the feldspar to red iron oxide to silica is 5 : 2 : 3 . The mass of the mixture is 1 kilogram 200 grams. Find the mass of each ingredient used to prepare the mixture.

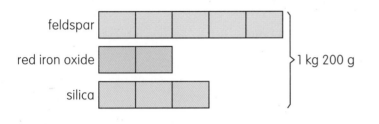

1 kg 200 g = 1,200 g

Total number of units = 5 + 2 + 3
= 10

10 units = 1,200
1 unit = 1,200 ÷ 10
= 120
2 units = 120 × 2
= 240

The mass of the red iron oxide is 240 grams.

3 units = 120 × 3
= 360

The mass of the silica is 360 grams.

5 units = 120 × 5
= 600

The mass of the feldspar is 600 grams.

> Add the mass of each ingredient to check that the total is 1 kg 200 g.
>
> 240 g + 360 g + 600 g
> = 1,200 g or 1 kg 200 g

© 2020 Marshall Cavendish Education Pte Ltd

TRY **Practice solving real-world problems involving ratios of three quantities**

Solve.

1 A school raised $18,000 at a charity event. The money raised was shared among three charities, A, B, and C, in the ratio 1 : 2 : 3. How much money did each charity receive?

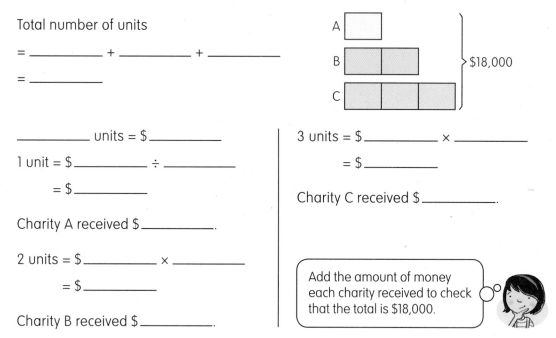

Total number of units

= _____ + _____ + _____

= _____

_____ units = $_____

1 unit = $_____ ÷ _____

= $_____

Charity A received $_____.

2 units = $_____ × _____

= $_____

Charity B received $_____.

3 units = $_____ × _____

= $_____

Charity C received $_____.

> Add the amount of money each charity received to check that the total is $18,000.

2 The number of coins collected by Dominic, Emilio, and Kiri is in the ratio 2 : 5 : 8. Emilio collected 85 coins.

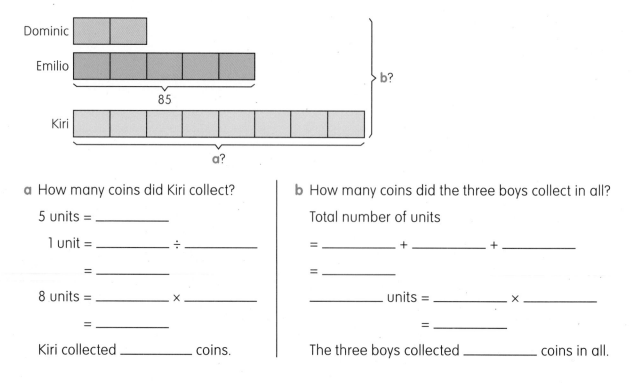

a How many coins did Kiri collect?

5 units = _____

1 unit = _____ ÷ _____

= _____

8 units = _____ × _____

= _____

Kiri collected _____ coins.

b How many coins did the three boys collect in all?

Total number of units

= _____ + _____ + _____

= _____

_____ units = _____ × _____

= _____

The three boys collected _____ coins in all.

The ratio of the mass of a rabbit to the mass of a cat is 1 : 2. The ratio of the mass of the cat to the mass of a fox is 4 : 7. Draw a bar model to find the ratio of the rabbit's mass to the fox's mass. Compare your bar model to your partner's. Now, if their total mass is 13 kilograms, how do you find the cat's mass? Explain your thinking.

LEARN Solve real-world problems involving two sets of ratios

1. The ratio of Emily's score to Gianna's score in a bowling game is 3 : 2. The ratio of Gianna's score to Liam's score is 4 : 5. Emily, Gianna, and Liam scored 360 points in all.

   a Find the ratio of Emily's score to Liam's score.

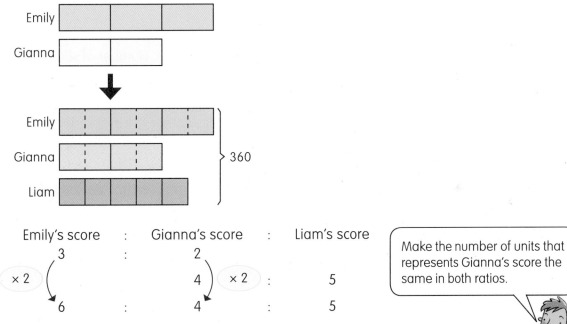

Emily's score	:	Gianna's score	:	Liam's score
3	:	2		
×2		4 ×2	:	5
6	:	4	:	5

> Make the number of units that represents Gianna's score the same in both ratios.

The ratio of Emily's score to Liam's score was 6 : 5.

   b How many points did Liam score?

Total number of units = 6 + 4 + 5
                      = 15

Method 1
15 units = 360
  1 unit = 360 ÷ 15
         = 24
5 units = 24 × 5
        = 120

Method 2
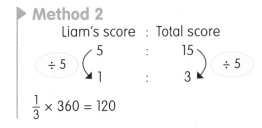

Liam's score : Total score
      5   :   15
÷5   :   ÷5
      1   :   3

$\frac{1}{3} \times 360 = 120$

Liam scored 120 points.

TRY Practice solving real-world problems involving two sets of ratios

Solve.

1 Ava, Cole, and Zane have a total of 175 stickers. The ratio of the number of stickers Ava has to the number of stickers Cole has is 5 : 3. The ratio of the number of stickers Cole has to the number of stickers Zane has is 2 : 3.

a Find the ratio of the number of stickers Ava has to the number of stickers Cole has to the number of stickers Zane has.

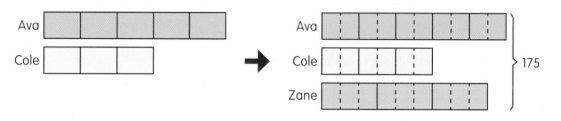

Number of stickers Ava has : Number of stickers Cole has : Number of stickers Zane has

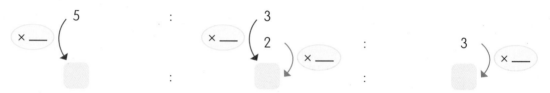

b How many stickers do Ava and Cole have in all?

▶ **Method 1**
Total number of units = _____ + _____ + _____

= _____

Number of units Ava and Cole have in all = _____ + _____

= _____

_____ units = _____

1 unit = _____ ÷ _____

= _____

_____ units = _____ × _____

= _____

▶ **Method 2**
Number of stickers Ava and Cole have : Total number of stickers

_____ × _____ = _____

Ava and Cole have _____ stickers in all.

Hannah had some blue and black pens. The ratio of the number of blue pens to the number of black pens is 2 : 1. Use three rectangular strips of paper of the same size to represent the ratio. Then, divide each strip into two equal parts using vertical lines. What ratio do you get?

Next, Hannah bought another 5 blue pens and the ratio became 5 : 2. How would you represent this situation? Draw a bar model to record your thinking. How many black pens did Hannah have? Explain your thinking.

LEARN Solve before-and-after problems involving changing ratios

1 Katherine placed some green and red apples in a basket. The ratio of the number of green apples to the number of red apples was 2 : 1. She placed 12 more red apples in the basket and the ratio of the number of green apples to the number of red apples became 4 : 5.

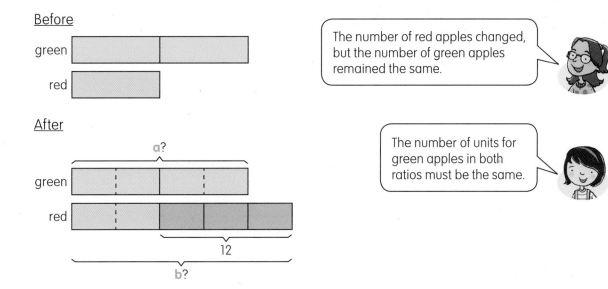

Before

green

red

The number of red apples changed, but the number of green apples remained the same.

After

a?

green

red

12

b?

The number of units for green apples in both ratios must be the same.

a How many green apples were there in the basket?

3 units = 12
1 unit = 12 ÷ 3
     = 4
4 units = 4 × 4
     = 16

There were 16 green apples in the basket.

b How many red apples were in the basket in the end?

5 units = 4 × 5
     = 20

There were 20 red apples in the basket in the end.

2. Sean and Michelle had some badges each. The ratio of the number of badges Sean had to the number of badges Michelle had was 4 : 3. Sean then gave 48 badges to Michelle. The ratio of the number of badges Sean had to the number of badges Michelle had became 2 : 3.

> The number of badges Sean and Michelle each had, changed. However, the total number of badges they had remained unchanged. So, the total number of units in both situations must be equal.

Before

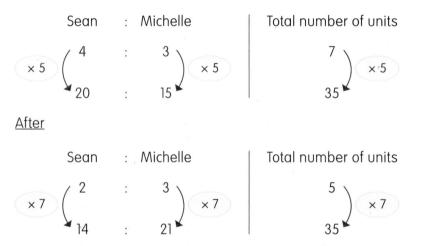

After

a How many badges did Sean have at first?

> After Sean gave Michelle 48 badges, the number of units Sean had decreased from 20 units to 14 units.

Difference in the number of units = 20 − 14
                                   = 6

6 units = 48
1 unit = 48 ÷ 6
        = 8
20 units = 8 × 20
         = 160

Sean had 160 badges at first.

b How many badges did Michelle have in the end?

21 units = 8 × 21
         = 168

Michelle had 168 badges in the end.

Activity Solving before-and-after problems involving changing ratios

Work in pairs.

① Read and solve the real-world problem.

> Nathan and Lilian shared some files in the ratio 5 : 7. Lilian gave Nathan 6 files. The ratio of the number of files Nathan had to the number of files Lilian had became 2 : 1. How many files were there in all?

② Discuss your solutions. Did you solve the same way? Why or why not?

③ Repeat the activity with the following word problem.

> Kaden and Jenna shared some cookies equally. After Jenna gave 12 of the cookies to her brother, the ratio of the number of cookies Kaden had to the number of cookies Jenna had became 5 : 3. How many cookies did Jenna have at first?

TRY Practice solving before-and-after problems involving changing ratios

Solve.

① Zara had some U.S. stamps and some foreign stamps. The ratio of the number of U.S. stamps to the number of foreign stamps was 3 : 4. She gave away 28 foreign stamps and the ratio of the number of U.S. stamps to the number of foreign stamps became 9 : 8.

Before

U.S.

foreign

After

a?

U.S.

foreign

b?

What remained the same? What changed?

a How many U.S. stamps did Zara have?

_____ units = _____

1 unit = _____ ÷ _____

= _____

_____ units = _____ × _____

= _____

Zara had _____ U.S. stamps.

b How many foreign stamps did Zara have in the end?

_____ units = _____ × _____

= _____

Zara had _____ foreign stamps in the end.

2 Henry and Nicole made some greeting cards. The ratio of the number of cards Henry made to the number of cards Nicole made was 5 : 2. Henry gave Nicole 46 cards. The ratio of the number of cards Henry had to the number of cards Nicole had became 6 : 7.

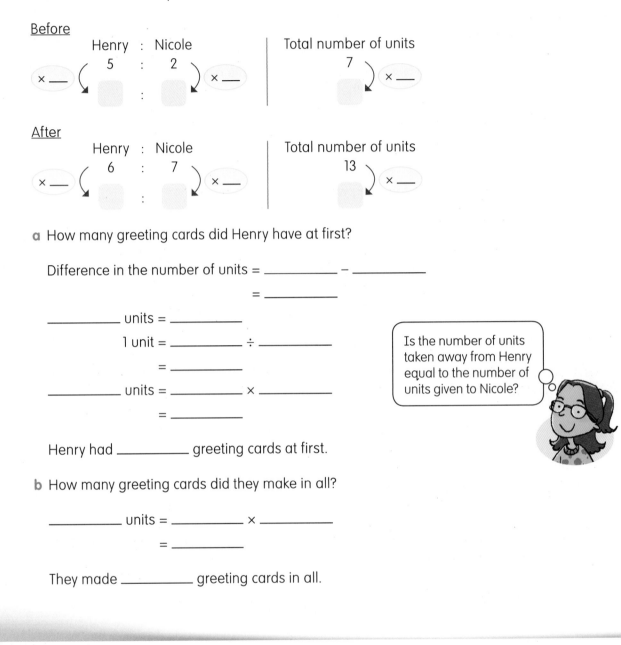

Before

Henry : Nicole

5 : 2

Total number of units

7

After

Henry : Nicole

6 : 7

Total number of units

13

a How many greeting cards did Henry have at first?

Difference in the number of units = _____ – _____

= _____

_____ units = _____

1 unit = _____ ÷ _____

= _____

_____ units = _____ × _____

= _____

> Is the number of units taken away from Henry equal to the number of units given to Nicole?

Henry had _____ greeting cards at first.

b How many greeting cards did they make in all?

_____ units = _____ × _____

= _____

They made _____ greeting cards in all.

Compare each ratio statement with the fraction statement. What pattern do you notice?
Similarly, how do you convert ratio statements in real-world problems to fraction statements?
Discuss some examples with your classmates.

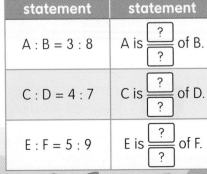

Ratio statement	Fraction statement
A : B = 3 : 8	A is $\frac{?}{?}$ of B.
C : D = 4 : 7	C is $\frac{?}{?}$ of D.
E : F = 5 : 9	E is $\frac{?}{?}$ of F.

Name: _____ Date: _____

Solve.

1. In a science experiment, Elizabeth mixes a salt solution and vinegar in the ratio 3 : 7. The total volume of the mixture is 260 milliliters. What is the volume of vinegar Elizabeth uses?

2. A rope is cut into three pieces, P, Q, and R. The lengths of the pieces are in the ratio 3 : 5 : 7. If the rope is 33 feet 9 inches long, find the lengths of P, Q, and R.

   P ▬▬▬▬
   Q ▬▬▬▬▬▬
   R ▬▬▬▬▬▬▬▬

3. Angelina, Briella, and Destiny shared some stamps in the ratio 8 : 9 : 18. Angelina received 184 stamps. Find the number of stamps that Briella and Destiny each received.

4. The number of points Chris, Noah, and Xavier scored in a video game was in the ratio 2 : 3 : 4. Xavier scored 114,400 points.

   a How many points did Noah score?

   b How many points did the three children score in all?

5. Madeline has three cats: Socks, Princess, and Luna. The ratio of Socks's weight to Princess's weight is 4 : 5. The ratio of Princess's weight to Luna's weight is 6 : 7. What is the ratio of Socks's weight to Luna's weight?

6. Benjamin poured 78 milliliters of water into Containers X, Y, and Z. The ratio of the volume of water in Container X to the volume of water in Container Y is 5 : 2. The ratio of the volume of water in Container Y to the volume of water in Container Z is 8 : 11.

   a How much water was poured into Container X?

   b How much more water was poured into Container X than Container Z?

7. The ratio of the number of mystery books to the number of science fiction books in a bookcase is 4 : 3. The ratio of the number of science fiction books to the number of biographies is 4 : 5. If there are 48 science fiction books, find the total number of books in the bookcase.

8 In a music room, the ratio of the number of clarinets to the number of flutes was 3 : 4. After the school bought another 24 flutes, the ratio became 3 : 8. How many clarinets were there in the music room?

9 At a book fair, the ratio of the number of students to the number of adults was 4 : 3. After 160 students left the book fair, the ratio became 4 : 5. How many adults were there at the book fair?

10 The number of chickens to the number of ducks on a farm was 6 : 5. After 63 ducks were sold, there were 3 times as many chickens as ducks left.

   a How many chickens were there on the farm?

   b How many chickens and ducks were there altogether on the farm in the end?

11 Last year, the ratio of the number of students in an art club to the number of students in a science club was 3 : 2. This year, 70 more students joined the science club and no students left either of the clubs. There are now 4 times as many students in the science club as the art club.

   a How many students are there in the art club?

   b How many students are in the art and science clubs this year?

12 Jessica and Sanjay collected some seashells. The ratio of Jessica's seashells to Sanjay's seashells was 3 : 1. Jessica gave Sanjay 21 seashells. The ratio of Jessica's seashells to Sanjay's seashells became 2 : 3. How many seashells did Jessica have at first?

13 The ratio of the number of stamps Sara has to the number of stamps Hunter has was 3 : 8. After Hunter had given 18 stamps to Sara, the ratio became 9 : 13.

   a How many stamps did Hunter have at first?

   b How many stamps did they have in all?

14 The ratio of the volume of fruit juice to the volume of smoothies served at a party was $4\frac{1}{2}$: 2.4. There were 35 liters more fruit juice served than smoothies. Find the volume of smoothies served.

15 A piece of ribbon is cut into two shorter pieces in the ratio 2.8 : 1.25. The difference in the length of the two shorter pieces is 80.6 centimeters. What is the length of the original piece of ribbon?

16 The ratio of Ricardo's age to his mother's age is 3 : 8. After 15 years, the ratio will become 6 : 11.

a Find Ricardo's age now.

b Find his mother's age after 15 years.

17. The ratio of Owen's savings to Lucas's savings was 4 : 3. After Owen saved another $120 and Lucas saved another $60, the ratio became 8 : 5. What was their combined savings before each of them saved the additional money?

18. Michael was reading a book. The ratio of the number of pages read to the number of pages unread was 2 : 5. After Michael had read 32 more pages, the ratio of the number of pages read to the number of pages unread became 18 : 17. How many pages were there in the book?

19. The ratio of the number of $5 and $10 bills in a box was 5 : 7. Four $10 bills were taken out from the box, changed into $5 bills, and put back in the box. The ratio of the number of $5 and $10 bills in the box became 9 : 5. What was the total value of all the bills in the box?

Name: _____ Date: _____

Mathematical Habit 2 Use mathematical reasoning

The ratio of the number of beads collected by Mia to the number of beads collected by Natalia was 7 : 3. Mia gave some beads to Natalia. Is it possible for both Mia and Natalia to have the same number of beads after Mia gave some beads to Natalia? Explain why you think so.

Problem Solving with Heuristics

1 **Mathematical Habit** **7** **Make use of structure**

ABCD is a rectangle. *BD* is a straight line that cuts the rectangle into equal halves. The ratio of the area of P to the area of Q is 2 : 5, and the ratio of the area R to the area of S is 4 : 3. The area of S is 9 square centimeters.

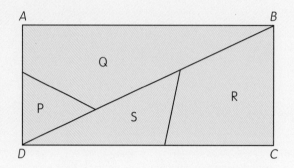

a Find the ratio of the area of R to the area of the rectangle.

b Find the area of the rectangle.

© 2020 Marshall Cavendish Education Pte Ltd

2 **Mathematical Habit 1** **Persevere in solving problems**

A farmer raises chickens and sheep on his farm. The ratio of the total number of legs of the chickens to the total number of legs of the sheep is 4 : 7. Find the minimum number of chickens and sheep on his farm. Use the table to solve the problem.

Number of Chickens	Number of Legs of Chickens	Number of Sheep	Number of Legs of Sheep	Number of Legs of Chickens : Number of Legs of Sheep
1	2	1	4	2 : 4 = 1 : 2

CHAPTER WRAP-UP

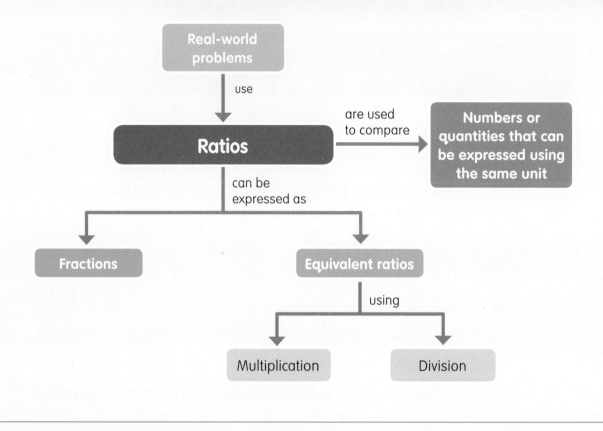

KEY CONCEPTS

- A ratio compares two or more numbers or quantities.
- When two quantities can be expressed using the same unit, you can compare them using a ratio without units.
- The ratio of two numbers, such as the ratio of 3 to 4 can be written as 3 : 4 or $\frac{3}{4}$.
- A ratio can be expressed as another equivalent ratio by
  - multiplying the terms of the ratio by the same multiplying factor.
  - dividing the terms of the ratio by a common factor.
- Given two equivalent ratios, you can find an unknown term given the other three terms.

Name: _____ Date: _____

Express each ratio in simplest form.

1 8 : 24

2 36 : 9

3 14 : 49

4 45 : 30

5 27 : 72

6 64 : 56

7 15 in. : 4 ft

8 2 L : 250 mL

9 550 m : 3 km

Find the missing term in each pair of equivalent ratios.

10 1 : 3 = 6 : [?]

11 4 : 7 = [?] : 21

12 25 : 15 = [?] : 3

13 54 : 36 = 18 : [?]

14 4 : [?] = 20 : 25

15 [?] : 9 = 48 : 72

16 28 : [?] = 4 : 6

17 [?] : 36 = 21 : 12

18 12 : [?] = 132 : 77

Solve.

19 There are 157 students in a dance club. 78 of them are in the sixth grade and the rest are in the seventh grade.

a What is the ratio of the number of students in the sixth grade to the number of students in the seventh grade?

b What is the ratio of the number of students in the seventh grade to the total number of students in the dance club?

20 A vase holds some roses and tulips. The number of roses is $\frac{7}{8}$ of the number of tulips.

 a Find the ratio of the number of roses to the number of tulips.

 b Find the ratio of the number of tulips to the total number of flowers.

21 The length of a ladybug is 9 millimeters. The length of a caterpillar is 45 millimeters.

 a How many times the length of the ladybug is the length of the caterpillar?

 b How many times the length of the caterpillar is the length of the ladybug?

22 A city has 28 ambulances and 36 fire trucks. Find the ratio of the number of ambulances to the number of fire trucks in simplest form.

23 Of the 80 students who signed up for after school clubs, 16 students signed up for the art club, and the rest signed up for other clubs. Find the ratio of the number of students who signed up for the art club to the number of students who signed up for other clubs. Express your answer in simplest form.

24 On Saturday, Jasmine used her cell phone for 36 minutes. On Sunday, she used her cell phone for 18 minutes more than on Saturday. Find the ratio of the number of minutes Jasmine used her phone for on Saturday to the total number of minutes she used it for on Saturday and Sunday. Express your answer in simplest form.

25 Elijah is 12 years old. John is 15 years older than Elijah. Kevin is 3 years younger than John. Find the ratio of Elijah's age to Kevin's age. Express your answer in simplest form.

26 The ratio of the number of left-handed batters in a team to the number of right-handed batters was 5 : 8. There were 45 left-handed batters.

a How many right-handed batters were there?

b Find the ratio of the number of left-handed batters to the total number of batters. Express your answer in simplest form.

27 Kaitlyn used the following table to prepare five mixtures of green paint using pails of blue paint and yellow paint. The pails she used are identical and she got the same shade of green for each mixture. Find the missing numbers in the table.

Mixture	A	B	C	D	E
Number of Pails of Blue Paint		10	15		25
Number of Pails of Yellow Paint	4		12	16	

a Find the ratio of the number of pails of blue paint used to the number of pails of yellow paint used for each mixture in simplest form.

b For each mixture, what fraction of the number of pails of blue paint used is the number of pails of yellow paint used?

28 Gabrielle mixes 6 cups of garden soil for every 5 cups of compost to make soil mixture for one flowerpot.

a Find the ratio of the amount of garden soil used to the amount of compost used.

b If Gabrielle wants to fill 7 flowerpots with the soil mixture, how many cups of garden soil and how many cups of compost does she need?

c If Gabrielle uses 45 cups of compost, how many cups of garden soil does she need?

29 The ratio of Pablo's age to Richard's age is 6 : 7. The ratio of Pablo's age to Tristan's age is 5 : 4. Find the ratio of Pablo's age to Richard's age to Tristan's age.

30 Ms. Murphy donated a sum of money to Charity A and Charity B in the ratio 5 : 6. Charity B received $2,400. How much did Ms. Murphy donate in all?

© 2020 Marshall Cavendish Education Pte Ltd

31 The ratio of the number of nonfiction books to the number of fiction books at a reading corner is 5 : 7. If there are 600 books at the reading corner, how many fiction books are there?

32 A sum of money was donated to Charities X, Y, and Z in the ratio 2 : 5 : 7. If Charity Z received $1,200 more than Charity X, what was the original sum of money donated?

33 The ratio of the number of beads Britney had to the number of beads Sofia had was 2 : 5. After Sofia bought another 75 beads, the ratio became 4 : 15. How many beads did each girl have at first?

34 Mr. Hill had some bottles of apple juice and orange juice. The ratio of the number of bottles of apple juice to the number of bottles of orange juice was 3 : 2. After he sold 64 bottles of apple juice, the ratio became 1 : 6. Find the total number of bottles of apple juice and orange juice Mr. Hill had in the end.

35 Christian and Yong had some stickers in the ratio 2 : 3. After Yong gave Christian 15 stickers, the ratio became 5 : 7. What was the total number of stickers they had?

Assessment Prep
Answer each question.

36 A library has fiction and nonfiction books. The ratio of the number of fiction books to the total number of books is 5 : 8. What is the ratio of the fiction to the nonfiction books in the library? Write your answer in the space below.

37 A class of 25 children shares 600 beads. On a day when 1 child is absent, what is the ratio of the number of children present to the number of beads? Write your answer in the space below.

38 This question has two parts.

A factory makes basketballs and volleyballs. The table below shows the factory production of basketballs for over two years.

Year	Number of Basketballs Made
2017	24,356
2018	30,164

Part A
The ratio of the total number of basketballs to the total number of volleyballs made in the two years is 5 : 3. What is the total number of volleyballs made in the two years? Write your answer and your work or explanation in the space below.

Part B
The ratio of the total number of basketballs and volleyballs made in the two years to the total number of basketballs and volleyballs made in 2019 is 4 : 3. The cost price of making each basketball or volleyball is $5. What is the factory's production cost in 2019? Write your answer and your work or explanation in the space below.

Name: _____   Date: _____

Baking Muffins

1 A group of sixth-graders baked muffins for a school fair. The ratio of the number of banana muffins to the number of blueberry muffins they baked was 3 : 5. The total number of muffins is more than 80 but fewer than 100. It is also not a factor of 3.

a How many muffins did the students bake in all?

b How many blueberry muffins did they bake?

2 A group of seventh-graders and a group of eighth-graders in the same school also baked muffins for the school fair. The ratio of the number of muffins the sixth-graders baked to the number of muffins the seventh-graders baked to the number of muffins the eighth-graders baked was 4 : 5 : 7. Find the total number of muffins the students baked. Show and explain your work.

3 The sixth-graders raised $\frac{2}{3}$ as much money as the seventh-graders at the school fair in the morning. In the afternoon, the sixth-graders continued to raise more money. In the end, they raised twice as much money as the seventh-graders. Both the sixth-graders and seventh-graders raised $324 in the end. How much more money did the sixth-graders raise in the afternoon? Show and explain your work.

© 2020 Marshall Cavendish Education Pte Ltd

Rubric

Point(s)	Level	My Performance
7–8	4	• Most of my answers are correct. • I showed complete understanding of the concepts. • I used effective and efficient strategies to solve the problems. • I explained my answers and mathematical thinking clearly and completely.
5–6	3	• Some of my answers are correct. • I showed adequate understanding of the concepts. • I used effective strategies to solve the problems. • I explained my answers and mathematical thinking clearly.
3–4	2	• A few of my answers are correct. • I showed some understanding of the concepts. • I used some effective strategies to solve the problems. • I explained some of my answers and mathematical thinking clearly.
0–2	1	• A few of my answers are correct. • I showed little understanding of the concepts. • I used limited effective strategies to solve the problems. • I did not explain my answers and mathematical thinking clearly.

Teacher's Comments

STEAM

Human Body Ratios

A ratio is a comparison of two or more values. For example, the ratio of the length of toes to the length of feet on a human body is approximately 1 to 5.

Although humans exist in all shapes and sizes, human body ratios generally tend to be similar and fit within certain ranges.

Task

Work in pairs to explore human body ratios and use the ratios to draw a picture.

① Collect a tape measure, paper, and pencil. Make a table to record measurements of the lengths of your big toe, foot, thumb, hand, arm span, height, thigh bone (or femur), and head. Round each measurement to the nearest whole number.

② Find the following ratios by comparing the lengths of:

- your big toe and your foot
- your thumb and your hand
- your arm span and your height
- your thigh bone and your height
- your head and your height

Write each ratio as a fraction in simplest form.

③ Explore additional human body ratios. Record your findings in your table.

④ Use the ratios you found to help you draw a full-body portrait of your partner.

How much is the postage?

With the postal service, you can mail a letter or a parcel anywhere in the world. The cost of postal services depends on the type and weight of an item as well as its destination.

Look at the illustration below. Suppose you want to mail something to a friend. You visit the post office to weigh the envelope and it measures 4 ounces. The first ounce costs $1.00, and each additional ounce costs 21 cents. This additional per-ounce cost is an example of a rate.

In this chapter, you will learn more about rates and how to apply them to solve real-world problems. Some rates you may have seen before include unit prices for food and gas, currency exchange rates, and parking fees.

Domestic Postage Rates		
	Weight Not Over (oz)	Price
Single-piece Letter (Stamped)	1	$0.50
	2	$0.71
	3	$0.92
	3.5	$1.13
Single-piece Letter (Metered)	1	$0.47
	2	$0.68
	3	$0.89
	3.5	$1.10
Single-piece Envelope (Flat)	1	$1.00
	Each additional ounce or part thereof	$0.21
Postcard	–	$0.35

How does the use of a rate help you compare one quantity to another quantity?

Name: _____   Date: _____

Multiplying whole numbers

Find 324×72.

$$
\begin{array}{r}
324 \\
\times \quad 72 \\
\hline
648 \\
22{,}680 \\
\hline
23{,}328 \\
\end{array}
$$

$324 \times 2 = 648$

$324 \times 70 = 22{,}680$

▶ **Quick Check**
Multiply.

1 54×471

2 75×698

Multiplying fractions or mixed numbers by a whole number

a $\dfrac{2}{15} \times 3 = \dfrac{2}{15} \times \cancel{3}^{1}$ Divide the denominator of the fraction and the whole number by their common factor, 3.

$= \dfrac{2}{5}$ Multiply.

b $2\dfrac{3}{5} \times 4 = \dfrac{13}{5} \times 4$ Express the mixed number as an improper fraction.

$= \dfrac{52}{5}$ Multiply.

$= 10\dfrac{2}{5}$ Express the improper fraction as a mixed number.

▶ **Quick Check**
Find each product in simplest form.

3 $4 \times \dfrac{5}{32}$

4 $9\dfrac{1}{2} \times 8$

Multiplying fractions

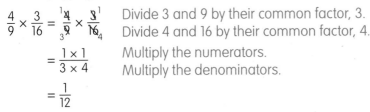

Divide 3 and 9 by their common factor, 3.
Divide 4 and 16 by their common factor, 4.

$$= \frac{1 \times 1}{3 \times 4}$$

Multiply the numerators.
Multiply the denominators.

$$= \frac{1}{12}$$

▶ Quick Check

Find each product in simplest form.

⑤ $\frac{2}{7} \times \frac{63}{84}$

⑥ $\frac{11}{18} \times \frac{3}{44}$

Dividing with fractions and whole numbers

Write as a multiplication expression.
Divide the numerator and denominator by their common factor, 3.

$$= \frac{1 \times 1}{4 \times 9}$$

Multiply the numerators.
Multiply the denominators.

$$= \frac{1}{36}$$

▶ Quick Check

Find each quotient in simplest form.

⑦ $\frac{6}{7} \div 30$

⑧ $72 \div \frac{9}{10}$

⑨ $\frac{7}{9} \div 49$

⑩ $56 \div \frac{8}{11}$

Dividing fractions

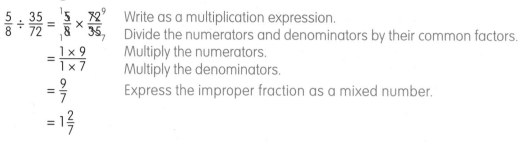

$\frac{5}{8} \div \frac{35}{72} = \frac{\overset{1}{5}}{\underset{1}{8}} \times \frac{\overset{9}{72}}{\underset{7}{35}}$ Write as a multiplication expression.
Divide the numerators and denominators by their common factors.

$= \frac{1 \times 9}{1 \times 7}$ Multiply the numerators.
Multiply the denominators.

$= \frac{9}{7}$ Express the improper fraction as a mixed number.

$= 1\frac{2}{7}$

▶ **Quick Check**

Find each quotient in simplest form.

(11) $\frac{4}{9} \div \frac{36}{135}$

(12) $\frac{77}{92} \div \frac{11}{42}$

Finding the quantity represented by a number of units

If 4 units represent 132 centimeters, find the value of 9 units.

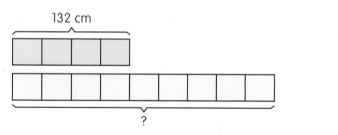

132 cm

?

4 units = 132
1 unit = 132 ÷ 4
      = 33
9 units = 33 × 9
      = 297

The value of 9 units is 297 centimeters.

▶ **Quick Check**

Find the value of each number of units.

(13) If 7 units represent 98 liters, find the value of 15 units.

(14) If 13 units represent 143 square meters, find the value of 24 units.

Finding ratios

You can use a ratio to compare two quantities that can be expressed as the same unit.

Find the ratio of length 47 centimeters to 2 meters.

47 cm : 2 m = 47 cm : 200 cm   Express as the same unit.
          = 47 : 200   Simplify.

This ratio can be expressed in three ways:
47 : 200, 47 to 200, and $\frac{47}{200}$.

▶ **Quick Check**
State whether each of the following can be expressed as a ratio.

15   3 m and 2 km

16   4 ft and 4 kg

Finding ratios in simplest form

a When you divide or multiply the terms of a ratio by the same number, you obtain equivalent ratios.

÷ 2 (12 : 18) ÷ 2
=   6 : 9
÷ 3 (   ) ÷ 3
=   2 : 3

12 : 18, 6 : 9, and 2 : 3 are equivalent ratios.
2 : 3 is in simplest form.

× 2 (6 : 7) × 2
= 12 : 14

× 3 (6 : 7) × 3
= 18 : 21

6 : 7, 12 : 14, and 18 : 21 are equivalent ratios.
6 : 7 is in simplest form.

b You can write a ratio in simplest form by dividing the terms by their greatest common factor.

10 g : 3 kg = 10 g : 3,000 g   Think: 1 kg = 1,000 g, so 3 kg = 3,000 g.
           = 10 : 3,000   Write ratio without units.
           = 10 ÷ 10 : 3,000 ÷ 10   Divide by their greatest common factor, 10.
           = 1 : 300

▶ **Quick Check**
Use division to find all whole-number ratios equivalent to each of the following.

⑰   24 : 54

⑱   130 : 50

Express each ratio in simplest form.

⑲   90 : 60

⑳   72 : 184

㉑   4 km : 370 m

㉒   66 L : 120 mL

㉓   15 in. : 5 ft

㉔   270 qt : 105 gal

Name: _____   Date: _____

Rates and Unit Rates

Learning Objective:
• Solve unit rate problems including unit pricing.

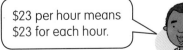

New Vocabulary
unit rate

THINK

When fully filled, Tank A contained 320 liters of water and Tank B contained 560 liters of water. The same amount of water was drained from each tank in 1 minute. After 4 minutes later, Tank A was half-empty. How long more would it take Tank B to be emptied?

ENGAGE

Austin types 39 words per minute. State the two quantities in the statement and explain what the statement means.

Now, use any two of these units to relate two quantities in a statement. Share your statements.

| mile | meter | dollar | gallon | pounds | minute | hour |

LEARN Identify a unit rate

1 Recall that you can use a ratio to compare two quantities that have the same unit.

A is 80 centimeters long. B is 92 centimeters long.
A and B are two lengths with the same unit.

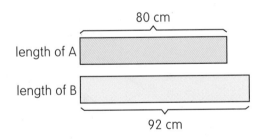

80 cm

length of A

length of B

92 cm

The ratio of the length of A to the length of B is 80 : 92 or 40 : 46 or 20 : 23.

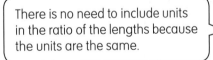

There is no need to include units in the ratio of the lengths because the units are the same.

2 You can use a rate to compare two quantities with different units, such as money and time.

For example, if Mai earns $23 in one hour, you can use the rate $23 per hour, or $\frac{\$23}{1 \text{ hour}}$ to

describe how much money she earns in one hour. This rate can also be written as $23/h.

The rate $23/h is an example of a unit rate.
A unit rate compares a quantity to one unit of a different quantity.

Math Note
The symbol / means per.

$23 per hour means
$23 for each hour.

TRY Practice **identifying** a unit rate

State whether each statement is expressed as a unit rate.

1 A monkey plucked 4 coconuts per minute.

2 Gabriella paid $2 for a bottle of orange juice.

3 A basketball team scored 294 points in 6 games.

4 Joseph reads 3 books in a week.

ENGAGE

Sue picked apples at a farm for 3 hours. She picked a total of 171 apples and put them equally in 9 baskets. Write two expressions (in unit rates) to relate any 2 quantities. Then, write statements for each expression.

LEARN Express and compute unit rates in terms of time and other quantities

1 A printer prints 750 pages in 10 minutes.

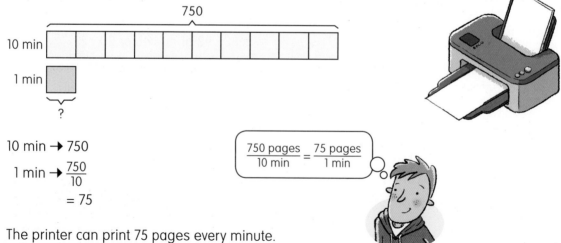

10 min → 750

1 min → $\frac{750}{10}$

= 75

$$\frac{750 \text{ pages}}{10 \text{ min}} = \frac{75 \text{ pages}}{1 \text{ min}}$$

The printer can print 75 pages every minute.
The printer prints at a rate of 75 pages per minute.

Practice expressing and computing unit rates in terms of time and other quantities

Solve.

1. Kimberly is paid $48 for working 6 hours. How much is Kimberly paid per hour?

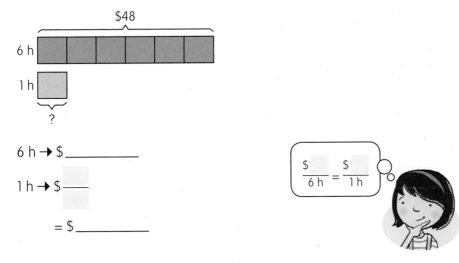

6 h → $ _____

1 h → $ [   ]

   = $ _____

$\frac{\$ \;\;\;}{6\;h} = \frac{\$ \;\;\;}{1\;h}$

Kimberly is paid $ _____ per hour.

ENGAGE

1. A stool cost $4.80. Farid had $12. Estimate the number of stools Farid can buy. Use unit rate to explain your estimation to your partner.

2. Mr. Young bought some bags of grain that cost $1.30 per bag. He had $12 and he wanted to use up as much money as possible. What is the greatest number of bags he could buy?

LEARN Find a unit rate

1. A school buys 2.75 acres of land for a new athletic field. What is the cost per acre if the school pays $275,000 for the land?

Cost per acre = Total cost ÷ Total number of acres

$$= \$275{,}000 \div 2.75$$

$$= \$\frac{275{,}000}{2.75}$$

$$= \$\frac{27{,}500{,}000}{275}$$

$$= \$100{,}000$$

Math Note

Multiply both the numerator and denominator of the fraction by the same number to make the divisor a whole number.

The unit cost of the piece of land is $100,000 per acre.

TRY Practice finding a unit rate

Solve.

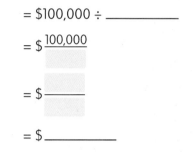 **1** A sports center buys 1.25 acres of land for a new swimming complex. What is the cost per acre if the sports center pays $100,000 for the land?

Cost per acre = Total cost ÷ Total number of acres

= $100,000 ÷ _____

= $ $\dfrac{100,000}{\boxed{}}$

= $ $\dfrac{\boxed{}}{\boxed{}}$

= $ _____

The unit cost of the piece of land is $ _____ per acre.

2 A few years ago, when the fuel tank in Jayla's car was completely empty, she paid $63 to fill the tank with 22.5 gallons of gasoline. What was the cost per gallon?

Cost per gallon = Cost of gasoline ÷ Volume of gasoline filled

= $ _____ ÷ _____

= $ _____

The unit cost of the gasoline was $ _____ per gallon.

ENGAGE

Store A sells yogurt at 12 packets for $5.40. Store B sells yogurt at 8 packets for $3.60. Which is a better buy? Explain.

LEARN Find and compare unit rates

① The table shows the cost of some fruit purchased at a farm stand.

Type of Fruit	Amount Purchased	Amount Paid	Cost Per Pound
Mango	2.00 lb	$2.60	?
Pear	2.50 lb	$3.50	?
Orange	2.25 lb	$2.70	?

Which fruit costs the most per pound?

To find out which fruit costs the most per pound, you can divide to find the unit cost for each fruit.

Cost of mangos per pound = Cost of mangos ÷ Weight of mangos
$$= \$2.60 \div 2$$
$$= \$1.30$$

The unit cost of the mangos is $1.30 per pound.

Cost of pears per pound = Cost of pears ÷ Weight of pears
$$= \$3.50 \div 2.5$$
$$= \$1.40$$

The unit cost of the pears is $1.40 per pound.

Cost of oranges per pound = Cost of oranges ÷ Weight of oranges
$$= \$2.70 \div 2.25$$
$$= \$1.20$$

The unit cost of the oranges is $1.20 per pound.

Comparing the unit costs of the three types of fruit, the unit cost of the pears is the greatest.

Unit cost of oranges < Unit cost of mangos < Unit cost of pears
   $1.20   < $1.30   < $1.40

So, the pears cost the most per pound.

TRY Practice finding and comparing unit rates

Solve.

1 The table shows the costs of some food items Benjamin bought from a supermarket.

Type of Food	Amount Purchased	Amount Paid	Cost Per Pound
Potato	5 lb	$4.00	?
Carrot	5 lb	$3.00	?
Onion	2 lb	$2.50	?

Which type of food costs the most per pound?

Cost of potatoes per pound = Cost of potatoes ÷ Weight of potatoes

= $_____ ÷ _____

= $_____

The unit cost of the potatoes is $_____ per pound.

Cost of carrots per pound = Cost of carrots ÷ Weight of carrots

= $_____ ÷ _____

= $_____

The unit cost of the carrots is $_____ per pound.

Cost of onions per pound = Cost of onions ÷ Weight of onions

= $_____ ÷ _____

= $_____

The unit cost of the onions is $_____ per pound.

Comparing the unit costs of the food items, the unit cost of the _____ is the greatest.

Unit cost of _____ < Unit cost of _____ < Unit cost of _____

$_____ < $_____ < $_____

So, the _____ cost the most per pound.

ENGAGE

Stephanie can tap her foot 2 times per second. Will she tap her foot more or less than 100 times in a minute? Explain how you use the unit rate to help you solve. If Stephanie taps her foot 240 times, how long would that take her?

LEARN Find a quantity given the unit rate

① Electrical consumption is measured in kilowatt-hours (kWh). The Harris family used 350 kilowatt-hours of electricity in April. The cost of electricity is 12¢ per kilowatt-hour. At this rate, how much did the Harris family pay for the electricity used in April?

$$1 \text{ kWh} \rightarrow 12¢$$
$$350 \text{ kWh} \rightarrow 12¢ \times 350$$
$$= 4{,}200¢$$
$$= \$42$$

The Harris family paid $42 for the electricity used in April.

② A pool is filled at a rate of 150 liters per hour. At this rate, how long will it take to fill the pool with 750 liters of water?

$$150 \text{ L} \rightarrow 1 \text{ h}$$
$$1 \text{ L} \rightarrow 1 \div 150$$
$$= \frac{1}{150} \text{ h}$$
$$750 \text{ L} \rightarrow \frac{1}{150} \times 750$$
$$= 5 \text{ h}$$

It will take 5 hours to fill the pool with 750 liters of water.

Activity Finding the rate, the total, or the number of units given the other two quantities

Work in pairs.

① Read and solve the real-world problem.

Allison rented a car at $450 for 5 days. Find the unit rate of renting the car.

② What information do you need to find the car rental rate? Discuss your answers.

③ What do you notice about the relationship between the information you need and the car rental rate?

④ Repeat the activity with each of the following real-world problems.

    a The cost of gasoline is $2.50 per gallon. Find the cost of 20 gallons of gasoline.

    b The cost of 1 pound of mixed nuts is $9. Lucas paid $36 to buy the mixed nuts. Find the weight of the mixed nuts he bought.

⑤ What do you notice about the relationship between the rate, the total amount, and the number of units?

TRY Practice finding a quantity given the unit rate

Solve.

① Water flows from a faucet at a rate of 10 liters per minute. At this rate, how many liters of water flows from the faucet in 4 minutes?

        1 min → _____ L

    _____ min → _____ × _____

           = _____ L

    _____ liters of water flows from the faucet in 4 minutes.

② Apples were sold at $3 per kilogram. At this rate, how many kilograms of apples did Kwan buy with $21?

INDEPENDENT PRACTICE

Solve.

1. A machine can print 300 T-shirts in 10 minutes. How many T-shirts can the machine print in 1 minute?

2. Audrey types 900 words in 20 minutes. How many words does she type per minute?

3. A 2-liter bottle is filled completely with water from a faucet in 10 seconds. How much water is filled into the bottle each second?

4. Tomas is paid $200 for 5 days of work. How much is he paid per day?

5. It takes 12 gallons of gasoline for a car to travel 300 miles. What is the rate of gasoline used in miles per gallon of gas?

6. The table shows the costs of three types of meat Isaiah bought at a supermarket. Find the missing numbers in the table.

Type of Meat	Amount Purchased	Amount Paid	Cost Per Pound
Fish	2.0 lb	$7.20	
Lamb	2.5 lb	$8.10	
Chicken	3.5 lb	$9.80	

Which type of meat costs the least per pound?

7 The room rate of a hotel is $136 per day. A tourist booked a room for 5 days in the hotel. How much money did she have to pay?

8 Brayden painted 95 square feet of the fence in his garden per hour. At this rate, how long did he take to paint 380 square feet of the fence?

9 Samantha can make 48 muffins per hour. Find the missing numbers in the table.

Number of Hours	Number of Muffins
1	48
2	
3	
	192
	240
6	

10 Faucet A flows at a rate of 100 liters per 5 minutes and Faucet B flows at a rate of 100 liters per 4 minutes into an empty pool. How many minutes do the two faucets take to fill a pool with 9,000 liters of water?

Real-World Problems: Rates and Unit Rates

Learning Objective:
• Solve real-world problems involving rates and unit rates.

THINK

A store sells juice in packets of 200 milliliters or 250 milliliters. The price of 10 packets of 200 milliliters is $2.50. The price of 8 packets of 250 milliliters is $2.20. Which option gives a better value for money?

ENGAGE

a   Cindy reads 5 pages of a book in 10 minutes. Use 2 different methods to find how long she will take to read 25 pages. Discuss your ideas with your partner.

b   How long will Cindy take to read 27 pages? Can both methods be used? Explain.

LEARN Solve simple real-world problems involving rates and unit rates

① A water pump can dispense 120 gallons of water into a tank in 15 minutes. At this rate, how much water will the pump dispense in an hour?

STEP 1 Understand the problem.

> What is the rate at which the water pump is dispensing water into the tank?
> What do I need to find?

STEP 2 Think of a plan.
I can draw a diagram.

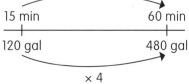 Carry out the plan.

1 h = 60 min

15 min → 120 gal
60 min → 120 × 4
           = 480 gal

The pump will dispense 480 gallons of water in an hour.

STEP 4 Check the answer.
I can work backwards to check my answer.

15 min → 480 ÷ 4
           = 120 gal

The water pump can dispense 120 gallons
of water into a tank in 15 minutes.
My answer is correct.

TRY Practice solving simple real-world problems involving rates and
unit rates

Solve.

1 A machine takes 10 minutes to seal 50 boxes. At this rate, how many boxes can the
machine seal in an hour?

1 h = _____ min

   10 min → _____

_____ min → _____ × _____

     = _____

The machine can seal _____ boxes in an hour.

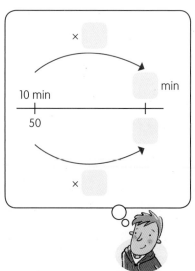

ENGAGE

Ms. Reed filled 100 water bottles equally using 50 liters of water. Find the number of bottles she could fill with 1 liter of water. Explain how you find the number of liters needed to fill 150 bottles.

LEARN Solve two-part real-world problems involving rates and unit rates

1 Mr. White painted an area of 450 square meters using 6 liters of paint.

a What is the area painted using 1 liter of paint?

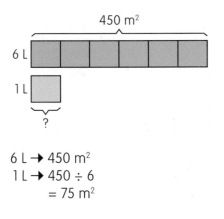

6 L → 450 m²
1 L → 450 ÷ 6
= 75 m²

The area painted using 1 liter of paint is 75 square meters.

b How many liters of paint does Mr. White need for an area of 600 square meters?

75 m² → 1 L
1 m² → 1 ÷ 75
= $\frac{1}{75}$ L

600 m² → $\frac{1}{75}$ × 600
= 8 L

Mr. White needs 8 liters of paint for an area of 600 square meters.

TRY Practice solving two-part real-world problems involving rates and unit rates

Solve.

1 A machine can fill 16 identical bottles with ketchup in 2 minutes.

 a At this rate, how many bottles can the machine fill per minute?

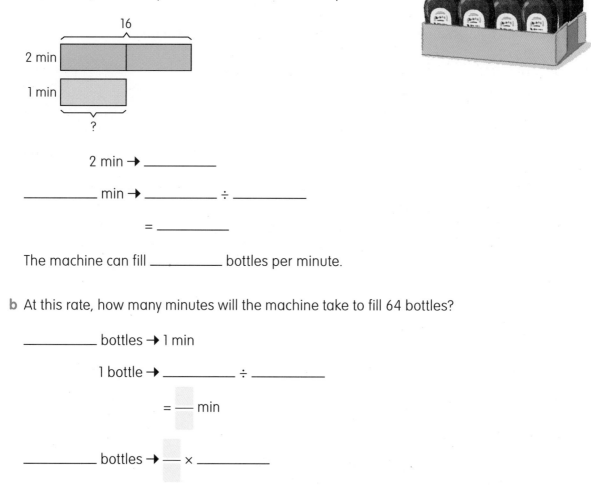

2 min → _____

_____ min → _____ ÷ _____

= _____

The machine can fill _____ bottles per minute.

 b At this rate, how many minutes will the machine take to fill 64 bottles?

_____ bottles → 1 min

1 bottle → _____ ÷ _____

= $\dfrac{}{}$ min

_____ bottles → $\dfrac{}{}$ × _____

= _____ min

The machine will take _____ minutes to fill 64 bottles.

ENGAGE

The table shows the postal charges for sending letters within Country Z. What are the possible weights of letters that you could send for less than $2.00?
Explain your thinking.

First Ounce	50¢
Per Additional 1 Ounce	21¢

LEARN Read a table to find the information to solve multi-step rate problems

1. The table shows the fees at a parking lot. Blake parked his car there from 9 A.M. to 2 P.M. on the same day. How much did he pay for parking?

First Hour	Free
Second Hour	$1.75
After the Second Hour	$2.50 per hour

Total number of hours = 5 h

Parking fee for first hour = $0

Parking fee for second hour = $1.75

Parking fee for last three hours = $2.50 × 3
                                  = $7.50

Total parking fee = $0 + $1.75 + $7.50
                  = $9.25

Blake paid $9.25 for parking.

TRY Practice reading a table to find the information to solve multi-step rate problems

Solve.

1. The table shows the charges for renting a bicycle. Tyler rented a bicycle from 10 A.M. to 2 P.M. on the same day. How much did Tyler pay for renting the bicycle?

First Hour	$3.00
For Every Additional $\frac{1}{2}$ Hour	$2.50

Total number of hours = _____ h

Charge for first hour = $ _____

Charge for each additional 1 hour
= 2 × Cost for each additional $\frac{1}{2}$ hour

= 2 × $ _____

= $ _____

Charge for last three hours

= $ _____ × _____

= $ _____

Total charge = $ _____ + $ _____

          = $ _____

Tyler paid $ _____ for renting the bicycle.

ENGAGE

Player A scored 15 goals in 10 soccer games and Player B scored 25 goals in 20 soccer games. Which player should win the award for the leading scorer? Explain your reasoning.

LEARN Solve multi-step real-world problems involving comparison of unit rates

1 A package of two Brand A batteries costs $3.20. The manufacturer claims the batteries will last for 20 hours. A package of two Brand B batteries cost $2.80. The manufacturer claims the batteries will last for 14 hours. Which of the two brands is a better buy? Explain your answer.

Brand A:
$3.20 → 20 h

$$\$1 \rightarrow \frac{20}{3.20}$$
$$= 6.25 \text{ h}$$

Brand A gives 6.25 hours of battery time per dollar.

Brand B:
$2.80 → 14 h

$$\$1 \rightarrow \frac{14}{2.80}$$
$$= 5 \text{ h}$$

Brand B gives 5 hours of battery time per dollar.

Since 6.25 hours > 5 hours, Brand A is a better buy.

Activity Comparing unit rates in a real-world situation

Work in pairs.

1 Press your fingers firmly on your wrist to feel your pulse. Count the number of times your heart beats in 15 seconds while your partner uses a stopwatch to take the timing.

2 Find your resting heart rate per minute. Compare your unit heart rate to your partner's unit heart rate. What do you notice?

3 Find your heart rate per minute after doing 30 jumping jacks. Compare your unit heart rate to your partner's unit heart rate. What do you notice?

Practice solving multi-step real-world problems involving comparison of unit rates

Solve.

① Haley scored 87 points in 5 basketball games, and Bianca scored 45 points in 2 basketball games. Which of the two players scored more points per game? Explain your answer.

Haley:

5 games → _____ points

1 game → _____ ÷ _____

= _____ points

Haley scored _____ points per game.

Bianca:

2 games → _____ points

1 game → _____ ÷ _____

= _____ points

Bianca scored _____ points per game.

Since _____ > _____, _____ scored more points per game.

ENGAGE

Look at the graph.

① What does each axis represent?

② Write 4 questions that you can ask using the information given in the graph. Exchange your questions with your partner and answer each other's questions.

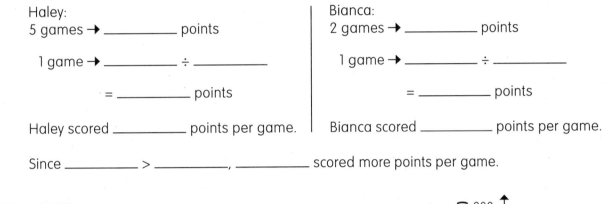

LEARN Read a graph to find the information to solve rate problems

① Gabriel saves an equal amount of money every week. The line graph shows the total amount of money Gabriel saves in 8 weeks.

a How much does Gabriel save every week?

2 weeks → $10

1 week → $\frac{10}{2}$

= $5

Gabriel saves $5 every week.

b How many weeks will Gabriel take to save a total of $80?

$5 → 1 week

$80 → $\frac{80}{5}$

= 16 weeks

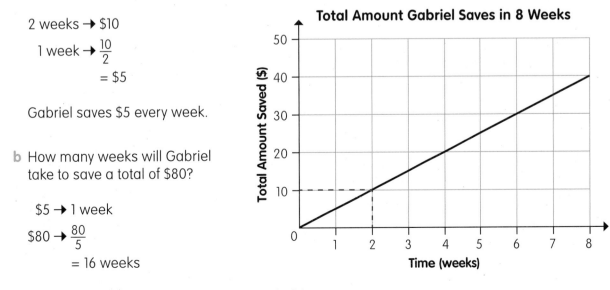

Gabriel will take 16 weeks to save a total of $80.

2 Weights of different masses were attached to the end of a spring. The line graph shows how the length of the spring changed with the mass of the weight attached.

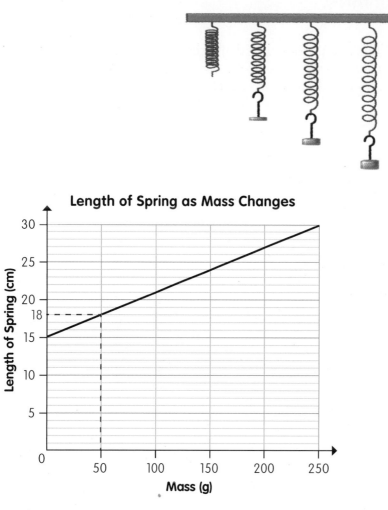

Length of Spring as Mass Changes

a What was the original length of the spring? Explain your answer.

The original length of the spring was 15 cm.
The original length of the spring was the length of the spring when no weight was attached to it.

b How much did the length of the spring increase for each gram of weight attached?

50 g → 18 − 15
　　　= 3 cm

1 g → $\frac{3}{50}$
　　　= 0.06 cm

> Length of spring when weight was 50 g = 18 cm
> Original length of spring = 15 cm
> Increase in length of spring = 18 − 15
> 　　　　　　　　　　　　　= 3 cm

The length of the spring increased by 0.06 cm for each gram of weight attached.

Practice reading a graph to find the information to solve rate problems

Solve.

1 The line graph shows the volume of water in a tank with a leaking faucet over 60 minutes.

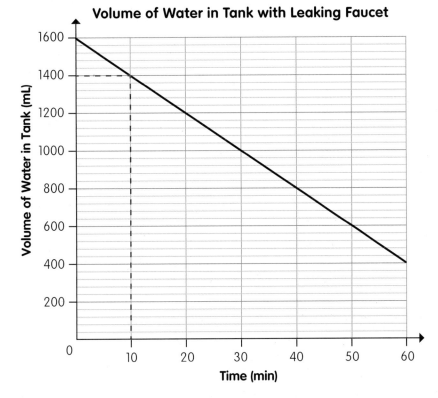

Volume of Water in Tank with Leaking Faucet

a Find the volume of water that leaks from the faucet each minute.

10 min → _____ − _____

        = _____ mL

1 min → _____

        = _____ mL

_____ milliliters of water leaks from the faucet each minute.

b Find the time, in hours and minutes, it will take for the tank to become empty.

_____ mL → 1 min

1,600 mL → _____

        = _____ min

        = _____ h _____ min

It takes _____ hour _____ minutes for the tank to become empty.

2 The line graph shows the conversion between the U.S. dollar and the Thai baht at a certain point in time.

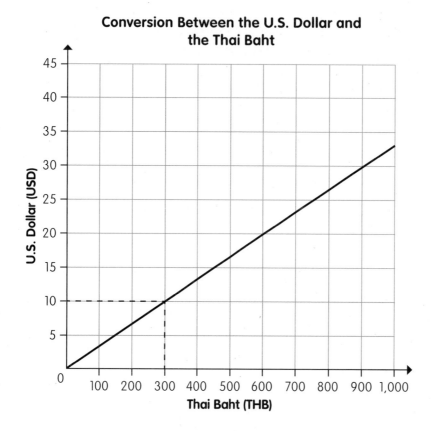

Conversion Between the U.S. Dollar and the Thai Baht

a Find the amount in Thai baht that can be exchanged for 1 U.S. dollar.

_____ USD → _____ THB

1 USD → _____ ÷ _____

= _____ THB

_____ Thai baht can be exchanged for 1 U.S. dollar.

b Aki paid 1,560 Thai baht for a full day tour in Bangkok. How much did he pay in U.S. dollars?

_____ THB → 1 USD

_____ THB → _____ ÷ _____

= _____ USD

He paid _____ U.S. dollars.

c Which exchange rate is more favorable for a tourist who wants to exchange U.S. dollars for Thai baht? Explain your answer.

Money Changer A: 100 USD = 3,000 THB
Money Changer B: 120 USD = 3,720 THB

INDEPENDENT PRACTICE

Solve.

1 A tennis ball machine can launch 60 tennis balls in 12 minutes. At this rate, how many tennis balls can it launch in an hour?

2 Water flows from a faucet at a rate of 5 liters every 25 seconds.

    a At this rate, how much water will flow from the faucet in 45 seconds?

    b At this rate, how long will it take to collect 60 liters of water?

3 A farmer uses 920 grams of grains to feed 8 chickens.

    a At this rate, how many grams of grains does he use to feed 100 chickens?

    b At this rate, how many chickens can he feed using 48.3 kilograms of grains?

4 The table shows the postal charges for sending letters to Country Y.

First 20 g	50¢
Per Additional 10 g	30¢

How much does it cost to send a letter weighing 60 grams to Country Y?

5 Car A travels 702 miles on 12 gallons of gasoline. Car B travels 873 miles on 15 gallons of gasoline. Hugo wants to buy a car with the lower fuel consumption. Find out the distance each car can travel per gallon of gasoline. Then, tell which of the two cars, A, or B, Hugo should buy.

6 A machine packs equal packets of vitamin tablets every minute. The line graph shows the number of packets of vitamin tablets packed by the machine over four minutes.

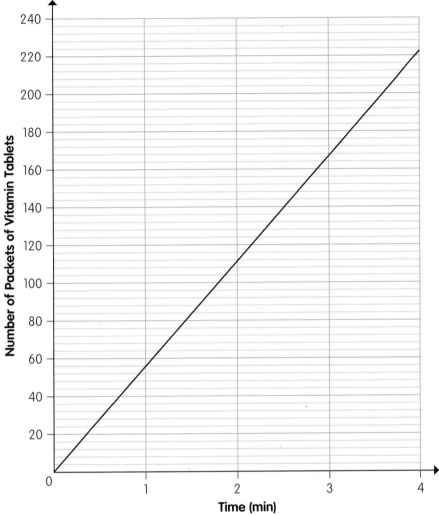

Number of Packets of Vitamin Tablets Packed

a How many packets of vitamin tables does the machine pack per minute?

b At this rate, how many minutes will the machine take to pack 672 packets of vitamin tablets?

7 Brooklyn's mother gave her an allowance at the beginning of a certain summer break. Brooklyn spent an equal amount of money each week from the allowance. The line graph shows her allowance over four weeks.

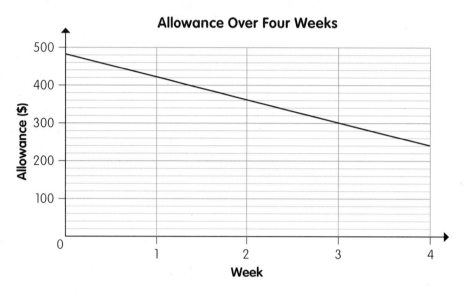

Allowance Over Four Weeks

a How much did Brooklyn spend from her allowance each week?

b How many weeks would it take Brooklyn to spend all her allowance?

8 A supermarket sells the three brands of rice shown in the table below.

Brand	Mass of Rice	Price
A	500 g	$1.20
B	5 kg	$9.80
C	10 kg	$18.90

Alexandra wants to buy 30 kilograms of rice.

a Which brand of rice should she buy to get the best deal, assuming that all three brands are of the same quality?

b How much will she save if she buys the cheapest brand of rice as compared to the most expensive one?

3 Distance and Speed

Learning Objective:
• Solve problems involving constant speed.

> **New Vocabulary**
> speed

💡 THINK

At 3 P.M., Carla walked from her school to a park at a constant speed of 60 meters per minute. 5 minutes later, Avery left the same school for the park along the same route. Avery did not change her speed throughout the journey and reached the park at the same time as Carla at 3:15 P.M. What was Avery's speed?

ENGAGE

Predict how many miles each of the following animals can run per hour.

> squirrel   elk   giraffe   brown bear   elephant

Place them in order from fastest to slowest. Compare your prediction to your partner's.

LEARN   Read, interpret, and write speed

1   Jaden traveled from Town A towards Town B. In 1 hour, he traveled 40 miles. Ang traveled in the same direction. In 1 hour, he traveled 50 miles.

> Jaden traveled at a speed of 40 miles per hour.
> Ang traveled at a speed of 50 miles per hour.

The speed tells us how fast Jaden and Ang were traveling.
You can write Jaden's speed as 40 mi/h.
You read 40 mi/h as 40 miles per hour.

TRY Practice reading, interpreting, and writing speed

Fill in each blank.

1. Callia cycles 9 kilometers in one hour. Her speed is _____ km/h.

2. Wyatt runs 200 meters in one minute. His speed is _____ m/min.

3. A bowling ball rolls 15 centimeters in one second. Its speed is _____ cm/s.

4. Martin swims at a speed of 2 m/s. He swims _____ meters in one second.

ENGAGE

Record the timing your partner takes to run 20 meters. Draw a bar model to show the distance ran and time taken. How do you find the distance your partner ran in 1 second? Explain your thinking.

LEARN Find the speed or rate of travel given the distance and time

1. Melanie ran 900 meters in 5 minutes. Find her speed in meters per minute.

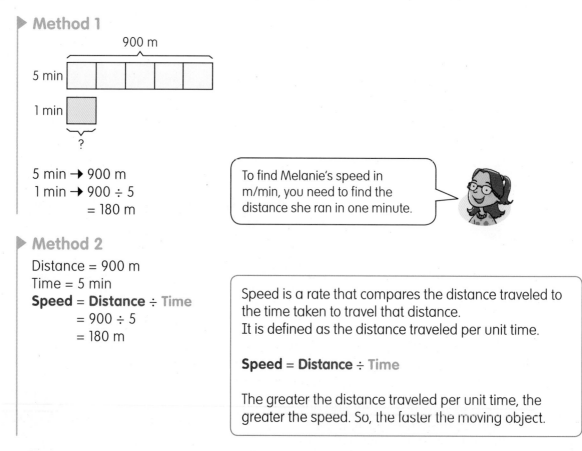

▶ Method 1

5 min → 900 m
1 min → 900 ÷ 5
        = 180 m

> To find Melanie's speed in m/min, you need to find the distance she ran in one minute.

▶ Method 2

Distance = 900 m
Time = 5 min
Speed = Distance ÷ Time
      = 900 ÷ 5
      = 180 m

> Speed is a rate that compares the distance traveled to the time taken to travel that distance.
> It is defined as the distance traveled per unit time.
>
> **Speed = Distance ÷ Time**
>
> The greater the distance traveled per unit time, the greater the speed. So, the faster the moving object.

Melanie's speed was 180 meters per minute.

TRY Practice finding the speed or rate of travel given the distance and time

Solve.

1. A truck traveled a distance of 280 kilometers in 4 hours. Find the speed of the truck.

▶ **Method 1**

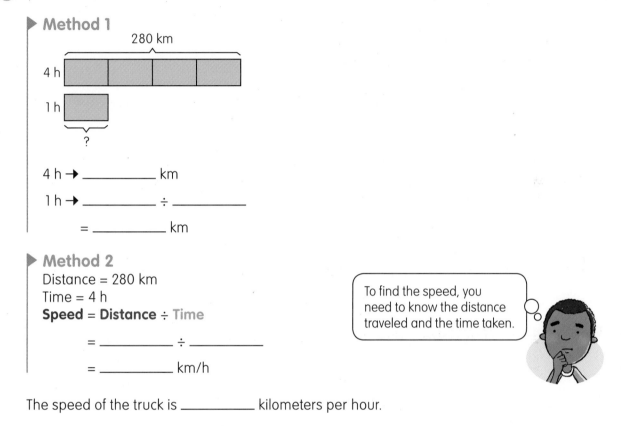

4 h ➔ _____ km

1 h ➔ _____ ÷ _____

= _____ km

▶ **Method 2**

Distance = 280 km
Time = 4 h
Speed = Distance ÷ Time

= _____ ÷ _____

= _____ km/h

To find the speed, you need to know the distance traveled and the time taken.

The speed of the truck is _____ kilometers per hour.

2. A scooter travels $\frac{1}{4}$ mile in $\frac{1}{2}$ minute. Find the speed of the scooter in miles per minute.

ENGAGE

a. A cyclist rides at a speed of 16 miles per hour. Create a table to show the distance he will travel in 1 hour, 2 hours, 3 hours, 4 hours, and 5 hours. What do you notice about the relationship among the speed, time, and distance? Share your observations.

b. Predict the distance that the cyclist ride in 7.5 hours. How do you find your answer? Explain.

LEARN Find the distance given the speed and time

1 Mr. Walker drives at a speed of 65 kilometers per hour.

a At this speed, how far does he travel in 2 hours?

In 1 hour, Mr. Walker travels 65 kilometers.

In 2 hours, Mr. Walker travels **65 × 2 = 130** kilometers.

Speed   Time   Distance

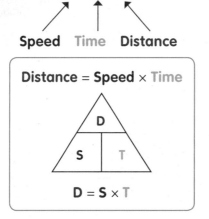

Distance = **Speed** × Time

D = **S** × T

b At this speed, how far does he travel in 5 hours?

In 5 hours, Mr. Walker travels 65 × 5 = 325 kilometers.

Math Note

The formula relating distance, speed, and time is often written as:

Distance = Speed × Time

2 A hamster runs at a speed of 16 meters per minute. How far does the hamster run in 1 hour?

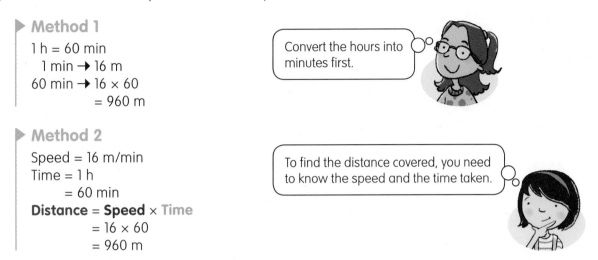

▶ **Method 1**

1 h = 60 min
  1 min → 16 m
60 min → 16 × 60
        = 960 m

> Convert the hours into minutes first.

▶ **Method 2**

Speed = 16 m/min
Time = 1 h
     = 60 min
Distance = Speed × **Time**
        = 16 × 60
        = 960 m

> To find the distance covered, you need to know the speed and the time taken.

The hamster runs 960 meters in 1 hour.

TRY **Practice finding the distance, given the speed and time**

Solve.

1 A train can travel at a speed of 120 kilometers per hour. How far can the train travel in 5 minutes?

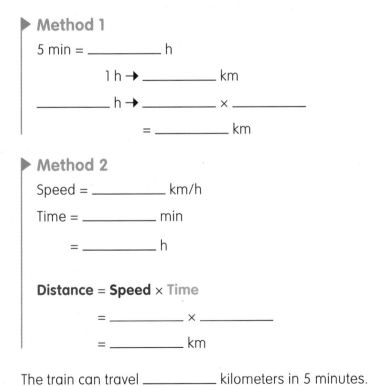

▶ **Method 1**

5 min = _____ h

        1 h → _____ km

_____ h → _____ × _____

        = _____ km

▶ **Method 2**

Speed = _____ km/h

Time = _____ min

     = _____ h

Distance = Speed × **Time**

        = _____ × _____

        = _____ km

The train can travel _____ kilometers in 5 minutes.

ENGAGE

a An ant moved at a speed of 2 inches per second. How do you find the time it took to travel 36 inches using the relationship among the speed, time, and distance? Explain your thinking.

b How long will it take the ant to move 45 inches?

LEARN Find the time given the distance and speed

① Christopher ran round a field at a speed of 6 meters per second. How long did he take to run 456 meters?

▶ **Method 1**

6 m → 1 s
456 m → 456 ÷ 6
= 76 s

▶ **Method 2**

Distance = 456 m
Speed = 6 m/s
Time = Distance ÷ Speed
= 456 ÷ 6
= 76 s

Christopher took 76 seconds to run 456 meters.

Activity Recognizing the relationship among the distance traveled, the speed, and the time taken

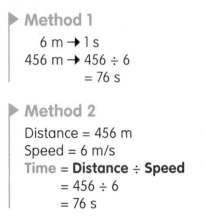 **Work in pairs.**

① Read and solve the real-world problem.

> Ms. Morgan takes 10 minutes to travel from her home to the community center, which are 6,500 meters apart. Find Ms. Morgan's speed.

② Tell your partner the information needed to find Ms. Morgan's speed. What is the relationship between the information you needed and Ms. Morgan's speed? Discuss.

③ Repeat the activity with each of the following word problems.

    a Mr. Howard took 45 minutes to drive from home to his office. He traveled at a speed of 60 km/h. Find the distance between Mr. Howard's home and his office.

    b Trinity cycled 36.4 kilometers at a speed of 28 km/h. Find the time Trinity took.

④ Discuss the relationship between distance traveled, speed, and time taken.

TRY Practice finding the time given the distance and speed

Solve.

① The distance between Town X and Town Y is 108 kilometers. Liam rides his motorcycle at a speed of 54 kilometers per hour. How long does he take to travel from Town X to Town Y?

▶ **Method 1**

    _____ km → 1 h

    _____ km → _____ ÷ _____

                    = _____ h

▶ **Method 2**

    Distance = _____ km

    Speed = _____ km/h

    Time = Distance ÷ Speed

          = _____ ÷ _____

          = _____ h

Liam takes _____ hours to travel from Town X to Town Y.

 Vanessa cycled from her home to the beach at a speed of 18 meters per second. The distance between her home and the beach is 1,350 m. How long did she take to cycle from her home to the beach?

Time = Distance ÷ Speed

= _____ ÷ _____

= _____ s

She took _____ seconds to cycle from her home to the beach.

 **Math Talk**

Two brothers, Justin and Jordan, left their home for their offices. Justin's office is further away than Jordan's office. Both of them traveled at the same speed. Who will take a longer time to reach the office? Explain.

MATH SHARING

Mathematical Habit 6 **Use precise mathematical language**

1 Search the internet to find out the fastest possible speed of each of the following:

- train
- car
- motorcycle
- airplane
- cheetah
- horse
- elephant

Compare the different speeds. Share your findings with your classmates.

2 What are the speed limits of the different types of vehicles traveling along roads, freeways, and tunnels in the country? Compare them and discuss why they are different.

INDEPENDENT PRACTICE

Solve.

1. Aubrey swims 450 meters in 5 minutes. Find her swimming speed in meters per minute.

2. A garden snail moves $\frac{1}{6}$ foot in $\frac{1}{3}$ hour. Find the speed of the snail in feet per hour.

3. A vehicle traveled at a speed of 54 kilometers per hour for 3 hours. Find the distance traveled.

4. A pigeon can fly at a speed of 84 kilometers per hour. How long does it take the pigeon to fly 7 kilometers?

5. Cameron walks home from school at a speed of 5 kilometers per hour. He takes 12 minutes to reach home. What is the distance between his school and his home? (Hint: Convert the time from minutes to hours.)

6 Isabelle ran from her home to a beach at a speed of 6 meters per second. The distance from her home to the beach was 756 meters.

a How long did she take to run from her home to the beach?

b If Isabelle wants to take 18 seconds less to reach the beach, at what speed must she run?

7 Adrian ran from his house to the park at a speed of 5 meters per second. He then ran back from the park to his house at a speed of 6 meters per second. The total time taken for Adrian to run the whole journey was 22 minutes. How many minutes did he take to run from his house to the park?

4 Average Speed

Learning Objective:
• Solve problems involving average speed.

New Vocabulary
average speed

THINK

Andrea and Caroline cycled from Point X to Point Y. Andrea cycled at an average speed of 20 meters per second. She cycled for 5 seconds before Caroline began. Caroline caught up with Andrea after 25 seconds. What was Caroline's average cycling speed?

ENGAGE

Diego ran 800 yards in 4 minutes. He then walked another 80 yards in 1 minute. Explain what it means to find Diego's average speed for the total distance he traveled. How do you justify your reasoning?

LEARN Find the average speed given the total distance traveled and total time taken

1. Tree A and Tree B are 9 meters apart. Tree B and Tree C are 21 meters apart. Andrew ran from Tree A to Tree B in 2 seconds. He then ran from Tree B to Tree C in 3 seconds. Find Andrew's average speed for the distance from Tree A to Tree C.

Distance = 9 m   Distance = 21 m
  Time = 2 s   Time = 3 s

A   B   C

? m/s

> It is not possible for an object or a person to move at the same speed all the time. You use average speed to describe how fast the object or person is moving.

Average speed is the average distance traveled per unit time.

$$\text{Average speed} = \frac{\text{Total distance traveled}}{\text{Total time taken}}$$

Total distance from Tree A to Tree C = 9 + 21
                                     = 30 m

Total time taken to run from Tree A to Tree C = 2 + 3
                                              = 5 s

Average speed
= Total distance traveled ÷ Total time taken
= 30 ÷ 5
= 6 m/s

Math Talk
Kylie computes average speed this way:
Average speed = Half of the sum of two speeds.
Is Kylie correct? Explain your answer.

Andrew's average speed was 6 meters per second.

2 Alexander swam for 100 s at a speed of 1.4 meters per second. He then swam another
360 meters. He took a total of 400 seconds to complete the swim.

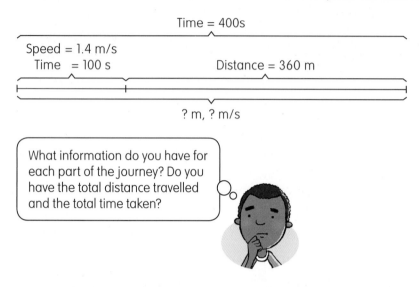

What information do you have for
each part of the journey? Do you
have the total distance travelled
and the total time taken?

a Find the total distance Alexander swam.

Distance Alexander swam in the first part = Speed × Time
= 1.4 × 100
= 140 m

Total distance Alexander swam = 140 + 360
= 500 m

The total distance Alexander swam was 500 meters.

b Find Alexander's average speed.

Average speed = Total distance traveled ÷ Total time taken
= 500 ÷ 400
= 1.25 m/s

Alexander's average speed was 1.25 meters per second.

TRY Practice finding the average speed given the total distance traveled and total time taken

Solve.

1 The distance between Town A and Town B is about 6 kilometers. The distance between Town B and Town C is about 15 kilometers. Farrah takes $\frac{1}{2}$ hour to cycle from Town A to Town B, and another 1 hour to cycle from Town B to Town C. Find Farrah's average speed for the journey from Town A to Town C.

Distance = ____ km   Distance = ____ km

Time = ____ h   Time = ____ h

Town A   Town B   Town C

? km/h

First, find the total distance traveled. Then, find the total time taken.

Total distance traveled = _____ + _____

= _____ km

Total time taken = _____ + _____

= _____ h

Average speed = Total distance traveled ÷ Total time taken

= _____ ÷ _____

= _____ km/h

Farrah's average speed for the journey from Town A to Town C was _____ kilometers per hour.

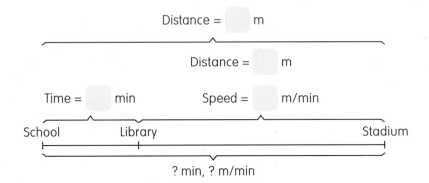

2 Mario's school was 897 meters away from the stadium. First, he took 4 minutes to walk from the school to the library. Then, he walked another 648 meters at a speed of 72 meters per minute from the library to the stadium.

Distance = ☐ m

Distance = ☐ m

Time = ☐ min   Speed = ☐ m/min

School   Library   Stadium

? min, ? m/min

a Find the total time taken for the journey.

Time taken to walk from the library to the stadium = Distance ÷ Speed

= _____ ÷ _____

= _____ min

Total time taken for the journey = _____ + _____

= _____ min

The total time taken for the journey was _____ minutes.

b Find Mario's average speed for the whole journey.

Average speed = Total distance traveled ÷ Total time taken

= _____ ÷ _____

= _____ m/min

Mario's average speed for the whole journey was _____ meters per minute.

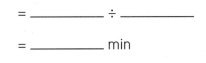**Math Talk**

Arianna walked at a constant speed of 80 centimeters per second from Point A to Point B. Mario walked at an average speed of 80 centimeters per second for the same distance. Did they walk at the same speed? Explain.

INDEPENDENT PRACTICE

Solve.

1. Post A and Post B are 120 meters apart. Post B and Post C are 300 meters apart. Brandon cycled from Post A to Post B in 15 seconds. He then cycled from Post B to Post C in 55 seconds. Find Brandon's average speed for the distance from Post A to Post C.

Distance = ☐ m   Distance = ☐ m

Time = ☐ s   Time = ☐ s

Post A   Post B   Post C

? m/s

2. A train moved at a speed of 95 miles per hour for 2 hours. It then slowed down and traveled another 136 miles for the next 2 hours.

Speed = ☐ mi/h   Distance = ☐ mi

Time = ☐ h   Time = ☐ h

? mi, ? mi/h

a Find the total number of miles the train traveled.

b Find the average speed of the train.

A family took 2 hours to drive from City A to City B at a speed of 55 miles per hour. On the return trip, due to a snowstorm, the family took 3 hours to travel back to City A.

a How many miles did the family travel in all?

b What was the average speed for the entire trip?

 Ms. Turner takes 5 hours to drive 390 kilometers from her home to the next city. If Ms. Turner's average speed for the first 2 hours is 60 kilometers per hour, find her average speed for the last 3 hours.

5 Real-World Problems: Speed and Average Speed

Learning Objective:
• Solve real-world problems involving speed and average speed.

THINK

Town A and Town B are 450 km apart. A van travels at a constant speed of 80 kilometers per hour from Town A to Town B. At the same time, a truck travels at a constant speed of 70 kilometers per hour from Town B to Town A. How far has the van traveled when they meet?

ENGAGE

a   Tiana walked from her home to school. She started her journey from her home at 7:30 a.m. and reached her school at 7:50 a.m. She walked at an average speed of 300 feet per minute. What distance did Tiana travel? Draw a diagram to represent this problem. Compare your diagram to your partner's.

b   If you wanted to travel from home to school in 15 minutes, find the average speed you needed to take to arrive at school.

LEARN Draw and use diagrams to solve real-world problems involving speed, distance, and time

1   Adam cycled from Town X to Town Y. He started his journey from Town X at 7:45 A.M. and ended at Town Y at 9:15 A.M. He cycled at an average speed of 14 kilometers per hour. What distance did Adam cycle?

STEP 1   Understand the problem.

At what time did Adam start his journey?
At what time did he end his journey?
What was his average speed?
What do I need to find?

STEP 2   Think of a plan.
I can draw a diagram.

STEP 3 Carry out the plan.

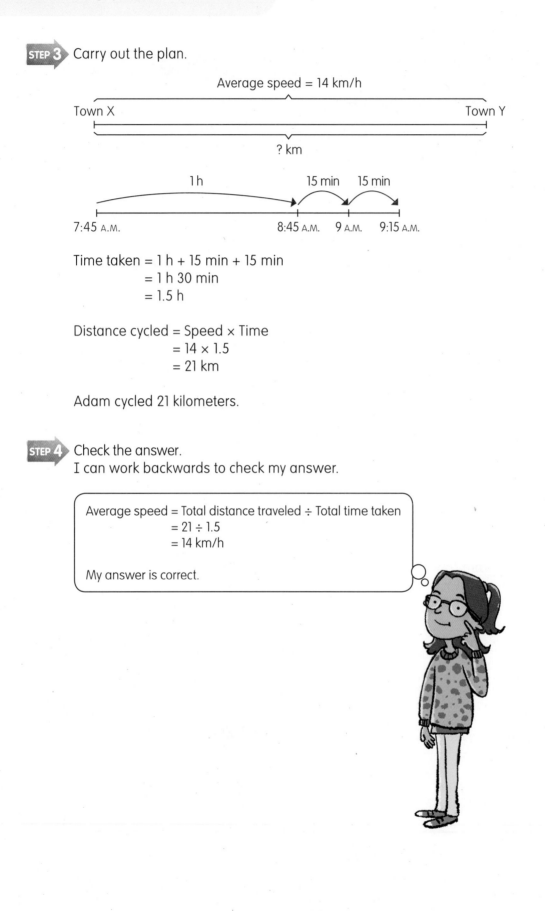

Time taken = 1 h + 15 min + 15 min
= 1 h 30 min
= 1.5 h

Distance cycled = Speed × Time
= 14 × 1.5
= 21 km

Adam cycled 21 kilometers.

STEP 4 Check the answer.
I can work backwards to check my answer.

Average speed = Total distance traveled ÷ Total time taken
= 21 ÷ 1.5
= 14 km/h

My answer is correct.

TRY Practice drawing and using diagrams to solve real-world problems involving speed, distance, and time

Solve.

1. Ms. Green started to drive at 7:50 A.M. to go to her office. She drove 30 kilometers at an average speed of 60 kilometers per hour. At what time did she reach her office?

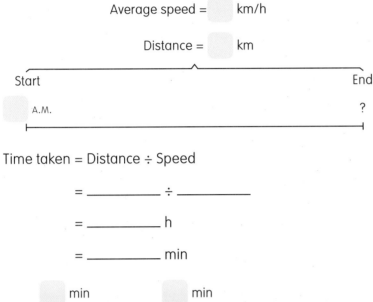

Average speed = ☐ km/h

Distance = ☐ km

Start   End

☐ A.M.   ?

Time taken = Distance ÷ Speed

= _____ ÷ _____

= _____ h

= _____ min

☐ min   ☐ min

7:50 A.M.

☐ A.M.   ☐ A.M.

She reached her office at _____ A.M.

ENGAGE

Victor rode a bicycle from Point A to Point B. He took an hour to complete $\frac{1}{3}$ of the journey. He rode the remaining 24 miles in 3 hours. What is Victor's average speed for the entire journey? Draw a diagram to represent this problem. Compare your diagram to your partner's. What are three questions you could ask about Victor's journey? Trade your questions with your partner and answer them.

LEARN Draw and use diagrams to find the average speed given the time taken and distance traveled for a proportion of the journey

1. Elena drove from City A to City B. She took 2 hours to complete $\frac{1}{4}$ of the journey. She drove the remaining 252 kilometers in 3 hours. Find Elena's average speed for the whole journey.

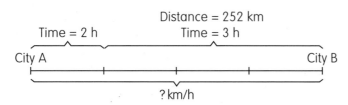

To find the average speed, you need to know the total distance traveled and the total time taken.

3 units = 252
1 unit = 252 ÷ 3
        = 84
4 units = 84 × 4
        = 336

Distance between City A and City B = 336 km

Total time taken for the whole journey = 2 + 3
                                       = 5 h

Average speed for the whole journey
= Total distance traveled ÷ Total time taken
= 336 ÷ 5
= 67.2 km/h

Elena's average speed for the whole journey was 67.2 kilometers per hour.

Practice drawing and using diagrams to find the average speed given the time taken and distance traveled for a proportion of the journey

Solve.

1. Carson took 20 minutes to cycle from his home to the park which was 1,314 meters away. He took 8 minutes to cycle from his home to a convenience store along the way. The distance between his home and the convenience store is $\frac{1}{3}$ of the distance between his home and the park. Find the average speed at which Carson cycled from the convenience store to the park.

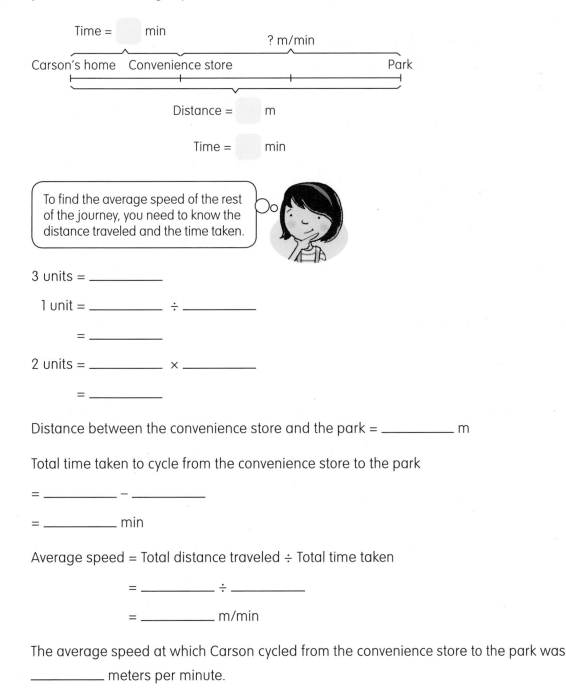

Time = ☐ min

? m/min

Carson's home   Convenience store   Park

Distance = ☐ m

Time = ☐ min

To find the average speed of the rest of the journey, you need to know the distance traveled and the time taken.

3 units = _____

1 unit = _____ ÷ _____

= _____

2 units = _____ × _____

= _____

Distance between the convenience store and the park = _____ m

Total time taken to cycle from the convenience store to the park

= _____ – _____

= _____ min

Average speed = Total distance traveled ÷ Total time taken

= _____ ÷ _____

= _____ m/min

The average speed at which Carson cycled from the convenience store to the park was _____ meters per minute.

A toy car took 30 seconds to travel from Point X to Point Y at an average speed of 150 centimeters per second. It then returned from Point Y to Point X in 45 seconds. Find the average speed at which the toy car took to return from Point Y to Point X. Draw a diagram to represent this problem. Compare your diagram to your partner's.

LEARN Draw and use diagrams to solve average speed problems involving a fixed distance

1 Jason took 10 minutes to run from Point A to Point B at an average speed of 180 meters per minute. He then ran from Point B to Point A in 15 minutes. Find the average speed at which Jason ran from Point B to Point A.

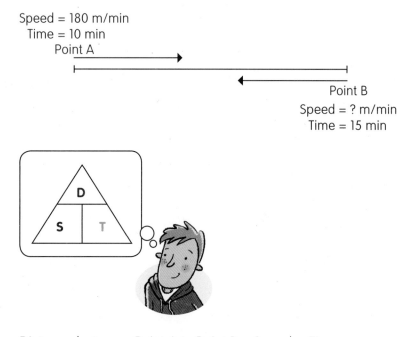

Speed = 180 m/min
Time = 10 min
Point A

Point B
Speed = ? m/min
Time = 15 min

Distance between Point A to Point B = Speed × Time
= 180 × 10
= 1,800 m

Jason's average speed from Point B to Point A
= Total distance traveled ÷ Total time taken
= 1,800 ÷ 15
= 120 m/min

The average speed at which Jason ran from Point B to Point A was 120 meters per minute.

TRY Practice drawing and using diagrams to solve average speed problems involving a fixed distance

Solve.

1. Mr. Hughes took 4 hours to drive from Town A to Town B at an average speed of 50 kilometers per hour. On his return journey from Town B to Town A, he traveled at an average speed of 80 kilometers per hour. How long did Mr. Hughes take on the return journey?

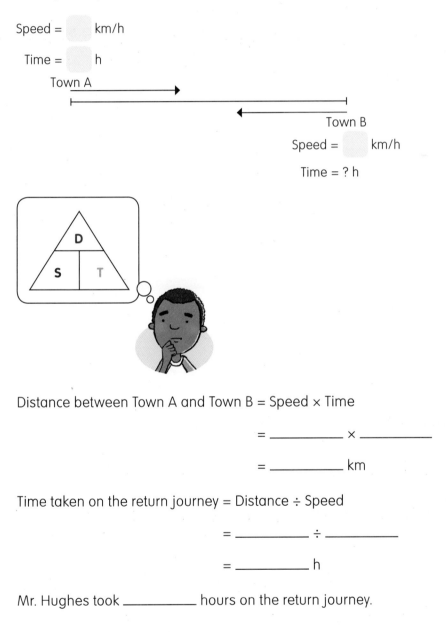

Speed = ___ km/h

Time = ___ h

Town A

Town B

Speed = ___ km/h

Time = ? h

Distance between Town A and Town B = Speed × Time

= _____ × _____

= _____ km

Time taken on the return journey = Distance ÷ Speed

= _____ ÷ _____

= _____ h

Mr. Hughes took _____ hours on the return journey.

ENGAGE

Maya's truck and Brian's truck both left the warehouse at 7 A.M. to start their delivery routes. When Maya arrived at the delivery site at 7:15 A.M., Brian was still 3 miles from the site. Maya drove at a constant speed of 60 miles per hour. Assume that Brian also drove at a constant speed. Find the speed of Brian's truck. Draw a diagram to represent this problem. Compare your diagram to your partner's.

LEARN Draw and use diagrams to solve constant speed problems involving two objects or persons moving towards the same end point

1 Bus X and Bus Y left a school at 2 P.M. for a stadium. Both buses did not change their speeds throughout the journey. Bus X traveled at a constant speed of 60 km/h. When Bus X arrived at the stadium at 2:30 P.M., Bus Y was 3 km from the stadium. Find the speed of Bus Y.

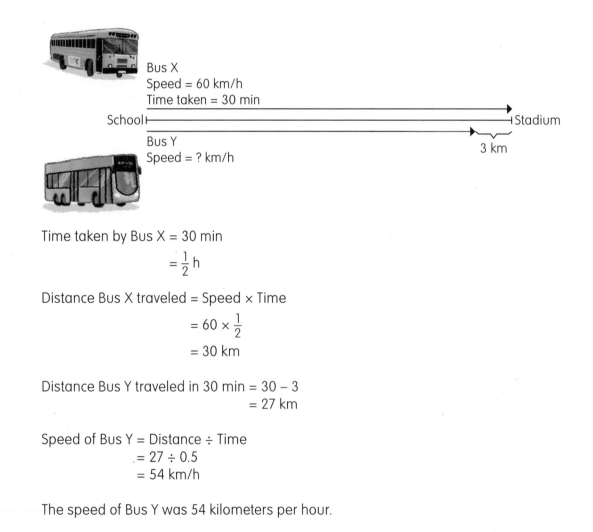

Time taken by Bus X = 30 min

$$= \frac{1}{2} \text{ h}$$

Distance Bus X traveled = Speed × Time

$$= 60 \times \frac{1}{2}$$

$$= 30 \text{ km}$$

Distance Bus Y traveled in 30 min = 30 − 3

$$= 27 \text{ km}$$

Speed of Bus Y = Distance ÷ Time

$$= 27 ÷ 0.5$$

$$= 54 \text{ km/h}$$

The speed of Bus Y was 54 kilometers per hour.

TRY Practice drawing and using diagrams to solve constant speed problems involving two objects or persons moving towards the same end point

Solve.

1. The diagram below shows the distance between Alexa's and Victoria's home from their offices.

```
              24 km                    48 km
        ┌───────────────┐   ┌─────────────────────┐
        ├───────────────┼───┼─────────────────────┤
   Alexa's office      Home              Victoria's office
```

Both of them drove from their offices to home at the same time. Alexa drove at a constant speed of 60 kilometers per hour. Victoria drove at a constant speed of 64 kilometers per hour.

a Who arrived home first?

Time taken by Alexa

= _____ ÷ _____

= _____ h

= _____ min

Time taken by Victoria

= _____ ÷ _____

= _____ h

= _____ min

_____ arrived home first.

b How many minutes later was it before the second person got home?

_____ − _____ = _____

It was _____ minutes later before the second person got home.

ENGAGE

Evelyn and Lola started running from a playground in opposite directions. Evelyn ran at a constant speed of 6 miles per hour. Lola ran at a constant speed of 8 miles per hour. How far apart were they at the end of 15 minutes? Draw a diagram to represent this problem. Compare your diagram to your partner's. What additional questions can be answered using the diagram you created? Discuss.

LEARN Draw and use diagrams to solve constant speed problems involving two objects or persons moving away from each other

1 Two classmates, Anthony and Hayden, started walking from their school in opposite directions. Anthony walked at a constant speed of 4 kilometers per hour. Hayden walked at a constant speed of 6 kilometers per hour. How far apart were they at the end of 15 minutes?

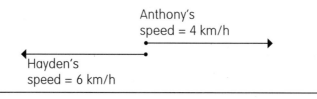

Anthony's
speed = 4 km/h

Hayden's
speed = 6 km/h

After 15 minutes, distance apart = ? km

$15 \text{ min} = \frac{1}{4} \text{ h}$

Distance Anthony walked = Speed × Time

$$= 4 \times \frac{1}{4}$$

$$= 1 \text{ km}$$

Distance Hayden walked $= 6 \times \frac{1}{4}$

$$= 1\frac{1}{2} \text{ km}$$

Distance apart $= 1 + 1\frac{1}{2}$

$$= 2\frac{1}{2} \text{ km}$$

They were $2\frac{1}{2}$ kilometers apart at the end of 15 minutes.

Work in pairs.

Activity 1

(1) Read the real-world problem. Draw a diagram to represent all the given information.

> Jade and Mariah started at the same point and ran in opposite directions. Jade ran at a constant speed of 120 m/min. Mariah ran at a constant speed of 160 m/min. How far apart would they be after 3 min?

(2) Solve the problem. Discuss your solutions.

(3) Repeat the activity with each of the following word problems.

   a Evan walked from his home to the post office, which is 550 meters away, at a constant speed of 80 meters per minute. How far away was he from the post office after 3 minutes?

   b A truck travelled for $1\frac{1}{2}$ hours from Factory A to Factory B at a constant speed of 50 miles per hour. It traveled from Factory B to Factory C at a constant speed of 60 miles per hour. The distance between Factory A and Factory B is $\frac{1}{4}$ of the total distance between Factory A and Factory C. How long did the truck take to travel from Factory B to Factory C?

TRY Practice drawing and using diagrams to solve constant speed problems involving two objects or persons moving away from each other

Solve.

1 Two siblings, Riley and Olivia, started jogging at constant speeds from their house in opposite directions. Riley jogged at a speed of 100 meters per minute. At the end of 20 minutes, they were 3,800 meters apart. Find Olivia's jogging speed in meters per minute.

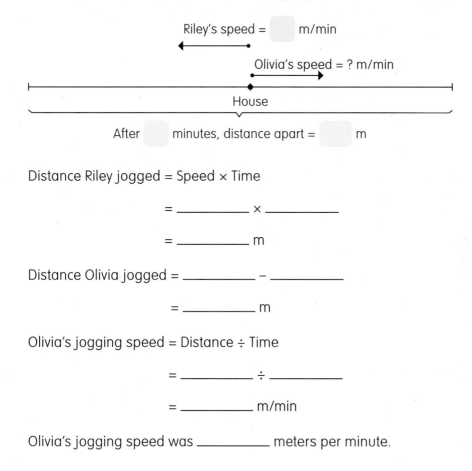

Distance Riley jogged = Speed × Time

= _____ × _____

= _____ m

Distance Olivia jogged = _____ − _____

= _____ m

Olivia's jogging speed = Distance ÷ Time

= _____ ÷ _____

= _____ m/min

Olivia's jogging speed was _____ meters per minute.

Name: _____   Date: _____

INDEPENDENT PRACTICE

Solve.

1. The distance between Station A and Station B is 4.8 miles. The distance between Station B and Station C is 16 miles. A train takes 4 minutes to travel from Station A to Station B and another 12 minutes to travel from Station B to Station C. Find the average speed of the train for the whole journey from Station A to Station C in miles per hour.

2. Aaliyah ran 100 meters in 30 seconds. She then ran another 150 meters at a speed of 3 meters per second.

   a Find the total time taken by Aaliyah for the distance she ran.

   b Find Aaliyah's average speed for the total distance she ran.

3. Mr. Moore drove the first half of his journey at an average speed of 96 km/h for 2 hours. He then drove the remaining half of his journey at an average speed of 80 km/h. How long did Mr. Moore take for the remaining half of his journey?

4 Lauren and Aidan left their offices at 6:15 P.M. and drove to meet at a restaurant the same distance away from their offices for dinner. Lauren drove at a constant speed of 39 miles per hour. Aidan drove at a constant speed of 42 miles per hour. Aidan reached the restaurant at 6:35 P.M. How far away was Lauren from the restaurant when Aidan reached?

5 Amanda and Franco left a library at the same time and cycled in opposite directions back toward their homes. Both of them cycled at constant speeds. Amanda cycled at a speed of 180 meters per minute. At the end of 15 minutes, they were 5,700 meters apart. Find Franco's cycling speed in meters per minute.

6 Morgan cycled from Town A to Town B at an average speed of 15 km/h. She reached Town B at 6 P.M. If she increased her average speed to 20 km/h, she would arrive at 5 P.M. At what time would she arrive at Town B if she cycled at an average speed of 25 km/h?

Name: _____   Date: _____

Mathematical Habit 2 Use mathematical reasoning

The table shows the data about distances and times for three sprinters.

Sprinter	Distance Ran	Time Taken
Caden	60 m	6.34 s
Lorenzo	100 m	10.23 s
Thomas	150 m	14.98 s

Who is the fastest sprinter? Justify your answer.

Problem Solving with Heuristics

1 **Mathematical Habit 4** **Use mathematical models**

The distance between Point A and Point B is 3,120 meters. Maria leaves Point A and Katelyn leaves Point B at the same time. The two girls cycle toward each other until they meet at Point C. Maria's speed is 7.2 meters per second, and Katelyn's speed is 8.4 meters per second.

a How long does Katelyn take to reach Point C?

b What is the distance between Point A and Point C?

(2) | Mathematical Habit 1 | **Persevere in solving problems**

Silas ran from his home to a park at an average speed of 5 km/h. He jogged back to his home using the same route at an average speed of 3 km/h. He took 1 hour in all.

a How long did he take to run from his home to the park?

b What is the distance between his home and the park?

CHAPTER WRAP-UP

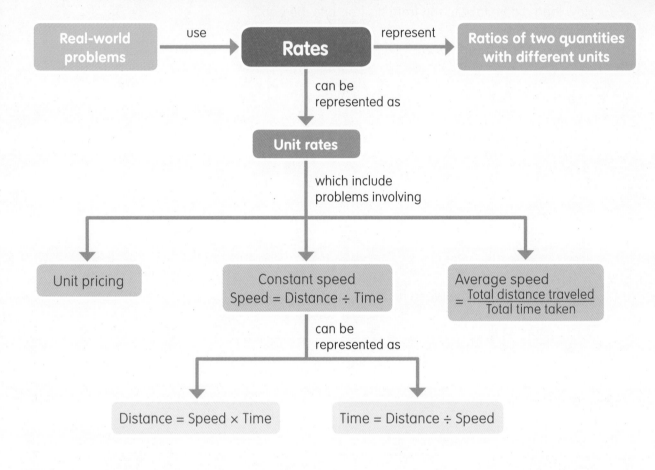

KEY CONCEPTS

- You can use a rate to compare two quantities with different units.
- A unit rate compares a quantity to one unit of another quantity.
- Speed is a special rate that expresses distance per unit time.

  Speed can be found using the formula: Speed = Distance ÷ Time.
- Distance traveled can be found using the formula: Distance = Speed × Time.
- Time taken can be found using the formula: Time = Distance ÷ Speed.
- Average speed is the average distance traveled per unit time.

  Average speed can be found using the formula: Average speed = $\dfrac{\text{Total distance traveled}}{\text{Total time taken}}$.

Name: _____   Date: _____

Solve.

1. A factory produces 300 video game disks in 15 minutes. How many video game disks can it produce in 1 minute?

2. Carolina is paid $336 for 7 days of work. How much is she paid per day?

3. A printer can print 25 pages per minute. At this rate, how long will it take to print 2,000 pages?

4. An empty bathtub is filled with water at a rate of 2.5 liters per minute. How long will it take to fill the bathtub with 30 liters of water?

5. $\frac{2}{3}$ cup of oatmeal is needed to make 10 granola bars. How many such granola bars can be made with 20 cups of oatmeal?

6 A machine takes 15 minutes to scan 1,125 pages. At this rate, how many pages can the machine scan in an hour?

7 150 grams of fertilizer is required for a land area of 6 square meters.

a At this rate, how many grams of fertilizer are required for a land area of 13 square meters?

b For what land area will 850 grams of fertilizer be sufficient?

8 A machine can stamp 36 bottle caps in 10 seconds. Find the missing numbers in the table.

Number of Seconds	Number of Bottle Caps Stamped
10	36
20	
30	
40	
50	
60	

a At this rate, how many bottle caps can the machine stamp in 5 minutes?

b At this rate, how many minutes will it take to stamp 24,408 bottle caps?

9 The table below shows the charges for using an internet service.

Plan A	Up to 10 hours	$6
	Every subsequent $\frac{1}{2}$ hour or part of $\frac{1}{2}$ hour	$1
Plan B	Up to 12 hours	$4
	Every subsequent $\frac{1}{2}$ hour or part of $\frac{1}{2}$ hour	$2

Alex used the internet service for 16 hours and 40 minutes last month.

a Under which plan would he have to pay less?

b How much less?

10 A tank was filled with water to its brim at first. Water was then drained from the tank at a constant rate. The line graph shows the volume of water in the tank over 30 minutes.

Volume of Water in a Tank Over 30 Minutes

a How much water was drained from the tank per minute?

b How many minutes will it take to drain all the water from the tank?

11 A cyclist rode a distance of 38 miles in 4 hours. Find the speed of the cyclist.

12 The speed of a car is 102 kilometers per hour. How far can the car travel in 20 minutes?

13 The distance between Sofia's home and the library is 360 meters. She walked from her home to the library at a speed of 1.2 meters per second. How many minutes did she take for the journey?

14 Jessica took 3 minutes to run a distance of 540 meters from Point X to Point Y. Rachel took 2 minutes to run a distance of 480 meters from Point Z to Point Y. Both girls ran at constant speeds.

Jessica
Distance = 540 m
Time = 3 min

Rachel
Distance = 480 m
Time = 2 min

X   Y   Z

a Find the speed of each girl.

b Which of the two girls ran faster?

15 The distance between Town A and Town B is 45 kilometers.

a If a train travels at an average speed of 60 kilometers per hour, how long will it take to travel from Town A to Town B?

b If a train takes 40 minutes to travel from Town A to Town B, what is its average speed in kilometers per minute? Round your answer to 1 decimal place.

16 At 7:30 A.M., a bus left Town P for Town Q at an average speed of 60 kilometers per hour. 15 minutes later, a car left Town Q and headed for Town P. The car reached Town P at 10:45 A.M. The bus reached Town Q at noon.

a What is the distance between Town P and Town Q?

b What was the average speed of the car?

Assessment Prep
Answer each question.

17 This question has three parts.

Ana can cycle 6 miles in 24 minutes. Zachary can cycle 5 miles in 30 minutes.

Part A
At her current rate, how many miles can Ana cycle in 14 minutes?

Ⓐ 2.5

Ⓑ 3.0

Ⓒ 3.5

Ⓓ 4.0

Part B
At his current rate, how many miles can Zachary cycle in 45 minutes?

Ⓐ 6.0

Ⓑ 6.5

Ⓒ 7.0

Ⓓ 7.5

Part C
Ana and Zachary both cycle from their homes to the library.

Ana's home   Library   Zachary's home

5 miles   3 miles

If both Ana and Zachary start cycling at the same time and they cycle at their current rates, how long will one have to wait for the other to arrive?

Ⓐ Ana will have to wait 1.5 minutes for Zachary.

Ⓑ Ana will have to wait 2 minutes for Zachary.

Ⓒ Zachary will have to wait 1.5 minutes for Ana.

Ⓓ Zachary will have to wait 2 minutes for Ana.

Name: _____ Date: _____

Postal Service

1 The table shows the postal charges for sending single-piece large envelopes within Country X.

Weight Not Over	Price
1 ounce	$1.00
Each additional ounce or part of an ounce	$0.21

How much does it cost to send a single-piece large envelope weighing 5 ounces within Country X? Show and explain your work.

2 A postman is paid a salary of $128 for 8 hours of work.

a What is the postman's hourly salary rate?

b At this rate, how much can the postman earn for 30 hours of work?

3 Robert drove his mail truck 250 meters uphill in 25 seconds. He then drove the truck downhill over the same distance in 12 seconds. What was his average driving speed for this whole journey? Round your answer to 1 decimal place. Show and explain your work.

Rubric

Point(s)	Level	My Performance
7–8	4	• Most of my answers are correct. • I showed complete understanding of the concepts. • I used effective and efficient strategies to solve the problems. • I explained my answers and mathematical thinking clearly and completely.
5–6	3	• Some of my answers are correct. • I showed adequate understanding of the concepts. • I used effective strategies to solve the problems. • I explained my answers and mathematical thinking clearly.
3–4	2	• A few of my answers are correct. • I showed some understanding of the concepts. • I used some effective strategies to solve the problems. • I explained some of my answers and mathematical thinking clearly.
0–2	1	• A few of my answers are correct. • I showed little understanding of the concepts. • I used limited effective strategies to solve the problems. • I did not explain my answers and mathematical thinking clearly.

Teacher's Comments

Percent

How much is a percent?

Whenever a book is sold, an author receives a percent of the price of each book. The payment is called a royalty. A cartoonist can also earn royalties based on comic books sales. One common practice to find the royalties amount is to calculate a percent of the earnings from the sales of the books. For example, a cartoonist may be paid 5% royalty on the earnings from the sales of his books.

In this chapter, you will learn how to calculate percents. The skill you learn will be useful for solving a variety of real-world problems. Two examples include finding the interests on deposits and sales tax.

How does the use of a percent help you compare quantities?

Name: _____ Date: _____

Finding equivalent fractions using multiplication

$$\frac{7}{20} = \frac{35}{100}$$

(× 5)

Multiplying the numerator and denominator of the fraction by the same number, 5, is the same as multiplying the fraction by $\frac{5}{5}$, or the number 1. It does not change the value of the fraction.

▶ Quick Check
Find each missing numerator and denominator.

1. $\frac{4}{5} = \frac{8}{\boxed{}} = \frac{\boxed{}}{100}$

2. $\frac{9}{25} = \frac{18}{\boxed{}} = \frac{\boxed{}}{100}$

Finding equivalent fractions using division

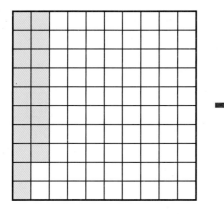

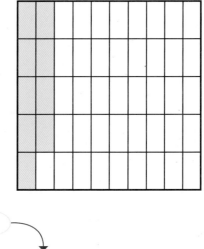

$$\frac{18}{100} = \frac{9}{50}$$

Dividing both the numerator and denominator of the fraction by the same number, 2, is the same as dividing the fraction by $\frac{2}{2}$, or 1. It does not change the value of the fraction.

A fraction is in simplest form when the numerator and denominator have no common factor, except 1.

▶ **Quick Check**

Express each fraction in simplest form.

③ $\frac{26}{100}$

④ $\frac{85}{100}$

⑤ $\frac{48}{100}$

⑥ $\frac{180}{240}$

Writing fractions with a denominator of 100 as a decimal

a $\frac{35}{100} = 0.35$

b $\frac{7}{25} = \frac{28}{100}$
$= 0.28$

c $\frac{25}{500} = \frac{5}{100}$
$= 0.05$

▶ **Quick Check**
Express each fraction as a decimal.

7 $\frac{15}{100}$

8 $\frac{2}{5}$

9 $\frac{39}{300}$

10 $\frac{25}{125}$

Multiplying fractions by a whole number

a $\frac{5}{6} \times 24 = \frac{5}{\underset{1}{6}} \times \overset{4}{24}$ Divide the denominator of the fraction and the whole number by their common factor, 6.

$= 20$ Multiply.

b $\frac{3}{8} \times 12 = \frac{3}{\underset{2}{8}} \times \overset{3}{12}$ Divide the denominator of the fraction and the whole number by their common factor, 4.

$= \frac{9}{2}$ Multiply.

$= 4\frac{1}{2}$ Express the improper fraction as a mixed number.

▶ **Quick Check**
Find each product in simplest form.

11 $\frac{3}{7} \times 42$

12 $\frac{6}{25} \times 40$

Name: _____   Date: _____

1 Understanding Percent

Learning Objective:
• Write equivalent fractions, decimals, and percents.

THINK

A box holds 125 blue balls and 35 red balls. How many blue balls needs to be replaced with red balls so that the blue balls takes up 75% of the box?

ENGAGE

Use a ten frame. Shade 7 squares. What fraction of the ten frame is shaded?
Now, use a 100-square grid. Shade 7 squares. What fraction of the 100-square grid is shaded? Are the two fractions the same? Explain your thinking.

LEARN Express a part of a whole as a fraction and a percent

1 Percents, like ratios, are used to compare two quantities.
Percents compare one quantity to 100.

> Percent is written as %, which means out of 100.

You can express a comparison such as 45 out of 100 as a fraction, ratio, or percent.

Fraction: Ratio: Percent:
$\frac{45}{100}$ 45 : 100   45%

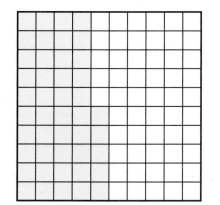

The large square is divided into 100 parts.

45 out of 100 parts are shaded.

So, 45% of the large square is shaded.

> What percent of the large square is not shaded?

55% of the large square is not shaded.

2 72 out of 100 cats are long-haired cats. What percent of the cats are long-haired cats?

72 out of 100 → $\frac{72}{100}$ Express the fraction as a percent.

= 72%

72% of the cats are long-haired cats.

3 A fruit display of 50 apples has 43 green ones. What percent of the apples are green?

43 out of 50 → $\frac{43}{50}$

= $\frac{43 \times 2}{50 \times 2}$ Multiply the numerator and denominator by 2 to make the denominator, 100.

= $\frac{86}{100}$ Express the fraction as a percent.

= 86%

86% of the apples are green.

4 Of the 2,000 people at a concert, 240 are teachers. The rest are students. What percent of the people at the concert are students?

240 out of 2,000 → $\frac{240}{2,000}$

= $\frac{240 \div 10}{2,000 \div 10}$ Divide the numerator and denominator by 10 to make the denominator, 200.

= $\frac{24 \div 2}{200 \div 2}$ Divide the numerator and denominator by 2 to make the denominator, 100.

= $\frac{12}{100}$ Express the fraction as a percent.

= 12%

12% of the people at the concert are teachers.

100% − 12% = 88%

88% of the people at the concert are students.

TRY Practice expressing a part of a whole as a fraction and a percent

Solve.

1 83 out of 100 students like to go to the movies. What percent of the students like to go to the movies?

83 out of 100 → ──────

= _____%

_____% of the students like to go to the movies.

2 Out of 25 chairs, 14 are brown. What percent of the chairs are brown?

14 out of 25 → ─────

$= \dfrac{ \times 4}{ \times 4}$

= ─────

= _____%

_____% of the chairs are brown.

3 Of the 400 animals in an animal park, 32 were monkeys.

a What percent of the animals were monkeys?

32 out of 400 → ─────

$= \dfrac{}{100}$

= _____%

_____% of the animals were monkeys.

b What percent of the animals were not monkeys?

_____% − _____% = _____%

_____% of the animals were not monkeys.

Sue was given some figures on percent. Explain and give reasons why the following do not show eight percent.

a 0.08%

b $\frac{8}{10}$

c 0.8%

LEARN Express percents as fractions or decimals

1 Express 80% as a fraction in simplest form.

▶ **Method 1**

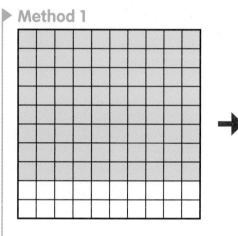 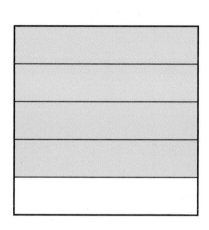

$80\% = \frac{80}{100}$ Express the percent as a fraction.

$= \frac{4}{5}$ Express the fraction in simplest form.

▶ **Method 2**

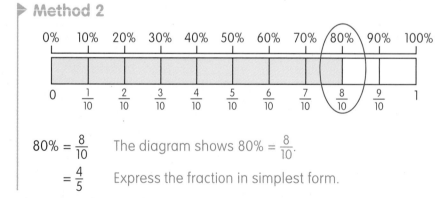

$80\% = \frac{8}{10}$ The diagram shows $80\% = \frac{8}{10}$.

$= \frac{4}{5}$ Express the fraction in simplest form.

2 Express 95% as a decimal.

▶ **Method 1**

$95\% = \dfrac{95}{100}$ Express the percent as a fraction.

$= 0.95$ Express the fraction as a decimal.

▶ **Method 2**

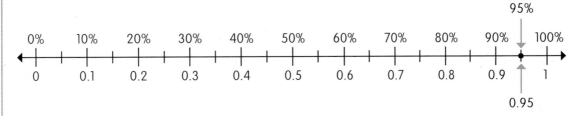

$95\% = 0.95$ The number line shows $95\% = 0.95$.

Activity Showing the relationship between percent and fraction, or percent and decimal

Work in pairs.

① Use the diagram below. Shade the parts to show 40%.

a How many parts make up the whole?

b How many parts are shaded?

② Express 40% as a fraction in simplest form.

③ Discuss your answers in ① and ②. Do you have the same answers? If not, explain why.

④ Repeat ① to ③ with each percent.

a 60%

0% 10% 20% 30% 40% 50% 60% 70% 80% 90% 100%

$0 \quad \frac{1}{10} \quad \frac{2}{10} \quad \frac{3}{10} \quad \frac{4}{10} \quad \frac{5}{10} \quad \frac{6}{10} \quad \frac{7}{10} \quad \frac{8}{10} \quad \frac{9}{10} \quad 1$

b 55%

0% 10% 20% 30% 40% 50% 60% 70% 80% 90% 100%

$0 \quad \frac{1}{10} \quad \frac{2}{10} \quad \frac{3}{10} \quad \frac{4}{10} \quad \frac{5}{10} \quad \frac{6}{10} \quad \frac{7}{10} \quad \frac{8}{10} \quad \frac{9}{10} \quad 1$

⑤ Use the number line and place a dot to show each percent. Then, express it as a decimal.

a 30%

0% 10% 20% 30% 40% 50% 60% 70% 80% 90% 100%

0 0.1 0.2 0.3 0.4 0.5 0.6 0.7 0.8 0.9 1

b 75%

0% 10% 20% 30% 40% 50% 60% 70% 80% 90% 100%

0 0.1 0.2 0.3 0.4 0.5 0.6 0.7 0.8 0.9 1

Do you have the same answers as your partner? If not, explain why.

TRY Practice expressing percents as fractions or decimals

Express each percent as a fraction or a mixed number in simplest form.

❶ $48\% = \dfrac{}{100}$

$= \dfrac{}{}$

❷ 85%

❸ 108%

Express each percent as a decimal.

❹ $13\% = \dfrac{}{100}$

$= \underline{}$

❺ 8%

❻ 126%

Name: _____ Date: _____

Solve.

1. Out of a total of 500 flowers, 65 are roses. What percent of the flowers are roses?

2. Of the 200 packages of bagels sold, 15 of them are sesame seed bagels. What percent of the bagel packages sold are sesame seed bagels?

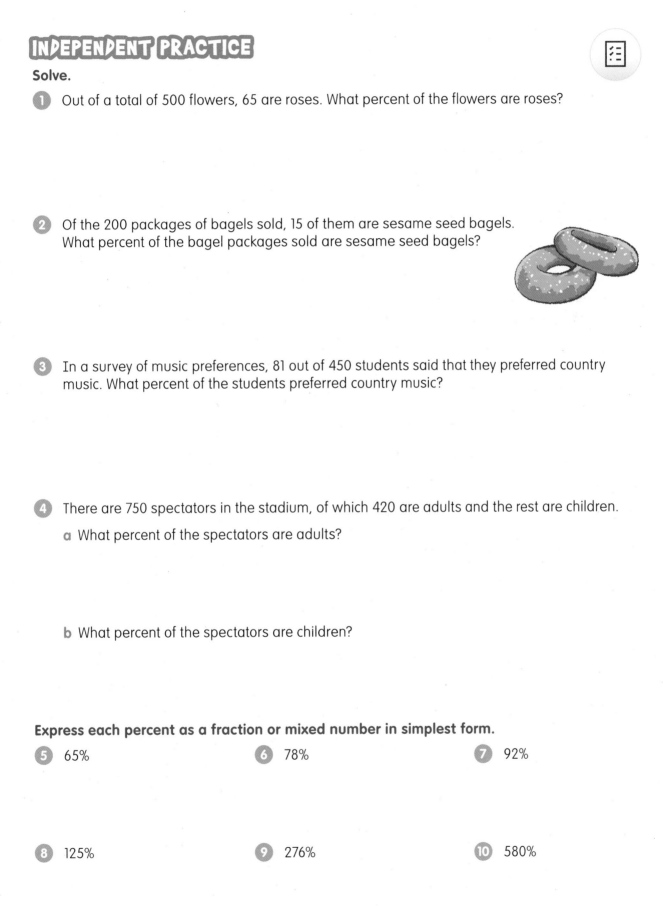

3. In a survey of music preferences, 81 out of 450 students said that they preferred country music. What percent of the students preferred country music?

4. There are 750 spectators in the stadium, of which 420 are adults and the rest are children.

   a What percent of the spectators are adults?

   b What percent of the spectators are children?

Express each percent as a fraction or mixed number in simplest form.

5. 65%   6. 78%   7. 92%

8. 125%   9. 276%   10. 580%

Express each percent as a decimal.

⑪ 6%

⑫ 43%

⑬ 80%

⑭ 367%

⑮ 579%

⑯ 854%

Solve.

⑰ The music for Savannah's dance routine lasts for exactly 4 minutes. When Savannah dances her routine, she starts with her music and finishes 12 seconds before the music ends. What percent of the time the music is playing is Savannah dancing?

⑱ **Mathematical Habit 2 Use mathematical reasoning**
In a practice session of darts, Amy hits the bull's eye 4 times out of 25 times. Jacob hits the bull's eye 8 times out of 100 times.

a Who hits the bull's eye more times?

b Whose aim is more accurate? Justify your answer.

Fractions, Decimals, and Percents

Learning Objective:
• Write more equivalent fractions, decimals, and percents.

THINK

Rafael writes $30\frac{1}{2}\%$ as 0.305 and Jack writes it as $\frac{61}{200}$. Who is correct? Explain your answer.

ENGAGE

Can you express each of the following fractions with 100 as the denominator?
Why or why not? Discuss.

a $\frac{3}{4}$ **b** $\frac{2}{3}$

Now, name three fractions that can easily be written as a percent and three fractions that cannot as easily be converted to a percent. What do you notice? Share your observations.

LEARN Express fractions or mixed numbers as percents

Activity Expressing fractions or mixed numbers as percents ─────────

Work in pairs.

Use these fractions and mixed numbers.

$$\frac{7}{9} \qquad \frac{3}{5} \qquad \frac{1}{2} \qquad \frac{7}{10} \qquad \frac{3}{4} \qquad \frac{7}{8} \qquad \frac{5}{6} \qquad 1\frac{2}{3} \qquad 2\frac{1}{4} \qquad 3\frac{2}{5}$$

① Find which of the fractions or mixed numbers can be expressed as percents using the method of writing an equivalent fraction. List the fractions that cannot be expressed as percents using this method.

Example:

$$\frac{3}{5} = \frac{3 \times 20}{5 \times 20}$$

$$= \frac{60}{100}$$

$$= 60\%$$

② If you want to use the method of writing an equivalent fraction to express a fraction as a percent, what must be true of the fraction or mixed number?

1 Express $\frac{3}{4}$ as a percent.

▶ **Method 1**

$\frac{3}{4} = \frac{75}{100}$ Express as a fraction with 100 as the denominator.

$\quad = 75\%$ Express the fraction as a percent.

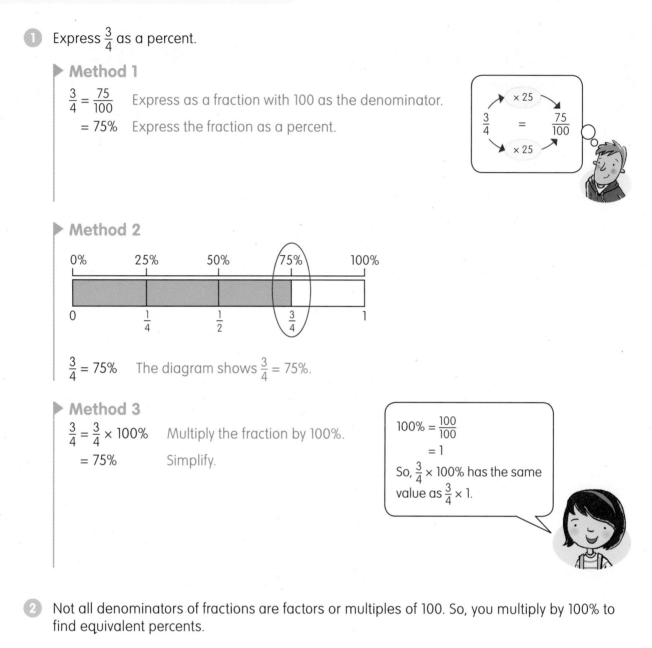

▶ **Method 2**

$\frac{3}{4} = 75\%$ The diagram shows $\frac{3}{4} = 75\%$.

▶ **Method 3**

$\frac{3}{4} = \frac{3}{4} \times 100\%$ Multiply the fraction by 100%.

$\quad = 75\%$ Simplify.

$100\% = \frac{100}{100}$
$\quad\quad = 1$
So, $\frac{3}{4} \times 100\%$ has the same value as $\frac{3}{4} \times 1$.

2 Not all denominators of fractions are factors or multiples of 100. So, you multiply by 100% to find equivalent percents.

$\frac{2}{3} = \frac{2}{3} \times 100\%$ Multiply the fraction by 100%.

$\quad = \frac{200}{3}\%$ Simplify.

$\quad = 66\frac{2}{3}\%$ Write the improper fraction as a mixed number.

TRY Practice expressing fractions or mixed numbers as percents

Express each fraction or a mixed number as a percent.

1 $\dfrac{4}{5} = \dfrac{\boxed{}}{100}$

   $= \underline{\hspace{2cm}}\%$

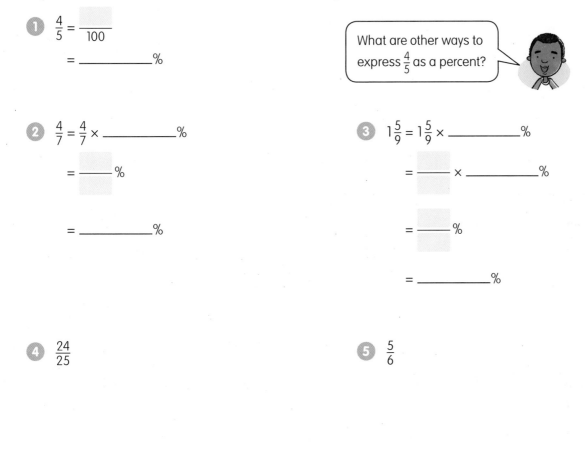

What are other ways to express $\dfrac{4}{5}$ as a percent?

2 $\dfrac{4}{7} = \dfrac{4}{7} \times \underline{\hspace{2cm}}\%$

   $= \dfrac{\boxed{}}{\boxed{}}\%$

   $= \underline{\hspace{2cm}}\%$

3 $1\dfrac{5}{9} = 1\dfrac{5}{9} \times \underline{\hspace{2cm}}\%$

   $= \dfrac{\boxed{}}{\boxed{}} \times \underline{\hspace{2cm}}\%$

   $= \dfrac{\boxed{}}{\boxed{}}\%$

   $= \underline{\hspace{2cm}}\%$

4 $\dfrac{24}{25}$

5 $\dfrac{5}{6}$

6 $1\dfrac{7}{8}$

7 $1\dfrac{5}{7}$

ENGAGE

Express each decimal as a fraction with 100 as the denominator.

a 0.07   b 0.17   c 1.07   d 0.017

Share your method with your partner. Then, show and explain how you can express each fraction as a percent.

What is another method to express a decimal as a percent? Use specific examples to explain your thinking.

LEARN Express decimals as percents

1 Express 0.9 as a percent.

▶ **Method 1**

$0.9 = \dfrac{9}{10}$ Express the decimal as a fraction.

$ = \dfrac{90}{100}$ Express as a fraction with 100 as the denominator.

$ = 90\%$ Express the fraction as a percent.

▶ **Method 2**

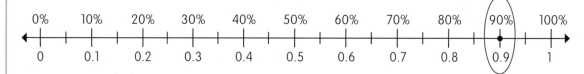

$0.9 = 90\%$ The number line shows 0.9 = 90%.

▶ **Method 3**

$\dfrac{9}{10} = \dfrac{9}{10} \times 100\%$ Multiply the fraction by 100%.

$\phantom{\dfrac{9}{10}} = 90\%$ Simplify.

$100\% = \dfrac{100}{100}$
$ = 1$
So, 0.9 × 100% has the same value as 0.9 × 1.

Express each decimal as a percent.

1 $0.82 = \dfrac{}{100}$

   $= \underline{\hspace{2cm}}\%$

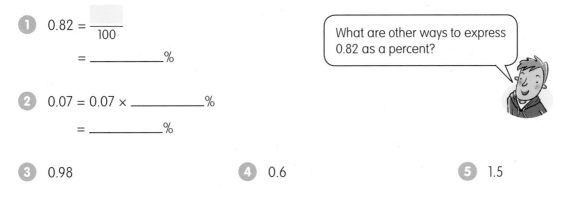

What are other ways to express 0.82 as a percent?

2 $0.07 = 0.07 \times \underline{\hspace{2cm}}\%$

   $= \underline{\hspace{2cm}}\%$

3 0.98

4 0.6

5 1.5

ENGAGE

17% written as a fraction is $\dfrac{17}{100}$. How can you write $27\dfrac{1}{2}\%$ as a fraction in its simplest form?

Now, consider this problem. In Grace's last examination, she had a grade of $85\dfrac{1}{2}\%$. What does that mean if the examination was worth 100 points? How do you express her grade as a fraction in its simplest form? Share your method.

LEARN Express percents as fractions

1 Express $33\dfrac{1}{3}\%$ as a fraction.

   $33\dfrac{1}{3}\% = \dfrac{100}{3}\%$ Express the mixed number as an improper fraction.

   $= \dfrac{100}{3} \div 100$ Divide by 100 to express the percent as a fraction.

   $= \dfrac{100}{3} \times \dfrac{1}{100}$ Rewrite using the reciprocal of the divisor.

   $= \dfrac{\overset{1}{\cancel{100}}}{3} \times \dfrac{1}{\underset{1}{\cancel{100}}}$ Divide the numerator and denominator by their common factor, 100.

   $= \dfrac{1}{3}$ Multiply.

To express $n\%$ as a fraction, divide n by 100. For example, $19\% = \dfrac{19}{100}$.

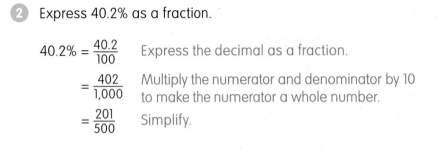

2 Express 40.2% as a fraction.

$40.2\% = \dfrac{40.2}{100}$ Express the decimal as a fraction.

$= \dfrac{402}{1,000}$ Multiply the numerator and denominator by 10 to make the numerator a whole number.

$= \dfrac{201}{500}$ Simplify.

TRY Practice expressing percents as fractions

Express each percent as a fraction in simplest form.

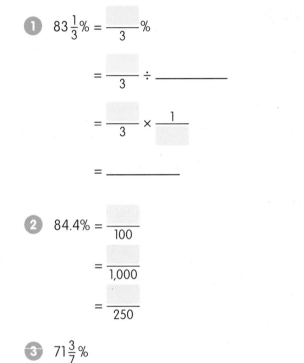

1 $83\dfrac{1}{3}\% = \dfrac{\boxed{}}{3}\%$

$= \dfrac{\boxed{}}{3} \div \underline{}$

$= \dfrac{\boxed{}}{3} \times \dfrac{1}{\boxed{}}$

$= \underline{}$

2 $84.4\% = \dfrac{\boxed{}}{100}$

$= \dfrac{\boxed{}}{1,000}$

$= \dfrac{\boxed{}}{250}$

3 $71\dfrac{3}{7}\%$ **4** 90.5%

Name: _____   Date: _____

INDEPENDENT PRACTICE

Express each fraction or mixed number as a percent.

1) $\frac{3}{5}$ 2) $\frac{3}{8}$ 3) $\frac{1}{3}$

4) $2\frac{1}{5}$ 5) $7\frac{3}{4}$ 6) $9\frac{7}{8}$

Express each decimal as a percent.

7) 0.46 8) 0.7 9) 0.06

10) 1.52 11) 6.03 12) 8.9

Express each percent as a fraction in simplest form.

13) 5.75% 14) 25.5% 15) 85.25%

16) $16\frac{2}{3}\%$ 17) $42\frac{3}{8}\%$ 18) $79\frac{5}{6}\%$

 **Express each fraction as a percent. Round your answer to the nearest whole number.**

19 $\dfrac{76}{125}$

20 $\dfrac{98}{230}$

21 $\dfrac{102}{350}$

Find the missing fractions and decimals.

22

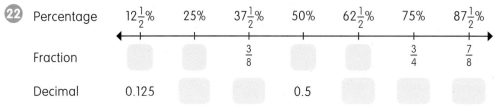

Percentage	$12\frac{1}{2}\%$	25%	$37\frac{1}{2}\%$	50%	$62\frac{1}{2}\%$	75%	$87\frac{1}{2}\%$
Fraction			$\dfrac{3}{8}$			$\dfrac{3}{4}$	$\dfrac{7}{8}$
Decimal	0.125			0.5			

Solve.

23 **Mathematical Habit 2** Use mathematical reasoning

School A has 450 seniors, and 432 of them plan to go to college. School B has 380 seniors, and 361 of them plan to go to college. In which school does a greater percent of seniors plan to go to college? Justify your reasoning.

3 Percent of a Quantity

Learning Objective:
• Find the percent of a number.

> **New Vocabulary**
> base (of a percent)

THINK

Find three pairs of possible missing numbers.

$$5\% \times \boxed{?} = \boxed{?}\% \times 1{,}500$$

ENGAGE

Use a 100-square grid. Shade 5% of the whole square. How many small squares are shaded? Draw lines on the grid to find 5% of 200. Share your method.

If 5% was represented by 10 squares shaded, what is the total number of squares? What if 5% was represented by 7 squares shaded? What if 5% was represented by 4 squares shaded? Discuss.

LEARN Find the quantity represented by the percent

1. 5% represents 5 units for every 100 units.

   5% of a whole quantity refers to the part of the quantity that represents 5%.

   A whole quantity (100%)

   How much is the part here? (5%)

   The bar model shows that 100% refers to the whole quantity, or the **base**.

> 5% represents 5 units for every 100 units. Explain how many units are represented by 5% if there are 200 units.

2 Find 5% of 160.

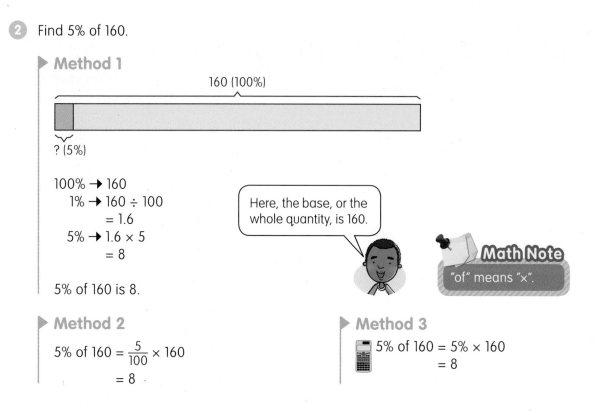

▶ **Method 1**

160 (100%)

? (5%)

$100\% \rightarrow 160$
$1\% \rightarrow 160 \div 100$
$\qquad = 1.6$
$5\% \rightarrow 1.6 \times 5$
$\qquad = 8$

5% of 160 is 8.

Here, the base, or the whole quantity, is 160.

Math Note
"of" means "×".

▶ **Method 2**

$5\% \text{ of } 160 = \dfrac{5}{100} \times 160$
$\qquad\qquad\quad = 8$

▶ **Method 3**

$5\% \text{ of } 160 = 5\% \times 160$
$\qquad\qquad\quad = 8$

TRY Practice finding the quantity represented by the percent

Find the percent of each whole.

1 40% of 720 cm

▶ **Method 1**

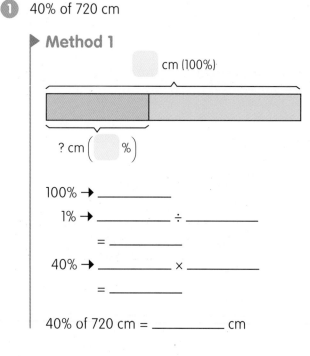

☐ cm (100%)

? cm (☐ %)

$100\% \rightarrow$ _____

$1\% \rightarrow$ _____ ÷ _____

$\qquad =$ _____

$40\% \rightarrow$ _____ × _____

$\qquad =$ _____

40% of 720 cm = _____ cm

▶ **Method 2**

$40\% \text{ of } 720 \text{ cm} = \dfrac{\boxed{}}{100} \times 720$

$= \underline{} \text{ cm}$

▶ **Method 3**

 $40\% \text{ of } 720 \text{ cm} = 40\% \times 720$

$= \underline{} \text{ cm}$

2 30% of 450

3 55% of 320

4 75% of 800 kg

5 110% of $550

ENGAGE

Daniel thinks of a number. 25% of the number is 78. Draw a bar model to show the information. Write the problem as an expression and solve it. Share your expression and solution with your partner.

LEARN Find the whole given a quantity and its percent

1 Julia has 15% of her DVD collection in a box. There are 60 DVDs in the box. How many DVDs are in Julia's collection?

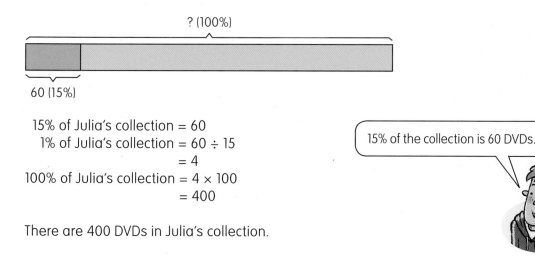

15% of Julia's collection = 60
1% of Julia's collection = 60 ÷ 15
= 4
100% of Julia's collection = 4 × 100
= 400

There are 400 DVDs in Julia's collection.

15% of the collection is 60 DVDs.

Activity Finding the whole given a quantity and its percent

Work in pairs.

① Read the real-world problem. Draw a bar model for the problem.

> Chloe places 48% of her hair clips in a box. There are 12 hair clips in the box. How many hair clips does Chloe have in all?

② Use the bar model to solve the problem. Check each other's answer using a calculator.

③ Repeat the activity with each of the following real-world problems.

  a 75% of a number is 708. Find the number.

  b At an amusement park, 60% of the people were adults and the rest were children. There were 720 adults. How many people were at the amusement park?

TRY Practice finding the whole given a quantity and its percent

Solve.

① 27% of the students in a school are in Grade 6. There are 540 Grade 6 students. How many students are there in the school?

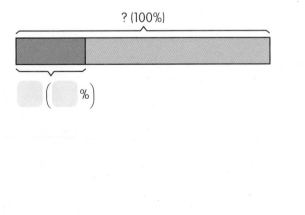

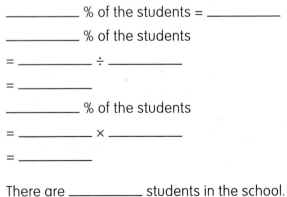

_____ % of the students = _____

_____ % of the students

= _____ ÷ _____

= _____

_____ % of the students

= _____ × _____

= _____

There are _____ students in the school.

② 20% of a number is 184. What is the number?

INDEPENDENT PRACTICE

Solve. Use the bar model to help you.

1 What is 15% of 12 meters?

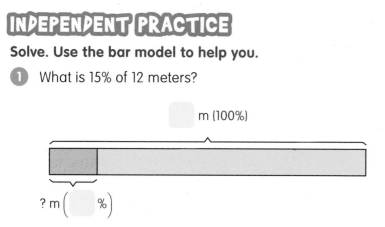

2 A park ranger finds that 35% of the park's visitors stay at the campground. If 105 visitors stayed at the campground one day, how many visitors did the park have that day?

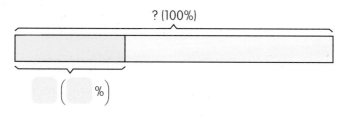

Find the quantity represented by each percent.

3 45% of $360

4 66% of 740 km

Solve.

5 There are 1,500 students in a school. 65% of them wear glasses. How many students in the school wear glasses?

6 A school raises $4,000 for its new library. 36% of the money is used to buy reference books. How much money is used to buy reference books?

7 Ms. Allen spent 55% of her savings on a television that cost $550. How much money did she have in her savings before she bought the television?

$550

8 75% of a number is 354. Find the number.

9 Ryan has 250 songs on his cell phone. 10% are country, 70% are pop, and the rest are hip-hop. How many songs are hip-hop?

10 There are 820 people at a stadium. 65% of them are adults, 20% of them are boys, and the rest are girls. How many girls are there at the stadium?

11 Mr. Peterson had 2,600 hens, ducks, and goats on his farm. 35% of them were hens, and 25% of them were goats. How many ducks did he have on his farm?

12 There are 1,505 pieces of fruit for sale at a farmer's market. 39% of them are apples, 28% are oranges, 13% are honeydew melons, and the rest are watermelons. How many watermelons are there?

13 120% of a number is 45. Find the number.

14 250% of a number is 60. Find the number.

15 400% of a number is 45. Find the number.

16 Last month, Diego spent 40% of his salary on a laptop. He then spent 30% of it on his bills and saved the remaining $1,200. What was his salary?

17 20% of the spectators at a tennis match wore black shirts. 10% of them wore red, 30% wore blue, and the remaining 3,600 spectators wore white shirts. Find the total number of spectators at the match.

18 Kaylee made 300 greeting cards. She sold 40% of the cards, gave 85% of the remaining cards to her friends, and kept the rest of the cards for herself. How many greeting cards did she keep for herself?

19 Owen saved $500. He received 25% of the money for his birthday, saved 30% of the remainder from his allowance, and earned the rest of it by mowing lawns. How much of his savings did he earn by mowing lawns?

4 Real-World Problems: Percent

Learning Objective:
• Solve real-world problems involving percent.

New Vocabulary
commission
interest rate

THINK

Kayla paid $102.60 for a meal for two at a restaurant, inclusive of an 8% sales tax. How much was the sales tax in dollars?

ENGAGE

Pedro scored [?] out of 45 points in a test. Choose a value for Pedro's score and draw a bar model to represent the situation. Trade with your partner. How do you find the percent of the total number of points he scored? Explain your thinking.

LEARN Solve real-world problems involving finding the percent represented by a quantity

1 In her last basketball game, Megan scored 18 of her team's 48 points.

   a What percent of her team's points did Megan score?

   b What percent of her team's points did the rest of Megan's team score?

   STEP 1 Understand the problem.

   How many points did Megan score?
   How many points did her team score?
   What do I need to find?

   STEP 2 Think of a plan.
   I can draw a bar model.

STEP 3 Carry out the plan.

a

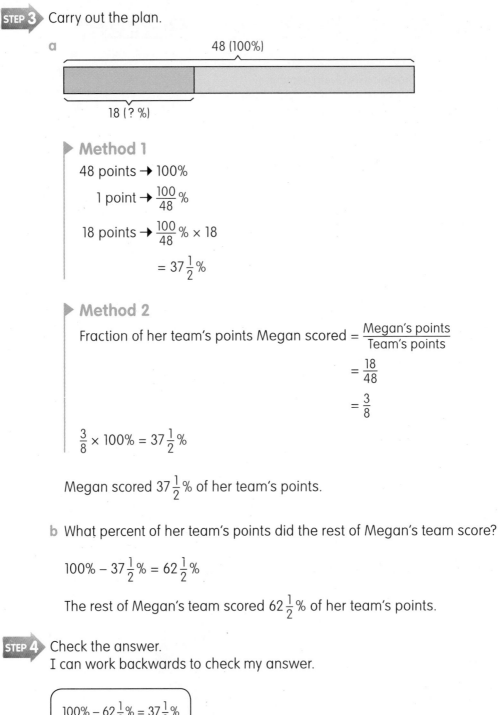

48 (100%)

18 (? %)

▶ **Method 1**

48 points → 100%

1 point → $\frac{100}{48}$%

18 points → $\frac{100}{48}$% × 18

$= 37\frac{1}{2}$%

▶ **Method 2**

Fraction of her team's points Megan scored $= \dfrac{\text{Megan's points}}{\text{Team's points}}$

$= \dfrac{18}{48}$

$= \dfrac{3}{8}$

$\dfrac{3}{8} \times 100\% = 37\frac{1}{2}\%$

Megan scored $37\frac{1}{2}$% of her team's points.

b What percent of her team's points did the rest of Megan's team score?

$100\% - 37\frac{1}{2}\% = 62\frac{1}{2}\%$

The rest of Megan's team scored $62\frac{1}{2}$% of her team's points.

STEP 4 Check the answer.
I can work backwards to check my answer.

$100\% - 62\frac{1}{2}\% = 37\frac{1}{2}\%$

$37\frac{1}{2}\% \times 48 = 18$

My answer is correct.

TRY **Practice solving real-world problems involving finding the percent represented by a quantity**

Solve.

1 Mr. Sanders is making 80 cups of fruit punch for the opening of his bakery. He uses 52 cups of fruit juice and the rest is sparkling water.

a What percent of the punch is fruit juice?

▶ **Method 1**

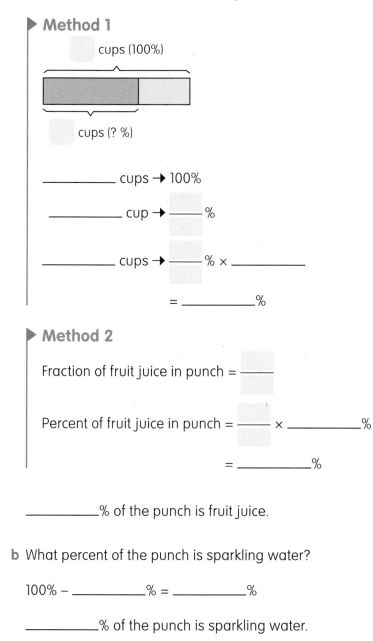

cups (100%)

cups (? %)

_____ cups → 100%

_____ cup → _____ %

_____ cups → _____ % × _____

= _____ %

▶ **Method 2**

Fraction of fruit juice in punch = ⬜⬜

Percent of fruit juice in punch = ⬜⬜ × _____ %

= _____ %

_____% of the punch is fruit juice.

b What percent of the punch is sparkling water?

100% − _____% = _____%

_____% of the punch is sparkling water.

A T-shirt costs $50. A sales tax of 7% will be added to the price. What is the total cost of the T-shirt? Draw a bar model to represent this problem. Compare your bar model to your partner's.

LEARN Solve real-world problems involving taxes

1. Dara and his family had dinner in a restaurant. The total cost of the food was $68.50, and an 8% sales tax was added to the bill. What was the total bill?

▶ **Method 1**

$100\% \rightarrow \$68.50$

$1\% \rightarrow \$\dfrac{68.50}{100}$

$8\% \rightarrow \$\dfrac{68.50}{100} \times 8$

$\qquad = \$5.48$

$\$68.50 + \$5.48 = \$73.98$

▶ **Method 2**

Sales tax $= 8\%$ of $\$68.50$

$\qquad = \dfrac{8}{100} \times \$68.50$

$\qquad = \$5.48$

$\$68.50 + \$5.48 = \$73.98$

The total bill was $73.98.

Check

Estimate the value of 8% of $68.50. 8% is close to 10% and $68.50 is close to $70, so the sales tax should be close to 10% of $70, or $7. The estimate shows a total bill of $70 + $7 = $77. So, the answer is reasonable.

2. A pair of shoes costs $52.00 and the sales tax is $2.60. The sales tax is calculated based on the cost of the shoes. What is the sales tax rate?

The cost of the shoes is 100%.

$\$52.00 \rightarrow 100\%$

$\$1.00 \rightarrow \dfrac{100}{52.00}\%$

$\$2.60 \rightarrow \dfrac{100}{52.00}\% \times 2.60$

$\qquad = 5\%$

The sales tax rate is 5%.

Check

Estimate the value of 5% of $52. $52 is close to $50, so the sales tax should be close to 5% of $50. 5% of $50 is half of $5, or $2.50, which is close to $2.60. So, the answer is reasonable.

Solve. Check that each answer is reasonable.

1. A laptop displayed at a shop costs $720. A sales tax of 7% will be added to the price. What is the total cost of the laptop?

   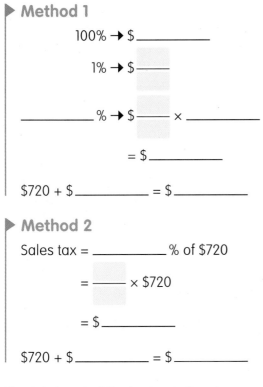

   ▶ **Method 1**

   100% → $_____

   1% → $ ——

   _____% → $ —— × _____

   = $_____

   $720 + $_____ = $_____

   ▶ **Method 2**

   Sales tax = _____% of $720

   = —— × $720

   = $_____

   $720 + $_____ = $_____

   The total cost of the laptop is $_____.

2. Lily went to lunch with her friends. The food cost $78.50, and a sales tax of $4.71 was added to the cost of the meal. What was the sales tax rate?

   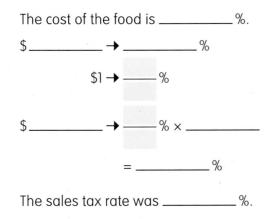

   The cost of the food is _____%.

   $_____ → _____%

   $1 → —— %

   $_____ → —— % × _____

   = _____%

   The sales tax rate was _____%.

ENGAGE

8% of the magazine sales made by a sixth-grade class will be donated to a charity. The class raised $400 for the charity. What is the total amount of the magazine sales in dollars? Draw a bar model to represent this problem. Compare your bar model to your partner's.

LEARN Solve real-world problems involving finding the whole given a quantity and its percent

1 Mr. Davis earns a 3% commission on all the furniture he sells. He receives $2,880 in commission. What is his sales amount in dollars?

$$3\% \rightarrow \$2,880$$
$$1\% \rightarrow \$2,880 \div 3$$
$$= \$960$$
$$100\% \rightarrow \$960 \times 100$$
$$= \$96,000$$

A commission is a percent of total sales earned by a salesperson.

His sales amount is $96,000.

Check

Estimate the value of 3% of $96,000. $96,000 is close to $100,000, so the commission, $2,880, should be close to 3% of $100,000, or $3,000. So, the answer is reasonable.

TRY Practice solving real-world problems involving finding the whole given a quantity and its percent

Solve. Check that each answer is reasonable.

1 A cartoonist earns 12% royalty on the retail price of his comic books. He receives $25,800 in royalties. What is the retail price of his comic books in dollars?

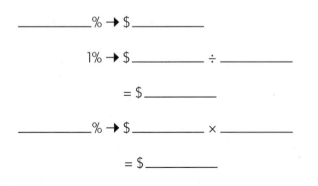

The retail price of his comic books is $_____.

Mr. Ortiz saves $1,000 in a bank account. The bank will pay him 4% interest at the end of a year. Ms. Collins saves $1,500 in a bank account. The bank will pay her 3% at the end of the year. Who will receive more interest? How do you know? Explain your thinking.

LEARN Solve real-world problems involving interest

1. Ms. Taylor deposits $1,500 in a savings account. The bank will pay her 5% interest at the end of a year. How much interest will Ms. Taylor receive?

Interest = 5% of $1,500 for 1 year

$$= \frac{5}{100} \times \$1,500 \times 1$$

$$= \$75$$

Ms. Taylor will receive $75 in interest.

> When you deposit money in a savings account, the bank pays you interest on the money. The interest rate is the rate at which your money earns interest in a given amount of time.

2. A basketball club has $24,000 in an account that has an interest rate of 3% per year. How much interest will it earn at the end of $\frac{1}{2}$ year?

Interest $= \frac{3}{100} \times \$24,000 \times \frac{1}{2}$

$$= \$360$$

The basketball club will earn $360 at the end of $\frac{1}{2}$ year.

TRY Practice solving real-world problems involving interest

Solve.

1. A firm has $30,000 in a bank account at the beginning of the year. Interest will be paid at a rate of 2% at the end of the year. How much interest will the firm receive for the year?

Interest $= \dfrac{}{} \times \$\underline{\hspace{2cm}} \times 1$

$$= \$\underline{\hspace{2cm}}$$

The firm will receive $\underline{\hspace{2cm}} in interest for the year.

2 A company has $500,000 in a savings account. The interest rate is 4% per year. How much interest will the company earn at the end of $\frac{1}{2}$ year?

Interest = ─── × $ _____ × ───

= $ _____

The company will earn $ _____ in interest at the end of $\frac{1}{2}$ year.

1 A bag costs $59 and the sales tax is $4.13.
The sales tax is calculated based on the cost of the bag.
What fraction of the price of the bag is the sales tax?
What percent of the price of the bag is the sales tax?
Are the fraction and percent equivalent?

2 Compare each fraction statement with the decimal and percent statements. What pattern do you notice? How do you convert fraction or decimal statements to percent statements?

Fraction statement	Decimal statement	Percent statement
P is $\frac{1}{2}$ of Q.	P is [?] of Q.	P is [?] % of Q.
R is [?] of S.	R is 0.6 of S.	R is [?] % of S.
X is [?] of Y.	X is [?] of Y.	X is 5% of Y.

INDEPENDENT PRACTICE

Solve. Check that each answer is reasonable.

1 Ashley had 25 hair clips. 7 of them were blue and the rest were purple.

    a What percent of the hair clips were blue?

    b What percent of the hair clips were purple?

2 Julian had $60. He spent $36 on a pair of shoes and the rest on a shirt.

    a What percent of the money did he spend on the pair of shoes?

    b What percent of the money did he spend on the shirt?

3 Ms. Nguyen bought a camera that cost $450. In addition, she had to pay 4% sales tax. How much did Ms. Nguyen pay for the camera?

4 Mr. Rogers bought a computer that cost $2,500. The sales tax rate was 7%. How much did he pay for the computer?

⑤ There were 320 adults and 180 children at a carnival. What percent of people were adults?

⑥ Kiara spent $36 and had $12 left. What percent of her money did she spend?

⑦ An artiste receives 20% royalty on the price of his recordings. He receives $36,000 in royalties. What is the price of his recordings in dollars?

⑧ A club deposited $50,000 in a savings account at the beginning of the year. Interest will be paid at a rate of 3% at the end of the year. How much interest will the club receive for the year?

⑨ Company X has $128,000 in a savings account that pays 6% interest per year. How much interest will it earn at the end of $\frac{1}{2}$ year?

Name: _____ Date: _____

Mathematical Habit 3 Construct viable arguments

Sara and Kyle checked some books out of the library. 20% of the books Sara checked out were fiction books, and 40% of the books Kyle checked out were fiction books. Your friend thinks that Kyle checked out more fiction books than Sara. Explain the error in your friend's thinking. Use an example to support your reasoning.

Problem Solving with Heuristics

1 **Mathematical Habit 2** Use mathematical reasoning

A florist had 1,800 roses, tulips, and orchids in her shop. 55% of the flowers were roses. After she sold some of the roses, the percent of the flowers that were roses became 10%. How many roses were sold?

2 **Mathematical Habit 7** Make use of structure

In the figure, the area of the shaded part is 40% of the area of Square P. It is also 20% of the area of Square Q. What percent of the figure is shaded? Round your answer to 2 decimal places.

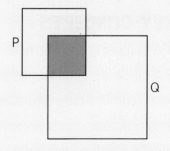

How does the use of a percent help you compare quantities?

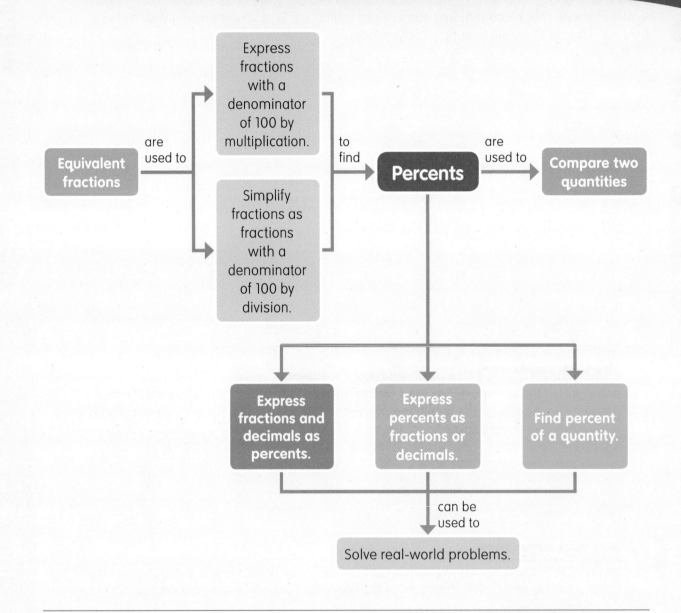

KEY CONCEPTS

- A percent is a part-whole comparison in which the whole is divided into 100 equal parts.
- A percent can be expressed as a fraction with a denominator of 100 or as a decimal.
- You can use diagrams to express percents as fractions, or fractions as percents.
- You can use number lines to express percents as decimals, or decimals as percents.
- 100% has the same value as 1. You can multiply a fraction by 100% to find the percent.
- You can use bar models to find a percent of a quantity.

Name: _____ Date: _____

Express each percent as a fraction in simplest form.

① 46%

② $16\frac{2}{3}$%

③ 8.8%

Express each percent as a decimal.

④ 34%

⑤ 60%

⑥ 9%

Express each fraction as a percent.

⑦ $\frac{17}{20}$

⑧ $\frac{21}{25}$

⑨ $\frac{270}{300}$

Express each decimal as a percent.

⑩ 0.02

⑪ 0.63

⑫ 0.9

Find the quantity represented by each percent.

13 35% of 500 kg

14 68% of $2,800

Solve.

15 There were 45 people on a bus. 60% of them were adults. How many adults were on the bus?

16 Ms. Torres had $900. She spent 22% of this amount on a mobile phone. How much did she pay for the mobile phone?

17 22% of a number is 44. Find the number.

18 125% of a number is 65. Find the number.

19 Steven had 1,400 stamps. He gave 350 of them to his brother and the rest to his sister.

    a What percent of the stamps did he give to his brother?

    b What percent of the stamps did he give to his sister?

20 There were 25 adults and 15 children at a restaurant. What percent of the people were children?

21 Anya paid $2,800 plus 7% sales tax on mountain bikes for a bike club. How much did Anya pay in total for the mountain bikes?

22 Ms. Wright opens a savings account with a deposit of $800. The bank will pay her 3% interest per year.

    a How much interest will Ms. Wright receive at the end of $\frac{1}{2}$ year?

    b How much interest will she receive at the end of 1 year?

Assessment Prep
Answer each question.

23 What is 70% of 3,600 gallons? Write your answer in the space below.

24 Alan brings 8 key chains to school. These represent 40% of Alan's key chain collection. What is the total number of key chains in Alan's collection? Write your answer in the space below.

25 This question has two parts.

At a shop, the sales tax rate for an item is a fixed percent of the cost of the item. A customer bought an item that cost $95 and paid a sales tax of $5.70.

Part A
Ms. Castillo bought an item that cost $120. What was the sales tax for the item? Write your answer and your work or explanation in the space below.

Part B
Mr. Stewart paid a sales tax of $51 for an item. What was the cost of the item? Write your answer and your work or explanation in the space below.

© 2020 Marshall Cavendish Education Pte Ltd

Royalties

1 A cartoonist is paid royalty based on the earnings from the sales of his books. He receives $1,250 in royalties and the earnings from the sales of his books is $25,000.

   a What fraction of the earnings from the sales of his books is the amount of his royalties?

   b What percent of the earnings from the sales of his books is the amount of his royalties?

2 Another cartoonist is paid 8% royalty on the price of the sales of her books. She receives $2,340 in royalties. What is the price of the sales of her books in dollars? Draw a bar model to explain and show your work.

3. Store A sells a comic book at $19, and a sales tax of 6% will be added to the price. Store B sells the same comic book at $18, and a sales tax of 7% will be added to the price. Which store gives a better deal to purchase the comic book? Show and explain your work.

Rubric

Point(s)	Level	My Performance
7–8	4	• Most of my answers are correct. • I showed complete understanding of the concepts. • I used effective and efficient strategies to solve the problems. • I explained my answers and mathematical thinking clearly and completely.
5–6	3	• Some of my answers are correct. • I showed adequate understanding of the concepts. • I used effective strategies to solve the problems. • I explained my answers and mathematical thinking clearly.
3–4	2	• A few of my answers are correct. • I showed some understanding of the concepts. • I used some effective strategies to solve the problems. • I explained some of my answers and mathematical thinking clearly.
0–2	1	• A few of my answers are correct. • I showed little understanding of the concepts. • I used limited effective strategies to solve the problems. • I did not explain my answers and mathematical thinking clearly.

Teacher's Comments

Glossary

A

- **absolute value**

  The distance of a number from zero on a number line.
  Examples: $|8| = 8$, $|-8| = 8$

- **average speed**

  The average distance traveled per unit time.
  Average speed
  $= \dfrac{\text{Total distance traveled}}{\text{Total time taken}}$

B

- **base (of a percent)**

  The whole quantity of which a percent is found.
  Example: In 20% of 85, the base is 85.

C

- **commission**

  A percent of the total sales earned by a salesperson.

G

- **greatest common factor**

  The common factor of two or more numbers that has the greatest value.
  Example:
  Factors of 12: ①, ②, ③, 4, ⑥, 12
  Factors of 30: ①, ②, ③, 5, ⑥, 10, 15, 30
  The greatest common factor of 12 and 30 is 6.

I

- **inequality**

  A mathematical statement that shows the relationship between two expressions that are not equal.

- **interest rate**

  The rate at which money earns interest.

L

- **least common multiple**

  The common multiple of two or more numbers that has the least value.
  Example:
  Multiples of 4: 4, 8, ⑫, 16, 20, ㉔, ...
  Multiples of 6: 6, ⑫, 18, ㉔, 30, 36, ...
  The least common multiple of 4 and 6 is 12.

N

- **negative number**

  A number that is less than zero.

O

- **opposite**

  Having the same numeral but different signs.
  Example: -6 is the opposite of 6.

P

- **perfect cube**

  The cube of a whole number.
  Example: 343 is a perfect cube because
  $343 = 7 \times 7 \times 7$.

- **perfect square**

  The square of a whole number.
  Example: 64 is a perfect square because
  $64 = 8 \times 8$.

- **positive number**

  A number that is greater than zero.

- **prime factor**

  A factor of a number that is also a prime
  number.

- **prime factorization**

  A composite number written as a product of its
  prime factors.
  Example: $18 = 2 \times 3 \times 3$

S

- **speed**

  A special rate that expresses distance per unit
  time.
  Speed = Distance ÷ Time

U

- **unit rate**

  A ratio that compares a quantity to one unit of a
  different quantity.

Index

A

Absolute value, **69**, 76
    to interpret real-world situations, 71–72, 83
    of number, 69–70, 73, 80

Addition, 125, 152–153
    with decimals, 86
        to solve real-world problems, 143–144
    multi-digit decimals, 121–122
    repeated, 127

Average speed, **271**–283, 289–290, 293–294, 299

B

Bar models,
    pictorial representations,
        comparison, *throughout, see for example,* 144, 168–169, 194–196, 201–207, 237
        part-part, *throughout, see for example,* 106, 112, 115, 128, 173–174
        part-whole, *throughout, see for example,* 110, 135–136, 146, 173–174, 323–327

Base,
    of expression, 23
    of percent, **323**–324

Blue cubes, 176, 183, 191

C

Commission, **336**

Common factors,
    greatest, 12
        with distributive property, 15
        of two whole numbers, 12–14
    of two whole numbers, 11–12

Common multiples
    least, 17–18
    of two whole numbers, 16–18

Commutative property of multiplication, 127

Comparison
    bar models, *see* Bar models
    numbers to 1,000,000, 44
    two numbers,
        whole numbers on number line and, 45–46
    two quantities
        with same unit, 169–170, 237
        with different units, 171–172, 237
    unit rates, 241–242, 252–253
    writing ratio to, 169–172

Composite number, 5, 34
    as product of prime factors, 5–6, 8

Constant speed, 261, 274, 284–286, 288, 294

Converting measurements, 167

Cube
    blue, 176, 183, 191
    connecting, 24
    green, 169, 176, 184–185, 196
    perfect, **24**
    red, 176, 183, 191, 196
    root, 25
    volume of, 24
    of whole number, 24–25, 34
    yellow, 169, 176, 196

D

Decimals, 152
    adding, 86, 143–144, 152
        multi-digit, 121–122
    denominator of 100 as, 306
    dividing, 151
        with one or more decimal places, 140
        to solve real-world problems, 146
        whole number by, 135–136
    multiplying
        with one or more decimal places, 131–132
        to real-world problems, 145
        by whole number, 127–130

> Pages in **boldface** type show where a term is introduced.

on a number line, 45, 48–52
percent and, 310–312, 314, 318–321, 342–343
real-world problems
addition, 143–144
division, 146
multiplication, 145
subtraction, 143–144
statements of inequality, 51–52
subtracting, 86
multi-digit, 123–124

Denominator of 100 as decimal, 306

Distance, *throughout, see for example,* 60, 69, 71,
143–144, 294
speed and time, 262–267

Distributive property
greatest common factor with, 15

Division, *throughout, see for example,* 4–5, 45, 152,
220, 306
decimals
with one or more decimal places, 140
to solve real-world problems, 146
whole number by, 135–136
equivalent fractions using, 166, 305
equivalent ratios by, 187–189, 197–198, 235–236
with fractions, 234
by improper fraction or mixed numbers,
99–100
by whole numbers, 88, 233
hundredths by hundredths, 138–140
with proper fraction
by proper fraction, 96, 98–99
by unit fraction, 93–95, 104–105
whole numbers by, 89–91, 97, 103–104,
108–110
real-world problems
fraction by fraction, 112–115
fraction by whole numbers, 105–107
proper fraction by unit fraction, 104–105
whole numbers by proper fraction, 103–104
whole numbers by fraction, 108, 110
tenths by tenths, 137–138
whole numbers by unit fraction, 88

Equivalent fractions, 315, 342
by division, 166, 305
by multiplication, 166, 304
writing, 167, 185–186

Equivalent ratios, 183–184, 186, 220, 235
by division, 187–189, 197–198, 235–236
missing term in a pair of, 189–190, 235–236
two sets of ratios, 196

Estimation, 144, 150

Evaluate
numerical expressions, 4, 25–26, 29

Exponents, 23
numerical expressions with, 25–26

Factors
common, 11
greatest common, 12
with distributive property, 15
ratio in simplest form, 188–189
for two whole numbers, 12–14
prime, **5**–8
numbers, 4

Formula
average speed, 294
distance, 264, 294
speed, 294
time, 294

Fractions, 152
using bar model to show, 175–177
with 100 as denominator, 306
dividing, 234
fraction by, 112, 115
by mixed numbers, 99–100
real-world problems, 103–108, 110, 112, 115
by whole number, 88, 233
as equivalent fractions
by division, 166, 305
by multiplication, 166, 304
improper, *see* Improper fractions
multiplying, 233
fraction by, 87
by whole numbers, 232, 306
on a number line, 48–51
and percent, 307–313, 315–320, 322, 342–343
proper, *see* Proper fractions
and ratio, 175–178, 187, 210, 230
real-world problems, 103–115
in simplest form, 87, 167
statements of inequality, 51–52

Fraction bar, 89

Fraction circle, 89–91

G

Graphs, 61, 73, 256, 259–260, 297
    line, *see* Line graphs
    to solve rate problems, 253–255

Greatest common factor (GCF), 12
    with distributive property, 15
    of two whole numbers, 12–14
    to write ratio in simplest form, 188–189, 236

Green cubes, 169, 176, 184–185, 196

H

Horizontal number lines, *throughout, see for*
    example, 50, 53, 55, 65, 77
    pictorial representations, *throughout,*
      see for example, 45–46, 48, 50, 59–61,
      76–78

Hundredths, 121, 123, 128, 130–132
    by hundredths, 138–140

I

Improper fractions
    dividing
      fraction by, 99–100
    and mixed numbers, 86–87, 234, 306,
      316, 319

Inequality, 64, 66–68, 73, 79–80, 171–172
    statements of, **46**, 51–52, 76

Interest
    rate, **337**–338, 340
    real-world problems, 337

Intervals, *throughout, see for example,* 45, 48, 63,
    77, 137–138

L

Least common multiple, 17–18, 20, 22, 34–35

Line graphs, 253–256, 259–260, 297

M

Manipulative
    fraction bar, 89
    fraction circle, 89–91

Measurements,
    converting, 167

Mixed numbers
    dividing, 99–100
    and improper fractions, 86–87, 234, 306
    on a number line, 48, 50
    by whole numbers, 232
    and percent, 315–317, 321

Multi-digit decimals
    adding, 121–122
    subtracting, 123–124

Multiples, 16–18, 178
    common, 16
    least common, 17–18, 34
    of whole number, 3

Multiplication, *throughout, see for example,* 12,
    89–90, 152, 220, 342
    equivalent fractions using, 166, 304
    expression, 88, 99, 234
    fractions, 233
      by fractions, 87–88, 96, 98–100, 130, 132, 233
      by whole numbers, 232, 306
    mixed numbers by whole numbers, 232
    decimals
      with one or more decimal places, 131–132
      real-world problems, 145
      by whole numbers, 127–130
    tenths by tenths, 130
    two decimal with one decimal place, 131
    of whole numbers, 3, 232

Multiplication dot, 7

Multiplying factor, 220

N

Negative numbers, 42, 65, 75–76, 79
    on a number line, 59–62
    in real-world situations, **57**–59, 64, 71–72, 83
    statements of inequality, 62–63

Number lines, *throughout, see for example*, 42, 47, 50, 54–55, 63
    horizontal, *see* Horizontal number lines
    pictorial representations, *throughout,*
        see for example, 45–46, 69–70, 82–83,
        127–129, 322
    vertical, *see* Vertical number lines

Numbers
    absolute value of, **69**–70, 73, 80
    composite, 5–6, 8
    mixed, *see* Mixed numbers
    negative, *see* Negative numbers
    positive, *see* Positive numbers
    to 1,000,000 compare, 44
    whole, *see* Whole numbers

Numerical expressions
    with exponents, 25–26
    using order of operations, 4

Opposites, **60**–62, 65, 67, 75–77

Order of operations, 25
    and numerical expressions, 4

Part-part bar model, *throughout, see for example*, 106, 112, 115, 128, 173–174

Part-whole bar model, *throughout, see for example*, 110, 135–136, 146, 173–174, 323–327

Paper strips, 89, 94, 207

Percent, 342
    base of, **323**–324
    expressing
        decimal, *throughout, see for example*,
            310–312, 318–319, 321, 338, 342
        fraction, 307–313, 315–317, 319–322
        mixed number as, 315–317
    of quantity, 323–327, 342, 344
        real-world problems, 331–333, 336

Perfect cube, **24**–25, 27

Perfect square, **23**, 25, 27

Pictorial representations
    bar models, *see* Bar models
    graphs, *see* Graphs
    number lines, *see* Number lines
    place-value chart, *see* Place-value chart
    tables, *see* Tables

Place-value chart, 44

Positive numbers, 45, 59–60, 62, 76

Prime factorization, 6–7, 12, 14–15, 17–18, 34

Prime factors, 5–8

Prime number(s), 4–7, 9, 34
    identifying, 4

Proper fractions
    with division
        proper fraction by, 96, 98
        by unit fraction, 93–95, 104–105
        whole number by, 89–91, 97, 103–104

Quantities
    percent of, 323–327, 331–333, 336, 342
    rate, 238–239, 243–244, 294
    ratio, *throughout, see for example*,
        169–172, 183–186, 192–194,
        203–204, 235

Rates, 237–238, 245–250, 294
    interest, *see* Interest rate
    real-world problems, 253–255
        graphs, 253–255
        multi-step, 251–253
        simple, 247–248
        two-part, 249–250
    sales tax, *see* Sales tax rate
    unit, *see* Unit rates

Ratios, 218, 230
    bar model using, 175–177
    before-and-after problems changing,
        207–209
    comparing, two quantities
        with different units, 171–172
        with same units, 169–170, 235, 237

equivalent, 196–198, 220, 236
    comparisons of numbers and quantities,
       183–186
    by division, 187–188
  finding, 177–178, 197, 222–223, 235
    quantities, 192–194
    in simplest form, 235
  involving two sets of ratio, 196, 205–206
  part-part or part-whole bar models,
    173–174
  real-world problems, 201–202
    involving two sets of, 205–206
    three quantities, 203–204
  in simplest form, 235
    expressing, 197, 222–223, 236
    greatest common factor, 188–189
  tables of, 190–191
  terms of, 169, 176, 220, 235

Real-world problems, 220
  absolute values, 71–72, 83
  average speed, 277–283, 289–290, 293, 299
  decimals
    adding, 143–144
    dividing, 146
    multiplying, 145
    subtracting, 143–144
  distance, 277–293
  dividing
    fraction by fraction, 112–115
    fraction by whole numbers, 105–107
    proper fraction by unit fraction, 104–105
    whole numbers by proper fraction, 103–104
    whole numbers by fraction, 108–110
  fractions, 113
  interest, 337
  negative numbers, 57–59, 64
  percent, 331–333
    quantity and, 326, 336
  rates
    graphs, 253–255
    multi-step, 251–253
    simple, 247–248
    two-part, 249–250
  ratios, 201–202
    involving two sets of, 205–206
    three quantities, 203–204
  speed, 266, 277–279, 284–288
  taxes, 334–335
  time, 277–279
  unit rates
    comparing, 252–253
    simple, 247–248
    two-part, 249–250

Reciprocal, *throughout, see for example*, 89,
  103–104, 135–137, 139–140, 319

Red cubes, 176, 183, 191, 196

Repeated addition, 127

S

Sales tax rate, 334–335, 339, 346

Simplest form
  fractions in, 86, 167, 305
  ratios in, 187–189, 197, 221–223, 230, 235

Speed, **261**, 294
  average, **271**–283, 289–290, 293–294, 299
  constant, 261, 274, 284–286, 288, 294
  distance and time, 262–267
  interpreting, 261–262
  reading, 261–262
  real-world problems, 266, 277–279
  writing, 261–262

Square, 34
  perfect, **23**, 25, 27
  of whole numbers, 23–24

Square root, 23

Statement of inequality, 46, 51–52, 76

Subtraction
  with decimals, 86, 152
    to solve real-world problems,
      143–144
  multi-digit decimals, 123–124

T

Tables, *throughout, see for example*, 5, 57, 190–191,
  241–242, 251

Tenths
  dividing tenths by, 137–138
  multiplying tenths by, 130–131, 152

Terms,
  missing, 189–190, 198, 221
  of ratio, 169, 176, 220, 235
  order of, 176
  with exponents, 26

Time, 294
    distance and speed, 262–267
    rates, 237–239

Unit cost, 239–242

Unit fraction
    dividing
        proper fraction by, 93–95, 104–105
        whole numbers by, 88

Unit rates, **237**–238, 294
    expressing and computing, 238–239
    finding, 239–240
        compare, 241–242
        quantity, 243–244
    identifying, 237–238
    real-world problems
        multi-step, 252–253
        simple, 247–248
        two-part, 249–250

Units of measure
    converting, 167

Vertical forms, 122–126, 128–134

Vertical number lines, *throughout, see for example,*
    42, 47, 50, 54, 66
    pictorial representations, 45–47, 49–50, 60–61,
        66, 76

Whole numbers, 34
    common factors, 11
    comparing, 44–47
    cube of, 24–25, 34
    dividing
        by decimal, 135–136
        fraction by, 88, 233
        by proper fraction, 89–91, 97, 103–104, 108–110
        by unit fraction, 88
    factors of, 2
    greatest common factor, 12–14
    least common multiple, 17–18
    multiples, 16–18, 178
    multiplying, 3, 232
        decimal, 127–130
        fractions by, 232, 306
        mixed numbers by, 232
    on a number line, 45–46
    real-world problems
        fraction by, 105–107
        by proper fraction, 103–104
    square, 23–24

Yellow cubes, 169, 176, 196

Zero, 42, 59
    distance from, 69, 76
    neither positive nor negative, 60
    opposite, 60

Photo Credits

NOTES

NOTES

© 2020 Marshall Cavendish Education Pte Ltd

Published by Marshall Cavendish Education
Times Centre, 1 New Industrial Road, Singapore 536196
Customer Service Hotline: (65) 6213 9688
US Office Tel: (1-914) 332 8888 | Fax: (1-914) 332 8882
E-mail: cs@mceducation.com
Website: www.mceducation.com

Distributed by
Houghton Mifflin Harcourt
125 High Street
Boston, MA 02110
Tel: 617-351-5000
Website: www.hmhco.com/programs/math-in-focus

First published 2020

ISBN 978-0-358-10189-5

Printed in Singapore

2 3 4 5 6 7 8   1401   25 24 23 22 21 20
4500799763   B C D E F

The cover image shows a barn owl.
Owls live in trees or sometimes in the top of barns. They are mostly nocturnal. They have large eyes that are fixed in place, so they rely on their ability to turn their necks 270° to scan their surroundings. Their ears are asymmetrically shaped and positioned, allowing their brains to calculate the exact location of their prey in total darkness. They are excellent hunters who eat mostly rodents.